THE WORLD'S MOST VALUABLE INVESTMENT STRATEGY

Power-Methods To Safely Multiply Your Money
(Even In Volatile Markets)!

by

B. BECK FISHER, JR.

WINDSOR BOOKS, P.O. Box 280, Brightwaters, N.Y.

Published by Windsor Books
P.O. Box 280
Brightwaters, N.Y. 11718

Manufactured in the United States of America

ISBN 0-930233-43-3

Contents

Introduction
And
Acknowledgments

This is basically a "how-to" book. It is a detailed plan for growing capital using stocks, bonds, and mutual funds.

The book uses a "building-block" approach. Each part of the book, beginning with Chapter 1, is a mandatory precedent for the parts which follow. I firmly believe that the book must be read from beginning to end in order to fully understand the detailed plan, and benefit from it. Please don't read the book piecemeal or read Chapters or pages nonsequentially. Even in Section VI, which discusses portfolio management in terms of the age of the investor, you are encouraged to read all Chapters even though you may not be in the specific Chapter's age bracket.

The style of this book is personal and informal. The first and second person pronouns are used to identify the author and the reader. Frequently I will use a two word phrase to identify myself, and this is explained in Chapter 1. If some of you find this in any way offensive, I am sorry. Certainly no offense is intended.

The writing of this book has been an unusual project. It has been an absolutely solitary endeavor.

My thirty year career in the financial services industry has enabled me to structure and write this book as though it was on the tip of my tongue. I have conducted no outside research; I have interviewed nobody. I have been able to write as the words flowed from my brain. From a professional standpoint it has been a satisfying experience. My only previous undertaking of this sort did involve considerable research. It was a much shorter academic Thesis written during my senior year in college, thirty-four years ago.

This book is not a scholarly monograph; it is a deeply personal exercise — I am communicating the ideas I have learned in my career. There are no footnotes in this book. I have written it in the Reference Room of the Public Library in Pompano Beach, Florida, near where I reside. Whenever I have needed to check a fact, figure, name, or date I have gotten it from one of three sources: The Encyclopedia Americana (International 1989 Edition); The Statistical Abstract of the United States, published by the U.S. Department of Commerce, both the 1988 edition and the "Colonial Times to 1970" edition; or from the standard investment publications which are discussed in some detail in Chapter 8. I thank the Reference Room staff for their assistance.

The real bibliography of this book is an extraordinary one. It is a list of literally hundreds of men and women with whom I've been in contact over my lifetime, mostly in my career - co-workers, clients, competitors, and customers - who have educated me to a point where I could write this book without a note of basic research. If I were to compile such a list, and I would like to, it would resemble in quantity of people the wall at the Vietnam Veteran's Memorial - there would be too many names. Some of these people are no longer here, and I revere their memory. To the rest I say: "You know who you are, and I thank you!"

There are, however, seven men whom I would especially like to acknowledge. I have been blessed, as I have been employed from coast to coast, with absolutely excellent bosses! They have been friends and teachers. They have been supportive and helpful, tough and demanding. They have been, each in his own way, a splendid influence on my professional (and personal) development. I love them all, and thank them for what they have given me:

The late Jim Murphy - 1959 to 1963 in California. I learned a bit about stocks and mutual funds and a lot about substance, style, and salesmanship.

Harold C. Adams - 1963 to 1973 in Wisconsin. Among thousands, the soundest banker I have ever met. I learned more from him than a briefcase full of MBA degrees would have given me.

Bob and Stewart Kester - 1973 to 1979 in Florida. Devoted brothers, good bankers, fine friends, and wonderful gentlemen. They taught me in arenas well beyond the doors of the bank.

Tom Snellgrove - 1979 to 1982 in Florida. Still a bank president, fighting some tough battles. Probably the most honorable human being I have ever known.

Andy Carroll - 1982 to 1985 in Florida. Calls himself a 'dinosaur of the investment business,' a stockbroker with few equals. A wonderful friend and companion.

And George Bloukos - 1986 to 1988 in Florida. He has forgotten more about bonds in his thirty year career of trading and selling them than most current professionals bring to their office each day.

My closest friend every year for more than half a century has been my father, now eighty-four years young. The quantity and quality of his love and paternal support have been beyond words. And my mother, long ago departed, first inspired me into the career of, to use her word, a financier. She bought me a subscription to the Wall Street Journal in 1957, when I was a bachelor Air Force officer and really could have cared less. Two years later I was off and running! I hope she is looking down at this book from her lofty perch and saying "Well done. I am proud!"

As a practical matter, this book would not be possible were it not for the initial encouragement and massive day-to-day support I have gotten during the writing of it from the two wonderful friends with whom I presently share my personal life. I thank each of them from very deep down.

Pompano Beach, Florida   B.B.F., Jr.
Summer, 1989

Disclaimer

This book presents a detailed plan for growing capital through the use of publicly traded stocks, bonds, and mutual funds.

The author has been employed in the financial services industry, both by commercial banks and NYSE and NASD investment firms, for thirty consecutive years. He has an absolutely unblemished record of compliance with all laws and regulations applicable to these industries. He currently holds NASD licenses (Series 7, Series 63, and Series 24) which qualify him as a securities salesman. He is not registered with the SEC as a licensed financial advisor. He is currently not affiliated in any way with any business entity in the financial services industry, and he has no present plans to become so affiliated.

This book's detailed plan for investment selection and portfolio management does not recommend any specific investment securities other than U.S. Treasury securities. It does offer very specific advice on the manner in which stocks, bonds, and mutual funds can be selected and best used to increase capital. The author believes the categories of securities recommended have, over time, the potential for reward that outweighs the risks that these categories of securities, except for U.S. Treasury securities, by definition possess. The author acknowledges that the detailed plan does have the potential for diminution of capital over any time period.

The detailed investment plan is offered in absolute good faith. The author does not hesitate to employ all the advices, concepts, techniques and strategies included in this book with his personal funds. The author must state, however, that he accepts no legal responsibility, monetary or otherwise, for losses of any sort that an investor might suffer as a result of reading this book and putting the detailed investment plan into effect.

This book is dedicated to
the memory
of a super friend and occasional colleague
whom I knew simply as
"The Z."
I miss him.

SECTION I.
THE ROAD MAP AND THE DRIVER

1
A Journey With The Seasoned Veteran

I want you to take a trip. A journey.

The journey is not going to be by airplane, nor by train, bus, steamship or spacecraft. It is not a real journey, in the geographic sense, but a journey of the mind. It can be likened to an educational journey.

It can best be compared to a cross-country trip by automobile, a "road trip" where you are the driver and the auto is your own.

Pretend that the starting point is in Maine, where the air and water are cold and the beaches are rocky, and the destination is San Diego, where the climate is glorious and the beaches are golden.

Imagine further that the trip cannot be accomplished in the usual week or ten days. It will take much longer than that. It will take years, many years, perhaps the rest of your lifetime. And there will be risks along the way. But the risks will be exceeded by rewards, and someday you will get to your destination. Once you get there, it will be very, very good. It will certainly not be Heaven on earth, but it will provide great satisfactions. It will be well worth the long time and the risks that must be taken to get there.

My involvement in the journey is similar to that of AAA or a very good travel agent: I will prepare you for the trip.

But you will be prepared for this trip in greater detail than AAA or a good travel agent ever contemplated or even dreamed of.

I will do these things, and more:

I will tell you in detail why you should take the trip in the first place. I will make a recommendation if I don't think you're qualified to make the trip. I will examine the time period I feel it will take you. (I feel I know you pretty well, even though we have never met.) I will tell you what type of auto you should be driving. I will prepare the auto for the trip: engine, tires, comfort systems, everything - even the appearance of it. I will tell you where to go for servicing along the way. I will tell you every highway to drive, equipping you for the bad roads and the good ones. I will prepare you for inevitable detours. I will tell you where to look for highwaymen, bad guys, flat tires, and overheated engines, and help you avoid them. I will tell you what the expenses of the trip are, and how to minimize them. And I will do even more than these things.

Even though I will be leading you on your journey, I will not be along with you on it. You will mostly be by yourself, although at one point early on you will pick up a guide who will be helpful to you for the duration of the journey. I will tell you where you can find this person, and he or she will prove to be a very good guide as well as travelling companion.

You will be doing all of the driving yourself.

You are probably saying at this point "What is this trip all about? Why should I take it? Why will it take so long? And is the destination really that much better than where I am now?"

Those are excellent questions.

I believe I can answer them.

The trip is about the business of making money. It is about using certain publicly traded financial instruments to accomplish this. It is about selecting the best of the publicly traded financial instruments. It is about what to do and what not to do in these areas. It is about certain techniques and strategies. It is about one very important financial concept that is as dependable as a law of nature. It is about history, some of it long ago but most of it fairly recent, that by studying it we can avoid mistakes and have reason for great optimism about the future.

It is about protecting capital and making it grow.

It is about the concept that great things take time, not epochs and centuries but rather years and decades. A corollary is that it is about patience.

It is about growing capital where the growing season is not so brief as a spring or a summer, but where the ultimate fruit is vastly larger than the initial seed. And the time frame is not so long that you can't enjoy the fruit in your lifetime.

It is specifically about taking an initial amount of capital. Just for an example, let's say it was $100,000. It would grow over your lifetime to make you easily a millionaire, and if you are a young person now, many times a millionaire.

"Wow!" you say. "That doesn't sound bad. Not bad at all. I think I might very well be interested! But tell me, who are you to think you can prepare me for such a trip? What are your qualifications? I don't have time, and certainly not capital, to waste on a pipe dream!"

Again, an excellent question. I believe I have a very good answer.

I have been to every hotel, motel, guesthouse, restaurant and service station along the way. I have been on every road and highway, and I have driven every conceivable type of auto. I have known and studied those who have attempted the journey, recently and some time ago. I have seen their mistakes and successes. I have worked side by side with the guides (I have been one myself!), and know the good ones from the bad ones. I have used numerous concepts, techniques, and strategies and I have employed the ones that work and rejected the ones that don't. And beyond just discovering the ones that work, I have refined them. I have visited all of these places over a lifetime.

Yes, I feel I am qualified. Let me begin to explain.

I am 55 years old. For the past five decades I have gotten up early every day. Twenty of my years were spent going to school and serving my country. And thirty of the years have been spent in employment in the financial services industry, with twenty years in banks and ten years in investment firms.

But you need to know even more about me, because my detailed educational and professional background is important in qualifying me to ask you to entrust your capital, not to me, but to my plan.

If I were looking for a job, and preparing a detailed resumé, it would look something like this:

1933. Born in Chicago.

1933-1947. A very constructive and comfortable childhood, first in Chicago, and in 1942 to the Fox Cities area of Wisconsin. Father worked his entire career in sales for a small paper manufacturer, sales manager in 1942 and Vice President in 1955.

1947-1951. Student at Wayland Academy. Campus leader, active in all sports; honor roll and Cum Laude; college preparatory courses.

1951-1955. Student at Princeton University. Majored in History, elective courses in Economics. Not a campus leader but popular on campus. Member of Tiger Inn, chairman of several committees. Wrote an Honors Thesis on a subject related to U.S. political history. Graduated (A.B.) in upper-third of the Class of 1955.

1955-1956. Trainee at a large grain merchandising company in Minneapolis. Exposed for the first time to the workings of the economic law of supply and demand.

1956-1959. Lieutenant, USAF. Air defense radar duty on Cape Cod. Officer-in-charge of a 25 man crew in the radar center, then Training Officer for the entire Squadron.

Then in April, 1959, my career in the financial services industry began.

1959-1963. Registered Representative (Stockbroker) in the San Francisco office of a large Wall Street-headquartered NYSE member firm. Sold common stocks and equity mutual funds, a few municipal bonds. "Growth stocks" were in vogue. Research a stock, convince clients to buy it, hope it goes up, then sell it and move on to the next one. Not much portfolio management or financial planning. Bear market in Spring, 1962. Became a believer in equity mutual funds.

1963-1973. Officer, mostly with the title of Vice President, of a commercial bank in the Fox Cities area of Wisconsin, tenth largest bank in the state, largest in the area.

1964-67: Director of Portfolio Investments, managed portfolio of $10 to $25 million in U.S. Treasuries and municipals. Director of Asset/ Liability Management. Counseled customers on all types of money market investments until Trust Department was established in 1966, when became member of Trust Investment Committee until 1973. This Committee managed portfolios of wealthy individuals and employee benefit plans, mainly using stocks and all types of bonds. Producing "income" was a large factor, as was portfolio "appreciation." Emphasis was on "balanced" investing.

Also, 1967-73: Vice President in the commercial loan department. Active in wide range of civic endeavors: Treasurer, United Way; Vestry-man, Episcopal Church; Trustee, local hospital; Director, Family Service, Children's Service, Taxpayer's Alliance, Goodwill Industries.

1973-1977. Executive Vice President, then quickly President and Director, of a small bank in southeast Florida, owned by a holding company. Responsible for all bank functions and operations, including investments, loans, deposit acquisition, and asset/liability management. Became a real student of interest rate volatility and various fixed income portfolio strategies. Experienced a transition from a manufacturing and agriculture oriented Wisconsin economy to a real estate, tourism, and service related Florida economy. During these years I was also a student for two weeks each of three summers at the Stonier Graduate School of Banking at Rutgers University.

1977-1979. The above bank was merged into the lead bank of the holding company, where I became Executive Vice President. This was a $250 million bank. The portfolio investment department reported to me, and I "called the shots" on a $35 to $50 million portfolio of U.S. Treasuries, U.S. Agencies, municipals, and a few corporates. I was Chairman of the Asset/Liability Management Committee. Seven branch managers reported to me, as well as the Comptroller's Department and the Business Development Department. I was on the Senior Officers Loan Committee. This was an exciting time in banking. The financial markets were having a difficult time adjusting to the phenomenon of inflation. I was there, both in my profession and in my personal accounts.

1979-1982. Executive Vice President and Director of a $100 million bank, located twenty miles from the above bank. The bank was owned by two extremely wealthy and elderly entrepreneurs. I had co-responsibility for virtually all aspects of the bank's day-to-day operations, with particular emphasis on the $40 million bond portfolio, daily money market activities, and asset/liability management. Trust Department investing policies and specific investments, both fixed income and equity, were matters for daily involvement. We purchased investment research from institutional sources outside the bank and I was involved with their inner workings. I was exposed to "wild and crazy" financial markets, with medium-term U.S. Treasuries selling for 70 and a prime rate at 21.50%. It was a terrific learning experience. I learned the real meaning of two new words: disintermediation and stagflation. I became absolutely fascinated by the world of investments and the marketplaces where they changed ownership. And I felt my banking career was leveling off.

So in the Spring of 1982 I made the decision to change my career path, not totally but still significantly.

July, 1982-September, 1983. Stockbroker with the Fort Lauderdale office of a small NYSE member firm headquartered in New York. Conducted public seminars that I organized myself; the first seminar was in late July, 1982, and it was called "The Coming Bull Market." I learned about put and call options, unit investment trusts, tax shelter oriented limited partnerships, fixed income mutual funds, financial futures, mort-gage-backed securities, index options - areas that were largely not in existence twenty-odd years before when I had last been a stockbroker. Developed an upscale clientele of well-off individuals. Sold many inter-mediate-term corporate bonds to the portfolios of underloaned commercial banks, where municipals were no longer attractive because of the 1982 Tax Act. The firm was heavily involved with the structure and distribution of limited partnership investments, tax shelters and venture capital, which I determined were not really "my cup of tea." My boss changed firms, and I followed him.

September, 1983-June, 1985. Stockbroker with the Fort Lauderdale office of a large and very good southeastern regional NYSE firm. Continued development of clientele of upscale individuals, employee benefit plans of small businesses, local bank trust departments and portfolio investment departments. Studied and sold several "market timing" plans, both equity and fixed income. Sold many municipal bond unit investment trusts, long and short-term, insured and uninsured. Studied the "junk bond" phenomenon, as well as the use and misuse of mortgage-backed pass-throughs. Studied and used floating rate bonds and C.D.'s. Participated in more than a few initial public offerings, both good ones and bad ones. The firm's equity research department got me very excited about a new high-tech computer company, and I placed tens of thousands of shares at prices below 10. I watched the company's business explode and the price start out on its trip above 100. I made a half dozen trips to my firm's headquarters 1000 miles away and saw how a good regional firm operates. I observed the activities of the 'financial planning' department, and became aware of the growth of 'financial planning' in the overall financial services industry.

June, 1985-June, 1988. After nearly two years with this fine firm, I determined that I was attempting to be a master of all things and was spreading myself too thin. I determined that I wanted to specialize, and that my current real interest was in the fixed income area, and my selling expertise should be concentrated on selling fixed income securities of all types to portfolio managers at banks, S&L's, insurance companies, credit unions, pension funds, and a few very wealthy individuals across the nation.

So that is what I have been doing for the last three years. I have been an "institutional bond salesman" at several NASD "bond houses." My products have been U.S. Treasuries; U.S. Agencies; C.D.'s; corporates and municipals of all ratings, coupons, and maturities; mortgage-backed securities (GNMA, FNMA, FHLMC, CMO, REMIC); and to a small extent, financial futures and bonds denominated in foreign currencies. During this period, I have developed a unique strategy for fixed income investing which you will learn about in Chapter 11.

And then, on June 15, 1988, I retired from this activity for the purpose of devoting my full energies to writing this book.

Over all the years of my life, I have been an ardent sports fan, particularly a fan of professional football.

I believe I attended my first game with my parents in Wrigley Field in 1940, watching the Bears play the Packers. Sid Luckman and Bulldog Turner. Cecil Isbell, Clark Hinkle, and Don Hutson.

Early on, I began reading the sports pages, the sports magazines, and the sports columnists, and I still do, almost fifty years later.

In the Sixties I resided only thirty miles from Green Bay, where I lived and breathed the Lombardi Packers. I had the pleasure of personally being friends with, and sometimes banker to, many of the players: Thurston, McGee, Dowler, Hornung, Willie Wood, Ray Nitschke and more.

In the Seventies, in Florida, my allegiance slowly transferred itself to the Shula Dolphins. Griese, Csonka, and Kiick. Warfield, Larry Little and the Kooch. Jake Scott and Dick Anderson, whom I got to know personally. Buoniconti and Fernandez. Garo Yepremian.

And there have been other players I've watched and like a lot. Y. A. Tittle and Leo Nomellini. Joe the Jet Perry. Harder and Hirsch. Unitas and Berry. Butkus and Sayers. Staubach and Pearson. The Juice. Fred Biletnikoff. The list could go on.

These are players who knew all of the nooks and crannies of their sport. They were the players that you could bet on. They had knowledge and experience. They didn't win every contest, but over time they were, as players, winners. Big winners.

The sportswriters that I read and have read are a varied breed; the best of them was the late Red Smith, but there are many other good ones. All of them tend to use a two-word phrase when they describe these players. At the time they are at the top of their game they are described as *seasoned veterans*.

In the world of late Twentieth Century finance and investments, I am a Seasoned Veteran. I sure am!

And I am at the top of my game!

But now the important part. *You.* Let's examine whether you have certain qualifications necessary for the challenges and opportunities of the journey.

2
Is This Journey
Really For Me?

The trip we are talking about, the journey, is really an Investment Plan. It calls for *permanently* dedicating an initial amount of *capital* to the Plan. The initial sum can certainly be added to (cash additions), and there will be some provisions made for subtracting from it (cash withdrawals), but it must be considered a rather inflexible Plan. The Plan will be successful only if the commitment to it is a continuous commitment over a period of time measured in years.

The success of the Investment Plan, the plan for growing capital, requires three basic ingredients. All of them can be acquired by a significantly large percentage of people. One is a basic amount of capital to start the Plan, and the other two are just as important. I call them the internal qualifications. They are: (1) a certain investor temperament, and (2) a certain amount of basic investment knowledge.

Let's consider each basic ingredient in turn.

INITIAL CAPITAL

First of all, there is a difference between *savings* and *capital*.

I believe that every person, or every family unit, should absolutely have an amount of *basic* savings equal to at least one year's living expenses. This amount of money should be liquid, readily available in an insured savings account, a reputable money market fund, very short-term insured C.D., or U.S. Treasury Bills. It should be available for all the real emergencies that might come up: a few of these might be medical, legal, family, or employment related. For most people this amount of savings is generated by having more after-tax income than expense, with the difference being saved. Thrift is certainly a word that comes to mind.

Over and above the *basic* need for savings, as just described, it frequently happens that money is accumulated for a near-term or intermediate-term major expense that is not really an emergency. I call this *earmarked* savings. A need of this type would be the acquisition of a residence, college tuition expense, the acquisition of an automobile, a planned trip around the world, a major gift to a family member, or the acquisition of very expensive art or jewelry. Whatever your need for earmarked savings might be, you cannot consider this money as part of the capital required for the Plan. These savings must be segregated and invested short-term, just like basic savings, so that they will positively be available when needed for the specifically earmarked purpose. Incidentally, it has been proven that federal deposit insurance can be absolutely relied upon, thanks only to the back-up provided by the American taxpayer.

Another thing that must be taken care of is *personal debt* apart from a real estate mortgage on your personal residence. Auto and boat loans, bank credit cards, department store revolving balances, and other personal loans all require the payment of interest at rates which today range from low double digits to the very high teens. In the next two Chapters, we will be setting an objective toward growing your capital at a compound rate that will be in the mid-teens (hopefully higher!). It is axiomatic that this is what financial professionals call "a wash." The growth rate is almost entirely offset by the expense rate, and the expense rate is no longer a tax deduction as it was. So before considering whether you have capital required to implement the Plan, personal debt should be paid in full and not ever incurred again. This is probably a good objective under any circumstance.

You will notice that I exempted a real estate mortgage on your personal residence. Yes, this form of debt is compatible with the Plan, although not a basic ingredient of it. Here is my reasoning. Your residence will normally be a non-depreciating asset from a monetary standpoint. And it can appreciate; we all have seen that. A mortgage creates leverage, which will enhance the return on your initial equity if there is appreciation. The monthly mortgage payment is really the equivalent of "rent" in the classic economic sense: it is perfectly appropriate to pay rent on basic shelter out of income. I hope you do not have a long-term mortgage with a fixed rate in the middle or high teens. If you do, you should definitely try to refinance with an adjustable rate loan with a "cap." Lastly, the interest you pay still qualifies as a full tax deduction, and this helps.

Now you say to me: "OK. I have provided for all my savings requirements, I have paid all my personal debt, and my personal residence is either rented, owned free and clear, or has a satisfactory mortgage loan. Over and above these things, I believe I have a sum of *capital*. My question is two-fold: How much capital must I have, at a minimum, and must it be in cash at the time I start the Plan?"

These are appropriate questions, and I have exact and well-thought-out answers.

You should have at least $10,000 of permanent capital, and it must be in cash. And you must not borrow it in order to start the Plan.

I hope you spent a moment or two with the Table of Contents before you began reading this book. If you did not, please do so now.

You have seen that the first three Sections are designed to tell you some of the specific reasons why the trip, or the Investment Plan, will be so good for you and why it will work. Section IV will prepare your informational belongings and your vehicle, and select your guide. The next two Sections are the trip itself, the investments, the strategies, and the structures. You will have certain categories of financial instruments, well selected, a specific vehicle for them to travel in, specific strategies on when to buy them and when to sell them, and then how to structure them into portfolios in accord with how far along on the journey you have traveled.

Our trip will never deviate off of one road, one interstate highway. The name of the interstate highway is: *Growing Capital.* It is ipso facto that the growth of capital presumes that the initial amount will be protected.

The prudent protection of capital demands *diversification.* It is only with an amount of capital equal to at least $10,000 that proper diversification of financial assets, or investments, can be attained. You will see that these investments will be *broadly* diversified. That will minimize the risks that are taken, and over time it will maximize the rewards.

To be attempting the Plan with less than $10,000 will not allow the broad diversification that the Plan requires. It is just that simple.

Perhaps, or even probably, many of you are saying "Well, that lets me out! I do not have $10,000 of capital. I might have it someday, but not now."

To you I say: *Work towards accumulating it.* The Plan will still be around in a year or three. Or longer. Its concepts, advices, strategies, and investments will still be good. You can save more. You can think about selling assets that are perhaps unproductive: paintings, unused second homes, heirloom jewelry that you never wear, perhaps a boat or a yacht. I have never owned a yacht, but I have owned several boats. I subscribe to the old saw that the second happiest day of one's life is the day one buys a new boat; the first happiest day is when one sells it! And while I am making a mild attempt at humor, let me also state that the sale of non-productive personal belongings does *not* include mothers-in-law, ex-spouses, present spouses, or children. You might sell an entrepreneurial business that has not been productive. Examine assets of this sort.

You might receive an inheritance. You might win the lottery!

In any event, do not put this book down. Keep reading. Finish the book! It will give you incentive to accumulate capital to start the Plan!

Some of you ask: "Why can't I borrow the $10,000?"

The answer here is easy, and it has already been given. The interest cost of your borrowing will largely offset the gain from the Plan. You will see that the Plan does include a leverage strategy, and this will be all the interest cost that the Plan allows. I have worked with numerous "for profit" endeavors that used borrowed money. To a large extent, that is what the banking business is all about. I believe that to leverage financial assets 100% and make a worthwhile positive return is the mark either of a person considerably smarter than anyone I have ever known or the luckiest person on earth. It may be possible in an inflationary scenario with real estate, energy-related assets, or precious metals. In Chapter 12 you will get some advice on how to do this, for a brief period and with maximum leverage. But over time, day in and year out, I believe it cannot be done.

Some of you say: "I already own stocks, bonds, and mutual funds in an amount over $10,000, and I meet all your requirements about savings and personal debt. Why can't I just contribute these to the Plan without selling them?"

A good question. There is an outside chance that some few of your presently owned stocks, bonds, and mutual funds will conform to the investment qualities and fit into the investment strategies that you will learn about in detail in Section V. So you will learn the answer for sure at that time. But in the meantime, you should proceed with the thought and assumption that you will have to sell all your present holdings, and pay applicable capital gains taxes, and come into the Plan with $10,000 cash minimum.

Still another person might ask: "I do not have $10,000 capital in cash, but I have some of it. And I do have an IRA (or a Keogh plan or a 401(K) plan with my employer) that is building up nicely. Can I count assets of this sort toward the capital requirement?"

The answer to this excellent question is "probably not" or "maybe" as to the IRA or Keogh. A further amplification gets fairly complicated, but the question is addressed in detail in Chapter 15. As to the 401(K) plan, the answer is "no." Chapter 15 will be helpful, and the asker of this question should read on.

Another good question might be: "I am a fairly wealthy person. I have well over $10,000 in cash in the bank. I own investment real estate, have an entrepreneurial interest in several businesses, and several large positions in stocks, bonds, and mutual funds that I just won't sell. Can I keep these activities and investments, and still participate in the Plan? And can

I start with more than $10,000?"

Absolutely, to both questions. All that is required is a minimum of $10,000 non-borrowed cash capital. And *any* amount over $10,000 is fine. Your portfolio will always be structured in terms of percent of assets allocated in the categories of stocks, bonds, and mutual funds. The results are to be measured in the same way. In other words, if $10,000 grows to $100,000 by long-term use of the Plan, in the same manner $500,000 will grow to $5,000,000 presuming the same investments over the same time period.

A CERTAIN INVESTOR TEMPERAMENT

I am not in any way a professional psychologist, but I believe my experience qualifies me to make certain judgments on personality characteristics that will go a long way toward contributing to your ability to make the Plan a success. And conversely, I believe I know certain of these characteristics that will doom the Plan to varying degrees of failure.

You must be able to put events into a long-term time perspective. This is difficult for some people. Results must be achieved *now*. Or next week. Or next month. Or at the very latest next year. These people lack the patience that is required. It has already been said the Plan's time frame is one of years and decades. You will be surprised how quickly they pass!

A corollary to the requirement of long-term patience is the requirement to see and interpret events away from what I call the "manic-depressive" syndrome. When good things happen, one tends to take them for granted, sometimes getting sloppy in disciplined adherence to the plan that is in effect, or to say "I'm going to quit while I'm ahead," thereby losing the long-term benefit. And when bad things happen, the discouragement, depression, or even despair tends to lead one to a relatively quick conclusion "What am I doing here? This is for the birds!" And then one abandons the plan. The "manic-depressive" syndrome must be totally avoided.

A few pages ago you learned quite a bit about me. For thirty years I have been through thick and thin in the financial markets. I absolutely believe in the Plan this book promulgates. You must join me in my belief that the Plan works against all types and conditions of markets, domestic and international events, and the various economic scenarios. You must adapt a deep sense of historical perspective. Hopefully, Section III will give you some tools for this. It deals largely with history, and remember: I am an old History major!

And then there are those among you who I call the "one investment" person. These are people who are, in a psychological sense, deeply committed to one investment area, and even if the investment area is stocks, bonds and mutual funds, they will concentrate on only one or two specific investments in the total spectrum. This psychological condition has been enhanced in recent years by the great success many of these people have had with this psychology. Let's examine it more closely.

Some of you are committed to real estate as an investment. This may take the form of commercial or residential property for income and appreciation, and until recently (but no more) for large tax benefits. Or building "spec" houses. Or the entrepreneurial activity of totally developing large real estate projects. Or "sitting on" unimproved land for appreciation. I have seen many people make veritable fortunes in these activities (I once tried the latter one myself, but did not make a fortune), and I do not disparage them. But it is not the name of my game nor is it the subject of this book. Those of you who have a deep psychological commitment to real estate as your primary investment method for growing capital will probably have some problems with the concepts, techniques, investment vehicles and strategies our Plan uses. You are, however, now aware of my caveat and you are most welcome as participants.

The same could be said of the basic entrepreneurs who run their own businesses. They will be tempted to siphon capital from the Plan for a variety of reasons, or they will say "I will make my investments in the Plan only in my own areas of expertise. I will select stocks (to the total exclusion of others) that I really know something about." This is a satisfactory approach only up to a very short point. The success of the Plan depends upon *broad* diversification. Sometimes I think that the successful entrepreneur, almost by definition, attains his success by "second guessing." He needs to be totally "in control." Again, the entrepreneurs of the world are encouraged to come aboard the Plan, but they also have a caveat: the Plan requires great long-term discipline in adhering to it. The Plan itself is really "in control."

Another category that must be addressed is life insurance. There are many people (although not as many as 20 or 30 years ago) who build their financial planning largely around life insurance policies. Most of us are familiar with the type of life insurance policy that is generically called an *endowment* policy, where the premiums are used to provide a death benefit and also a cash build-up which is called a cash surrender value, and then paid-up insurance. (Author's Personal Aside: I have owned many of these policies but I long ago cashed them in and discontinued them.) You should seriously consider cashing them in with the surrender proceeds becoming a possible source of capital for the Plan.

These days there are two newer types of life insurance that are investment and even market related. One is called a *variable* life policy, or a variable *annuity* policy, where the benefits are related to the changes in market values that the life insurance company's management produces by and with its investments. It is similar to (but not equal to) a mutual fund plus a death benefit. Then there is the *single payment deferred annuity,* where the policy owner places a lump sum of cash with the insurance company. This sum of cash grows at a compounded floating rate of interest, usually with an established "floor," and there is a death benefit which is an amount greater than the initial lump sum, the amount depending on age at time of purchase. This type of life insurance can also be purchased with a provision that makes its benefits variable, depending on market performance. This type of life insurance policy is not too bad. One advantage on the SPDA policies, as they are called in the trade, is that up until now the growth of the corpus is tax-free during the period of compounding. (There is a discussion in Congress, as this is being written, which might very well remove the tax-free provision.) But there are, in my opinion, certain characteristics of these market-oriented life insurance policies that make them unsuitable investments for our Plan. There is frequently *not* total liquidity, and there frequently *are* large sales commissions and management fees, some of which are rather well hidden. And I have seen very few of these policies that have produced a total return which is competitive with those of other mutual funds that are available at lower cost. Life insurance salesman tend to be the very best salesmen in the world, and they can be very persuasive in selling you on the merits of their company's investment plans. Simply put, our Plan is a lot better than theirs.

And while on the subject of life insurance, there is, of course, *term* insurance. These policies are low cost, and they simply provide a death benefit. Pure and simple. These policies can and should be used by those of you with family responsibilities so that if the proverbial streetcar runs you over, and it might (for all of us walk a thin line), your family will have money available for its living expenses over a period of many years. The cost of these policies is a living expense in the same category as food, clothing, and shelter. Term life insurance is in no way an ingredient in *your* capital formation. This Plan, our Plan, is to provide for you while *you* are alive!

Now we can turn to certain investor temperaments that *are* related to financial investments - stocks, bonds, and mutual funds. Here, too, you must be flexible enough to adapt to the Plan's inflexibility!

Many investors lack the mental capacity to diversify their investments to the extent that the Plan requires.

They might believe that bonds are the only suitable investment, that stocks are "too risky." I say that this is *sheer and utter nonsense!* Section V will give my detailed reasons for this position.

Many investors might say "I cannot be trusted to pick my own stocks. I will buy only mutual funds." This is a much more appropriate temperament than the one described in the previous paragraph, but it cannot be adapted to the Plan. In Chapter 10 and following Chapters you will see why.

Many investors choose their investments only because the dividend-related or interest-related current yield on the investment is high, and they get nice checks in the mail. This is worse than nonsense, it is *total baloney,* and in Chapter 3 and nearly every following Chapter you will see why.

Many investors, for various good reasons, are committed to what I call "single stock" investing. This situation frequently comes about by reason of employment, where the investor invests only in the company where he or she works. Stock options and employee stock purchase plans play a role in this. Or it comes about by reason of geography, where a particular company is local and well known, easy to follow, and where the investor feels he might be privy to "inside" information. Or it comes about by reason of inheritance. Many very wealthy people walk the streets today whose wealth has developed in this way. (Author's Personal Aside: I believe I could write another book, as lengthy as this one, which chronicled these stories using *only* the case histories of people *I personally know!*) It would be easy for me to say simply that these people are lucky. Yes, they *are* lucky. There is obvious risk in having all your chips on the same number, all your eggs in the same basket.

This book is about a Plan that vastly improves the odds for accumulating wealth. We do not hear too much about the many people who lacked diversification, although the Hunts and Connallys have recently been seen in the bankruptcy courthouses. And down the street from where I live a man named Leo Goodwin went bankrupt for about $70 million in 1976 when the large auto insurance company his father had founded all of a sudden had large underwriting losses and saw its stock go from 55 to 2, and the SEC suspended trading for two months. I remember this one well: I was one of Leo's many bankers, and had made loans in support of his rather unsuccessful entrepreneurial ventures that were collateralized by his inherited insurance company stock. We eventually came out whole, but Leo Goodwin was ruined. It was both a real mess and an attorneys' bonanza. In any event, many very intelligent people would argue the point with me that "single stock" investing is perfectly all right if one knows what he is doing. I would argue right back that diversification is essential and vastly improves the odds. And I believe I would win the debate.

Another investor temperament is displayed by the "trader." The trader uses stocks, options, futures, bonds, and now even mutual funds with hourly pricing. He or she hopes to buy low and sell high, or sell short high and buy back low, over periods of time ranging from a few minutes to a few weeks. I have seen and served dozens of these people. They are excellent commission generators for a broker! I have seen money doubled in a day, tripled in a week, quadrupled in a month. In our present computerized world the software whizzes and the market technicians have developed on-line programs that assist the traders with split-second readings on such things as stochastic oscillators, relative strength indices, moving average trendlines, compression ratios and expansion ratios, and more mathematical gobbledygook than Albert Einstein would have dreamed possible. The technical approach to investing, as opposed to the fundamental approach, does have a place, and we will address it in some of our strategies in Section V.

But I believe that it is easier to predict an investment's price for next year than it is for tomorrow or next week. For every successful trade that a trader has, the chances are excellent that he or she will have three, or five, or seven losers. I have never, *ever,* in a thirty year career, seen a trader consistently grow capital over anything resembling a long term. There is an inside joke in an investment firm. Broker A: "How is your trader doing?" Broker B: "Well, two out of three is not bad." Broker A: "What do you mean?" Broker B: "The firm is making money, and I am making money!" Those of you who have a trader's temperament will have trouble grasping the long term, value oriented Investment Plan that this book offers. I hope you come aboard because our Plan can help you (or even save you!). But be aware that you will need to completely change your investment and market orientations.

One or two steps removed from the market traders are the groups of people who, with varying degrees of compulsiveness, believe capital can be grown via casino gambling, sports betting, pari-mutuel wagering, or buying large quantities of lottery tickets. The last sentence of the previous paragraph applies to these poor souls, in spades!

A CERTAIN INVESTMENT KNOWLEDGE

This book is not an investment primer.

On the other hand, it does not require that the reader, or participant in the Plan, have a Ph.D. in finance nor even anywhere near the knowledge required to pass the six-hour NASD Series 7 examination that a fledgling stockbroker must pass before he writes his first "buy" or "sell" ticket.

But I believe a certain basic level of investment knowledge is required. And, certainly, the more basic knowledge you have the better off you will be.

I am going to give you a test! It is a list of investment words, phrases, and acronyms. This book does not have a glossary, and I am presuming you know what these words, phrases, and acronyms mean. The list is not all-inclusive; it is a sample of what lies ahead. I want you to understand what you are reading - that is absolutely essential. I want you to honestly score yourself on the list. Check off the ones you are unsure of. Use a red pencil. I will advise you after you have scored yourself of some steps you might take if you have a lot of red marks.

Here we go with the list:

stock	call date and price
bond	a point (on a bond)
open-end fund	equity investment
closed-end fund	your equity or N/W
put	yearly range
option premium	front-end load
NASD	NYSE
S&P 500	NASDAQ
quarterly report	pink sheets
monthly statement	margin buying power
price-earnings ratio	margin loan value
EPS	CPI
debt-equity ratio	GNP

book value

cash account

margin account

at the market

limit order

GTC order

Moody rating

par value

basis point

yield to maturity

current yield

sector fund

bid and asked

price spread

futures market

futures contract

daily limit

stop loss order

yield spread

interest

dividend

cash flow

ROE

AMBAC and MBIA

"takeover" stock

sell short

index option

cold call (on the phone)

hedge

covered call writing

socialism

crash

market circuit breakers

foreign exchange

coupon rate

street name

book entry

ex-dividend

market multiple

research department

dealer

yield curve

balanced fund

growth fund

debit balance

credit balance

proxy

LBO

GO bond

revenue bond

investment grade

junk bond

default

EPS trend

Treasury Long Bond

P/E multiple

premium (bond)

discount (bond)

SIPC

"penny" firm

rear-end load

GNMA pass-through

NYSE member

program trading

global village

OPEC

SEC	zero coupon
Fed	quality of earnings
12 (b) 1	IPO
capital gains tax	Fed funds rate

How did you do? There were 100 on the list.

If you checked off fewer than 10 that you did not know or feel comfortable with, you are in good shape with good basic investment knowledge.

If you checked off from 11 to 20 on the list, you have satisfactory basic knowledge, but you would do well to investigate the meaning of those that you checked. I am sure the reference librarian at your local public library can refer you to an investment glossary that will be very helpful.

If you scored less than 80, my *strong* suggestion is to do one or both of the following:

Have your reference librarian refer you to one or several *recently published* books on the subject of basic investing, and read on this subject before proceeding further with this book. I frankly admit I have not read such a book for many years, so I can't help you with a current specific recommendation. Your librarian can!

And/or sign up for the next basic investment class at the adult/ vocational night school that is available in most communities. These are usually excellent. They are frequently taught by moonlighting stockbrokers who do it for two reasons: small extra income and large extra contacts, with potential clients like you!

Then come back, score yourself again on the list, and I'm certain you will be ready to proceed.

Because the journey awaits! You are on the verge of learning why and how you can grow your capital. The Seasoned Veteran is ready, and so are you!

Onward!

SECTION II.
THE HIGHWAYS

3
The Eighth Wonder
of the World

A very long time ago, in the centuries B.C. known as the Alexandrian
epoch of the Greek and Roman world, there were built a selection of seven
works of art and architecture that came to be known as the Seven Wonders
of the World. Only one of them survives to this day, the pyramids of Egypt,
but for their time and for many decades and even centuries after they were
built they were regarded with awe by all who looked at them and studied
their amazing detail. It was believed that there were no possible additions
that could be made to the list of Seven, that they were absolutely unique and
not subject to improvement or even duplication. They were truly Wonders.

As works of art and architecture that may or may not be true.

But there is in fact an Eighth Wonder of the World.

It is not made of stone, brick, or mortar. It is not crafted by artisans nor
designed by architects. And it is not subject to destruction by wind, fire,
earthquake, or armies, as were six of the ancient Seven.

Some would call it a concept. Others might call it a theory. The
Seasoned Veteran calls it a Fact, an Absolute Truth. In a moment I will tell
you what the Fact is. But first let me digress. I want to first build up to the
Fact and talk about lawn grasses.

During my years in the midwest I occasionally planted a lawn. I threw
grass seed on the prepared soil, trying to distribute it uniformly. After a

week or so of good temperature and diligent watering, from each tiny little seed a tiny little sprout would emerge across the area, and as they took root they got thicker and healthier. After a month or so I had a nice lawn.

I moved to south Florida in 1973 and bought a house. The lawn was pretty spotty. In fact, it was worse than that. There were wide areas, *very* wide areas, where there wasn't any grass at all.

One Saturday morning, I got up early and prepared the soil. I went to the garden store to buy some grass seed. The man at the garden store was very nice.

"I need some grass seed."

"We don't have any."

"Well, I'll go someplace else."

"What are you trying to do?"

"Well, my lawn has some bare places. Some very big bare places. I'm afraid I need to sow a lot of seed."

"Are you from up north?"

"Yes, I just moved here."

"I thought so."

Then there was silence. Finally, he said:

"Look. Down here the only place that grows grass from seed is the sod farm, and they know how to do it. Nearly all the grass down here is St. Augustine grass. It's different from Bluegrass which you had up north. Grass down here grows from runners. All you really need is a couple pieces of sod. The pieces are about 2' by 2'. Just put them down on your soil about every fifteen feet or so, water them, and the runners will start running and pretty soon you'll have a nice lawn. Maybe I'll get an invitation to come over for a game of croquet!"

I thanked him and bought several pieces of sod. I took them home and did as he said. Sure enough, after about a week little *runners* started emanating from all sides of the sod squares, about six inches apart. Pretty soon there were *runners* going out from the *runners*. Pretty soon I had a magnificent lawn.

It occurred to me I could have probably accomplished the same magnificent lawn from just one tiny piece of sod, presuming it was a healthy one to start with, watering conditions were good, and I had lots of time. In fact, over the years now that I have lived in south Florida I have indeed seen this happen. The *runners*, which incidentally are technically called *rhizomes,* really know how to grow!

We have all heard from earliest childhood that money does not grow on trees. Unfortunately, it does not grow from *rhizomes*, either.

But just as a beautiful, wide, thick, green, magnificent, award-winning lawn can be grown from a small piece of sod, so can money be grown from a small aggregate of capital.

That is the Fact! That is the Absolute Truth! That is the Eighth Wonder of the World!

THE CONCEPT OF COMPOUND INTEREST

In my high school years, back in the late Forties, I would have summer jobs. I recall that I worked two summers as a "gardener" for several friends of my mother. One summer I worked at an ice cream stand in a local park where the manager was a slightly older friend of mine. I was paid an hourly wage for these endeavors, somewhere around sixty to seventy cents per hour. I had virtually no living expenses, so I was able to save some money.

I established a passbook savings account at the local bank. The balance built up to several hundred dollars.

I soon became aware that the bank liked my deposits, or balances, so much that they paid me for them. They paid me *interest.* I believe the per annum interest rate they paid me was 1.00%, and they credited my account with interest every six months. There was a very complicated formula they used to determine on what specific balance they would compute my interest. It certainly wasn't an average daily balance. The 'cards were stacked' in their favor. I recall that any withdrawal was deducted very quickly, but a specific deposit wasn't credited until perhaps the first day of the next month. But I did have an asset on which I was enjoying a return, because the first time I came to the bank after six months, the teller would post a few cents of interest to my passbook balance.

I had an asset that was returning me 1.00%, compounded semi-annually.

You have seen that about fifteen years later, I became a professional banker. Over these years I became dimly aware that compound interest really meant that one got *interest on interest* when one had a compounding asset. And that this was really a pretty good thing. But I still didn't really have any conception of how good a thing it was.

Soon after I began my work as a professional banker in 1963, I got to know the man at the bank who was Vice President in charge of the mortgage loan department. He had worked there all his career. He was more than a seasoned veteran; he was a grizzled veteran, a year or so from retirement age. He was gruff; he was opinionated; he didn't have all that much time for me, but we did get to know each other. I noticed some rather interesting things about him. He drove a new Cadillac, trading his old one in every two years. He helped his grown children a lot. He vacationed for three weeks in Arizona. His wife had a mink coat. He had a savings account at the bank. One day I surreptitiously went over to the savings account ledgers and looked up his balance. It was very much higher than I expected.

Soon I felt I had gotten to know this man well enough to ask him a few questions. I said:

"Dick, you really seem to live pretty well. As far as I can see, you are not a speculator, trader, or investor in stocks or other things, and I'm pretty certain you aren't an embezzler. And you have lived all your life on a small town banker's salary. Do you mind my asking how you've done it?"

He looked at me and smiled.

"Until about five years ago, I lived very frugally. I saved a significant amount out of every paycheck for forty years. That's where the money has come from. But then, too, there's been *the compounding.* That has really helped an awful lot."

I will always remember him saying that. I began to seriously investigate what compounding is all about. I soon had a good grasp of it. I have continued my study of compounding every year as my career in finance has moved along. Every year, I have learned more about it and developed more respect for it.

Its power is absolutely awesome. *It is the Eighth Wonder of the World.* Here is how it works:

Let's use a savings account that starts out with $100.00. Interest is 5.00% compounded annually. No deposits or withdrawals are made for ten years.

The balance is $105.00 at the end of the first year.

During the second year, interest is figured on $105.00, so that at the end of the year the interest credited is $5.25, making the balance $110.25.

During the third year, the interest is figured on $110.25 and it is $5.51, so at the end of three years the balance is $115.76.

And so on.

At the end of the tenth year, the principal balance stands at $162.89.

In this exercise, the interest rate has produced $50.00, which is of course 5.00% on $100.00 for ten years.

And the annual compounding has produced the extra $12.89.

This may not sound like any great big deal to you. But it is. It is 12.89% of what we started out with, and that is significant. But even more significant, it is the $12.89 that is now part of principal that will itself earn interest over the next time periods that is even more significant.

This example has been 5.00% compounded annually.

In our search for portfolio power, we will do better than that.

Let's change it to 15.00% compounded annually, and see what happens.

At the end of one year, the balance is $115.00.

At the end of three years, the balance is $152.09.

At the end of five years, the balance is $201.13 (doubling our initial capital).

And at the end of ten years, the balance is $404.57 (quadrupling our initial capital).

In this exercise, the increase of $304.57 has come $150.00 from the interest rate (15.00% on $100.00 for ten years) and $154.57 from the compounding! More has been made from the compounding than from the interest rate!

Let's now take the same exercise out *thirty* years, at 15.00% compounded annually.

Our $100.00 turns into $6,621.10! $450.00 of the $6,521.10 increase has come form the interest rate, and *$6,071.10 has come from the compounding!*

We are now at a point where the Seasoned Veteran will state the Fact, the Absolute Truth:

An amount of principal will grow at a compound rate of interest. The higher the interest rate, the better. The faster the compounding, the better. There comes a time, however, when the *compounding* of the interest rate becomes more important than the interest rate itself. Once that point in time is reached, the growth of principal becomes vastly faster than an arithmetic progression. The longer the principal is left to grow, the better.

This seems like a good time to give you a tool that will be of small mechanical help in connection with our effort to grow capital. It is a way to calculate how fast money will double at a certain rate of interest, and it is quite accurate. It is called The Rule of 72. It states:

Divide the rate of interest into 72 to find out the number of years the initial principal will double.

At 10.00%, principal will double in 7.2 years; at 12.00%, 6 years; at 16.00%, 4.5 years.

The Rule of 72 is only to be used to determine when principal will double. It cannot be used to determine when principal will triple or quadruple. In these equations the compounding becomes increasingly more important than the rate itself, and the Rule of 72 is increasingly inaccurate.

THE CONCEPT OF TOTAL RETURN

It is apparent from our just-completed discussion of compound interest that the principal would not grow as well or as fast if withdrawals were made from it along the way. Conversely, it will grow better and faster if additions are made to it along the way.

It is also apparent that *time* in the absolute sense is very important. The longer the time frame, the better.

Now we are in position to take our concepts a step or two further.

The previous discussion entirely used a savings account for an example. The interest was added to the savings account every time it was paid. Further, there was no change in the *market price* of the asset. A dollar was a dollar and is a dollar (although one can argue inflation is a factor; this is true, but it is too pedantic for our discussion right now.) Let's consider a concept where changing market price is an added factor. And let's assume that interest is any cash return the asset "throws-off." It might be interest or it might be dividends. And let's assume our objective with this asset is to grow capital from its employment.

We are at a point where we can look at a definition of total return, break it down so that we understand it for certain, and then use examples to show how it works.

The definition is:

The total return of an invested asset is the arithmetic result of its cash "throw-off" and the fluctuation of its price in the marketplace. It is expressed as an annualized percentage from a point in time that is a fixed starting place. Its parts can be either "realized" or "computational."

PLEASE! DON'T LEAVE ME! It is not that complicated!

Let's break it down.

Cash "throw-off" is either interest or dividends that the asset pays. It is "realized," and unless the "throw-off" is interest from a municipal bond, it creates a *taxable event*.

The fluctuations in the market price are easy to understand. They create a *taxable event* only when the asset is sold. A capital gain or loss is then "realized." Otherwise, it is "computational."

The best way to positively understand all of this is to use examples. Please get out your pocket calculators and follow along with me.

In all examples to follow, the asset starts out with a market price of

$1,000 on January 1 of any year, and it is *not* a municipal bond.
Let's go!

Example 1. The asset pays dividends of $50 the first year and is sold on December 31 of the first year for $1,100. The total return is 15.00%, and it has all been realized.

Example 2. The asset pays dividends of $50 the first year, and is still owned on December 31 when its market price is $1,100. The total return is 15.00%, of which 5.00% has been realized and 10.00% is computational. In other words, income taxes must be paid on the 5.00% *but not on the 10.00%*.

Example 3. The asset pays dividends of $50 the first year, and is sold on December 31 for $900. The total return is a *negative* 5.00%, all of which has been realized.

Example 4. The asset pays dividends of $50 the first year and $75 the second year. It is sold on December 31 of the second year for $1,225. This asset has produced a total return over the two year period of 35.00%, or 17.50% per annum. 2.50% of this has been realized in the first year and 15.00% has been realized in the second year.

Example 5. This asset has no cash "throw-off" whatsoever. It has a market value of $1,100 at the end of the first year, $1,200 at the end of the second year, and $1,400 at the end of the third year, when it is sold. The total return is a computational 10.00% the first year; a computational 9.09% the second year, and a computational 16.67% the third year. The average *annual* return has been 11.92% for three years, which has been realized at the end of the third year.

Example 6. The asset in Example 5 does pay a $50 cash dividend each year. Everything else is the same. The asset has a total return of 15.00% the first year (5.00% realized and 10.00% computational); a total return of 13.63% the second year (4.54% realized and 9.09% computational); and a total return of 20.84% the third year (4.17% realized and 16.67% computational). The sale at the end of the third year creates a realization, or taxable event, on the parts of the total return that had previously been computational. This asset has had an average annual total return of 16.47%, and at the end of the third year it has been fully realized.

Example 7. The asset pays $100 in cash "throw-off" each year for five years. The market price does not change at all until the end of the fifth year, when it goes down to $900 and is then sold. This asset has produced a 10.00% realized total return each year for the first four years. In the last year there is a zero total return. The average annual total return of the asset over the five year period is 8.00%, even though it is finally sold at a capital loss.

Example 8. The asset pays $50 in cash "throw-off" each year for two years. The market price is $1,300 at the end of the first year, and $2,000 at the end of the second year, when it is sold. The total return is 35.00% the first year (5.00% realized and 30.00% computational) and the total return is 57.70% the second year (3.85% realized and 53.85% computational). This asset has produced an average annual total return of 55.00%, all of it now realized. Notice how the average annual total return is higher than the arithmetic average of the two years taken individually. That is *compounding* at work!

Now let's change the scenario.

We now have a *portfolio* of assets (which does *not* include any municipal bonds). The portfolio has a total market value of $100,000 on January 1 of any year, as a starting point. The individual assets of the portfolio are all "long" in an account at an investment brokerage firm. All of the cash "throw-off" produced by the assets is credited to a money market fund *which is part of the portfolio*. The proceeds of all asset sales are credited likewise. Any new assets purchased are paid for from the money market fund. And both income and capital gains will be taxed at 30%, just to pick a number.

And very importantly, the purpose of this portfolio is to grow capital for its owner.

Example 1. The portfolio has produced a cash "throw-off" of $5,000 during the year. Nothing has been sold or purchased. The owner has made no cash or securities additions nor has he made any withdrawals. On December 31 of the first year the market value of the assets in the portfolio add up to $120,000. This portfolio has had a total return of 20.00% during the year, 5.00% realized for tax purposes and 15.00% computational. After paying taxes on the realized portion, the after-tax total return is 18.50%, which is available for compounding the next year.

Example 2. Everything is exactly the same as in Example 1, except that the owner of the portfolio decides on December 30 to withdraw $30,000 from the money market fund portion of the portfolio so that he or she can take a trip around the world. This withdrawal means that the portfolio stands at $90,000 on December 31, and after paying taxes of $1,500 the next April 15 (30% of the $5,000 "throw-off"), the bottom line is that the portfolio had an after-tax total return of a *negative* 11.50% for the year.

We cannot grow capital in that manner! At least not for that year.

Example 3. The portfolio "throw-off" is $10,000. Individual assets have been bought and sold during the year creating net realized capital gains of $10,000. No cash withdrawals have been made. The market value of the assets on December 31 is $120,000. After paying taxes of 30% on $20,000 ($10,000 "throw-off" plus $10,000 realized capital gains) the portfolio has had an after-tax total return of 14.00%, which is available for compounding next year.

Example 4.   Everything is the same as Example 3, except there have been no purchases or sales. Except for receiving the cash "throw-off," the portfolio has been dormant all year. The after-tax total return is 17.00% ($10,000 minus income taxes plus $10,000 unrealized appreciation on which no taxes need be paid).

Example 5.   The portfolio consists of growth stocks that pay no dividend whatever. There is no "throw-off." The portfolio is dormant all year. The market value on December 31 is $140,000. The return is 40.00%, and all of it is computational; all of it is available for compounding next year.

Example 6.   The portfolio is all invested in high yield, or "junk," corporate bonds that have a coupon interest rate of 15.00%. On December 31, the portfolio has a market value of $115,000. We can immediately see there was no price appreciation or depreciation at all. All of the market value increase came from "throw-off," which is taxable. The portfolio has an after-tax total return of 10.50%.

Example 7.   The portfolio has no "throw-off" and increases in price contribute to a total market value of $110,000 on December 30. On December 31 the owner makes a cash addition of $10,000 in new money. The portfolio has had a computational 10.00% total return from performance, and the cash addition has the effect of making the total return a computational 20.00% in terms of compounding for the next time period.

Example 8.   The portfolio has a "throw-off" of $7,000. The owner needs cash for living expenses and makes regular monthly withdrawals of $500 each month. On December 31 the market value of the portfolio is $110,000.

This portfolio situation is very important to analyze in detail. The owner has used 86% of the income to live on ($6,000 out of $7,000). Still, the portfolio has had a total return of 10.00% for the year, and after paying taxes of 2.10% (30% of the $7,000 "throw-off"), the after-tax return is 7.90% which is available for compounding next year.

Example 9. There is cash "throw-off" of $5,000. It is a particularly active year for portfolio turnover. Long-term gains of $31,000 are realized and long-term losses of $16,000 are also realized. The owner withdraws $10,000 cash in June, and later makes a "new money" contribution of $5,000. On December 31, the market value of the portfolio is $125,000.

This portfolio has had a before-tax total return of 25.00%. Taxes (at 30% of $5,000 "throw-off" plus $15,000 net realized capital gains) will take away 6.00%, leaving the after-tax total return at 19.00%, available for next year's compounding. The cash withdrawal and addition are both reflected in the final December 31 market value.

DRAWING SOME
VERY IMPORTANT CONCLUSIONS

You have been good students! I'm sure some of the material was tough going for some of you. And very easy for others.

We are ready to draw some very important conclusions. You should be mentally prepared to agree with the Seasoned Veteran that:

(1) Compounding is very powerful, similar to an absolutely dependable law of nature.

(2) Compounding works best the longer the period of time.

(3) Total return is what we are trying to compound.

(4) Taxes must frequently be paid on a portion of the total return but not on all of it. There is an important difference between realized total return and computational total return.

(5) The fewer taxes we have to pay on our total return, the more we have available for the next period of compounding.

(6)   Our individual assets should be entirely regarded as one single entity, or portfolio, domiciled at an investment firm, which can be regarded as the "vehicle" for compounding.

(7)   All cash "throw-off" by the individual assets, and all new cash contributed by the owner, are credits to the portfolio vehicle. All cash withdrawals, for whatever purpose, are debits to the same portfolio vehicle.

(8)   A cash withdrawal from the vehicle has the same impact on total return and compounding as an after-tax capital loss. A cash infusion to the vehicle has the same impact as an after-tax capital gain.

(9)   When all assets of the portfolio vehicle are publicly traded marketable securities, the owner will always be able to determine the exact current market valuation and know exactly how fast the vehicle is going and growing.

(10) We have, in fact, discovered the Eighth Wonder of the World.

Onward! This gets much better!!

4
Indians and Opportunities: The Magic Number

A Parable

The place was Boston, and the time was the early 1840's.

Averill and Archibald were both 33 years old, and they were scions of two of Boston's leading families. They had been friends since childhood and had been classmates at Harvard, each of them graduating in the Class of 1831. They were bright, attractive, gregarious, well-dressed, and had no problem securing the wonderful companionship of both genders.

They were well connected through their families, and it had been no problem for both Averill and Archibald to secure positions in the prosperous local economy, one of them in the maritime trade and the other in the new textile manufacturing industry. In their leisure they dabbled in the flowering downtown musical and theatrical activities. They had income from their employment, and in addition a generous stipend from their parents, who were very proud. Their futures seemed assured.

But, alas, it was not to be. For Averill and Archibald developed an extreme fondness for the brightest gaslights in Boston. They caroused. They wenched. They stayed out very late at night. They embarrassed their friends. They overspent their incomes. They were, to their horror, involved in some paternity-related unpleasantness. They were not strangers to the local constabulary.

And soon it happened that they lost their employment situations. They attempted several entrepreneurial ventures, one of them as partners, but everything failed. Everything failed miserably.

Over time their parents became distraught, and finally, with regret, the announcement was made by both sets of parents that effective July 1, 1843, the monthly parental allowances to Averill and Archibald would cease entirely.

One morning in late May, Averill and Archibald were in their favorite taproom having, as was their wont, a little taste of the hair of the dog that had bitten them rather severely until the early hours of the present day. They were contemplating the inequities of the world in general and the disaster that would befall them, in a financial sense, five weeks hence when there would be no income. Unless a miracle occurred.

The miracle began occurring at precisely 11:35 A.M.

Into the taproom walked a man that Averill and Archibald had never seen before. He was a stranger. He took up a bar stool next to them, and they noticed he was very peculiar in every respect. He was dressed in cowboy boots and a string tie. He had buckskin fringes on his waistcoat. He had weird jewelry and trinkets adorning his fingers and wrists. And he was not friendly. He had a strange focus to his eyes. After a moment, it was apparent to Averill and Archibald that the man had, attached to his belt under his waistcoat, a holster with an extremely large pistol in it. All of this was indeed unusual.

But the strangest thing about this man was his conversation, or lack of it. During the entire hour that he was in the taproom, he said only one thing, but he said it with regularity, to no one in particular, every sixty seconds. So he said it sixty times. And then he left.

The peculiar stranger had sixty times said: "There's a fortune to be made in Indian scalps."

This encounter made an enormous impression on Averill and Archibald. At first they chuckled over the weirdness and absurdity of the experience. *But then it hit them.* They ordered more ale. They discussed the possibility. They realized they had little to lose. The sense of adventure began to overtake them. They ordered more ale. They discussed the logistics. They organized a going-away party. They contemplated the nature of the expenditures they would make once their fortunes were in hand. They ordered more ale.

In the week that followed, they sold or gave away all their possessions, and outfitted themselves in western attire. They took riding lessons. They learned marksmanship. They bought a small tent and bedrolls, knapsacks, and canteens. They bought rifles, handguns, and large, very sharp hunting knives. They learned how to hunt small game. They learned how to skin a rabbit and a squirrel. They learned how to cook over an open fire.

And they practiced, with their newly acquired sharp hunting knives, the gruesome task that they were going to have to be soon performing, using up several dozen large cantaloupes in the process.

The adventure and their ultimate fortune was at hand!

Six weeks later, after an arduous journey by rail, steamboat, horseback, stagecoach, and the soles of their feet, Averill and Archibald were in remote South Dakota. They had not yet seen any Indians, but they knew they were close. They were in the land of the Sioux. They were very excited.

That evening, it was so beautiful, and the temperature so benign, that they decided to sleep under the stars, foregoing the shelter of their small tent. They cooked a rabbit dinner over their fire, enjoyed it to its bones, contemplated how close they were to acquiring their fortunes, and went to sleep in their bedrolls.

Archibald was the first to awake, just after dawn. He rose to his feet, and stretched. He blinked in the early light, and was amazed at what he saw. *Absolutely amazed.*

For he was surrounded by Indians. Twenty-five Indians formed a circle around him, strong young men with strange paint on their faces and long feathers stuck to their headbands. Each had a large knife in hand, clenched in a striking pose. Beyond this circle was another one, concentric with the first, with one hundred Indians similarly adorned and attired, although this group possessed spears with sharp points rather than knives. And then still another circle, with five hundred Indians, looking the same although these possessed bows and arrows, and each of them was taking an arrow from his quiver, looking directly at Archibald.

It occurred to Archibald that a large percentage of the entire Sioux nation was at hand, and he could barely contain his excitement. He reached down and shook his partner and companion. He tried to keep his voice as low as possible, but he was as excited as he had ever been in his thirty-three years.

"AVERILL! AVERILL! WAKE UP! WAKE UP! TODAY IS THE DAY WE GET RICH!!"

The story of Averill and Archibald is a nice little story. I first heard it only about a year ago, told by a friend at a time in a social evening when the group of friends were trying to prove to each other that each did know a cute and "clean" story or joke. Perhaps you have heard it before.

You may argue that it has nothing to do with our subject at hand.

But it definitely does. There are several morals to the story.

First of all, the two protagonists had everything going for them in their early careers. They had solid childhoods, even the proverbial silver spoon in their mouths. They each had an excellent formal education. They had the backing of family and friends. They had splendid career opportunities, one in trade and the other in manufacturing. They had an appreciation for the arts. They had the beginnings of extremely productive and satisfying lives.

But they got detoured. They did not establish solid priorities and measurable objectives. They did things that they probably knew were detrimental, but they thought that they as individuals were good enough that they could overcome. They liked to have fun. But it is difficult to have true fun when it involves lawsuits, criminality, and successive business failures, not to mention loss of family, employer, and peer group respect and support.

So they were in trouble. Financial trouble, family trouble, social trouble, career trouble, legal trouble, girlfriend trouble, even trouble with their health.

And then they saw an *opportunity*. But their analysis of it was dreadful. There is nothing wrong with the fact that it was presented under bizarre circumstances when they least expected it. But they lacked clear heads to analyze it. They did not have any knowledge of the man's background who presented the opportunity. It is certain that they did not have any knowledge of how the product, the Indian scalps, might be acquired. Their practice with the cantaloupes was scarcely a real life situation. They did not investigate the risks of the venture. They saw the potential reward, but they lacked a Plan.

The only thing they really had going for them was tremendous enthusiasm and spirit. And they truly wanted to make a fortune, to get rich.

Although we do not know for an absolute certainty how the parable ended that early morning in South Dakota, we can all make a guess that is very accurate. Because of their lack of organized planning and methodical analysis, the opportunity was, to put it mildly, not realized.

Now, how do we relate the parable and the morals that can be drawn from it to our specific situation.?

First, I do not mean in any way to equate you with the dire circumstance and recent history of Averill and Archibald as they sat in the taproom that morning. The comparison is hyperbolic to the largest degree! But all of us, as they did, miss major opportunities. All of us see our hopes and plans go awry. All of us get sidetracked in attaining our goals.

The idea of using capital to grow more capital is certainly not proprietary to the Seasoned Veteran. The idea has been around since Adam and Eve! But how easy it is for most of us to get confused, to try one thing that works only moderately or perhaps doesn't work at all, and then go on to another idea or thing. Or to achieve a success or two, and think how easy this is, only to then get careless and even sloppy and lose the successes and even then go backward a step or two. To feel that you have a lot of the tools, vehicles, concepts, and strategies, and even a grand master plan, but then things go a bit wrong, lack of confidence or even sheer fright sets in, we cannot see the forest for the trees (most of which seem to be falling down), and the entire plan, the noble vision, is lost in smoke. The capital that we are trying to grow looks like a patch of weeds. And then, to recoup, we feel we must take larger risks, which is almost always a mistake.

The Seasoned Veteran does not present himself to you as the stranger in the taproom did. I have attempted in the first Chapter to tell you quite a bit about myself, quite probably more than you wanted to hear. The reason is I have attempted to establish my professional qualifications. I have attempted to establish that I am neither a weirdo nor a charlatan. I am not a salesman, either, in this instance.

I am a professional who for thirty years has been in the business of helping other people with their money. As you have seen, I have worked with many different types of investments. And I have observed and studied many different investment marketplaces, where the prices of investments are determined mostly in accord with the law of supply and demand every working day around the clock and around the global village. I have been a student of history and a student of economics, both in formal learning environments and in the real world. I have acquired knowledge and facts and I have developed concepts, techniques, and strategies. I have seen economic expansions and economic recessions, and I believe there will be more of both. I have seen high interest rates and low interest rates, and I believe there will be more of both. I have seen inflation and disinflation, and I believe there will be more of both. I have seen bull markets and bear markets, and I believe there will be more of both. And I, like you, have seen a real honest-to-goodness Crash, and there will probably be more like it.

In short, I feel I have seen it all. And I don't believe I am surrounded by Indians, as were poor Averill and Archibald.

But like them, I believe I am surrounded by an unbelievable opportunity to get rich!

And you are, too!

The remainder of this book is my attempt to tell you specifically why and specifically how I believe a lot more capital can be grown.

It is time you ask: *"How much more capital?"*

OK. I am prepared to quantify.

The Seasoned Veteran believes that for the ten year period from 1990 to 1999 capital can be compounded at an average annual after-tax rate of 15.00% per annum. Some years will be better than that; some years will be worse; but that will be the average, at a minimum.

And the Seasoned Veteran believes that such an average annual after-tax compound rate of capital growth can be attained for the years beyond 2000, presuming the world and its civilization on earth performs about like it has since 1945, which now is far enough behind us to afford excellent historical perspectives.

But you say: "This Seasoned Veteran guy always wants to talk about percent! I want to talk about dollars. Good old-fashioned George Washingtons. What kind of dollars does 15.00% mean? Why is it such a Magic Number?"

OK again. That is a fair question. The answer is on the next page, where you will see the only Table that this book contains. It is a Table that shows what $1,000 will grow to if it can be compounded annually at 15.00% per annum for up to 50 years.

Take a good look at it. Study it closely. Spend five minutes with it. Put a paper clip on the top of the page and leave it there, so you can come back to it for quick reference. And for quick inspiration!

Is your question answered? I thought so! You have seen the Magic Number!

Onward! The journey has begun. We will now learn about the future by studying the past.

TABLE 1.

The effect on $1,000 of compounding annually at 15.00% per annum.

End of Year		End of Year	
1	$ 1,150	26	$ 37,857
2	1,322	27	43,535
3	1,521	28	50,066
4	1,749	29	57,575
5	2,011	30	66,211
6	2,313	31	76,144
7	2,660	32	87,565
8	3,059	33	100,700
9	3,518	34	115,805
10	4,046	35	133,176
11	4,652	36	153,152
12	5,350	37	176,125
13	6,152	38	202,543
14	7,075	39	232,925
15	8,137	40	267,864
16	9,358	41	308,043
17	10,761	42	354,250
18	12,375	43	407,387
19	14,232	44	468,495
20	16,368	45	538,769
21	18,821	46	619,585
22	21,645	47	712,522
23	24,891	48	819,401
24	28,625	49	942,311
25	32,919	50	1,083,657

SECTION III.
THE LESSONS OF HISTORY

5
The Past: 1776, 1945, 1954, 1980

I have never worked as a professional historian. Nor have I worked as a professional economist. But I was a very good student of both subjects for four intensive years at one of our leading universities, and have been a student of these subjects in the real world every day since graduating from the University thirty-four years ago.

For the purpose of what we are to accomplish, i.e. using financial instruments and markets to grow capital, it is imperative that we have a background on what has happened in the past so that we can make an intelligent forecast of what will happen in the future.

Specific events occurred in 1776, 1945, 1954, and 1980 that vastly and profoundly influence where we are today.

1776

In 1776, there were published two written documents that provide the framework for the very essence of our American Society as we have it today. These documents are in the realm of Absolute Truth.

One of the authors was a thirty-three year old patriot and wordsmith, by the name of Jefferson. His choice of language in the *Declaration of Independence* is a masterpiece of eloquence in stating the tenets and philosophies of our democratic society, where all men are created equal; where a God-given right exists to life, liberty, and the pursuit of happiness (think about that last word!); where the power of a government comes from all its people; where there are "Laws of Nature" which transcend everything and provide an objective standard against which the laws of men can be measured. These tenets and philosophies came to be embodied eleven years later in the U.S. Constitution, which with few amendments has provided our nation a structure for political stability for over 200 years. Our past, present, and future degrees of economic prosperity would not be possible without this. In the entire history of the world, no other country can match us over such a long period in consistent stability.

It is magnificent historical happenstance that absolutely simultaneous with Jefferson's writing, several thousand miles away in Glasgow, Scotland, a fifty-two year old Professor of Logic and Moral Philosophy was publishing a treatise called *An Inquiry Into The Nature and Causes of the Wealth of Nations*. His name was Adam Smith. Whereas feudalism had largely given way to mercantilism several hundred years before, Smith correctly and logically destroyed mercantilism by proving out theories which we know today as capitalism and free enterprise. He spoke of the division of labor in production; he provided a definition of capital in its several types; he pointed up the importance of productivity, competition, transportation, free trade without tariff, the law of supply and demand, and paper and metal money; theories of consumption; the existence of an 'invisible hand' that guides free markets toward societal betterment; the roles of ownership, management, and labor; the differences between subsistence, convenience, and luxury; the roles of urban centers and rural areas; the function of government in providing roads, bridges, armies, and education; and the role of taxation to pay for these. Smith's specific theories were very much on the table eleven years later in Philadelphia when our Constitution was drafted.

By the end of 1776, therefore, a capitalistic, free enterprise, democratic society had been defined. For over two hundred years since then entrepreneurs, investors, managers, and workers have been performing within this structure to provide themselves with subsistence, convenience, and luxury. It has by and large worked very well.

1945

The Seasoned Veteran now wants to take you to 1945. I was eleven years old during most of this year, but I remember it well. Franklin D. Roosevelt died on April 12. There are historians who will dispute this, but my statement is that on that day the Twelve Year Experiment with Socialism that this country had embarked upon with FDR's 1933 inauguration also died. The first week in May, the War in Europe ended. On August 6 an atomic bomb was dropped on Hiroshima, and three days later one was dropped on Nagasaki; on August 14 the Japanese surrendered and World War II was over.

The long awaited Post-War world was at hand. The serious problems were now behind us. The Depression was history. The New Deal was dead. Fascism and militarism had been crushed. We controlled the atomic bomb; it was our technology and our secret. Eager veterans returned to get educated at a grateful taxpayers' expense, have babies, and join the work force. Utopia was walking up to our front door.

So, what has happened in the years since 1945? Well, there have been a few problems. Quite a few problems. A veritable avalanche of problems.

Domestic Problems. Six recessions; the assassination of a President and several other national leaders of great symbolic importance; inflation at unprecedented levels; the largest companies paying 21.50% for short-term loans; race riots killing hundreds; the veritable demise of several of our largest industries to foreign competition; a scandal that toppled a President; monstrous federal budget and trade deficits; severe strikes and work stoppages; the worst stock market crash in our history; eight bear markets of various magnitude; Wall Street and White House leaders packed off to the slammer; the dangerous step of our government rescuing several of our largest private companies; imprudent lending by the leading banks, threatening to bankrupt them; high rates of alcoholism, drug addiction, and suicide; low personal savings and high personal debt; a national debt expanding tenfold; a Congress that has self-perpetuation as its major goal; double digit unemployment; ill-conceived handgun laws making our neighborhood streets run with blood; industrial and consumer pollution of the air, waters, and earth itself, with billions of conventionally unproductive dollars needed to cleanse the nation; a killer health epidemic, from out of nowhere; the impairment of the traditional family structure, with millions of children being raised in single-parent households; and there are more.

International Problems. Two large scale wars on the other side of the world that we didn't win; a cold war with an aggressive and powerful adversary, nuclear armed, whose structure of government and society is absolutely and diametrically opposed to ours; sovereign nations in the political control of terrorists, torturers, embezzlers, crooks, dope dealers, racists, and hate-obsessed lunatics; a Communist country, allied with our major adversary, located ninety miles from our shore for thirty of the years; nuclear technology in the hands of third-world countries; an eyeball-to-eyeball missile stand-off, our President against theirs; a well organized cartel controlling the world's supply and price of energy; sovereign nations unable to pay hundreds of billions in debts; a sovereign government in a large, populous nation that stubbornly continues policies of total racism, with the horrible oppression of about 80% of its citizens; a fanatic sovereign leader who kidnapped dozens of American diplomats for over a year, and who reigned until his death ten years later; inflation over 100% in many nations; wildly fluctuating currency exchange rates; our squadrons flying thousands of miles to try to kill a man who lives in a tent.

And so it goes in our Post War Utopia. Problems, problems, problems. Well, it could be worse. Somehow we have muddled through.

The Dow Jones Industrial Average closed on December 31, 1945 at 193. As this is written in Summer, 1989, it has gotten to 2752.

The Seasoned Veteran hopes the obvious point does not escape you.

1954

On November 29, 1954, a man named John M. Templeton did two things. He celebrated his forty-second birthday, and he started an open-end, diversified management investment company, or mutual fund, called the Templeton Growth Fund.*

The investment objective of this mutual fund, which is very much still in business, has never deviated. According to its Prospectus, it is "to provide long-term capital growth, which (it) seeks to achieve through a flexible policy of investing in stocks and debt obligations of companies and governments of any nation. Any income realized will be incidental."

Of humble and deeply religious Tennessee origins, Templeton had been a scholarship student at Yale, graduating *summa cum laude*. He was then a Rhodes Scholar at pre-war Oxford and came back to work for several years at a geophysical firm in Texas. In 1940 he went to Wall Street and, with several partners, hung out his shingle as an investment counselor.

Templeton was aware that the open-end mutual fund industry had started in this country in 1924. A handful of operating funds had survived the Depression with some distinction, and this same handful had come under well-conceived federal regulation, and in fact received increased credibility, with the passage of the Investment Company Act of 1940 (which, incidentally and importantly, is still operative today).

The Seasoned Veteran has been aware of the Templeton philosophy of investing only since early 1979, when I made my first investment, after careful study, in shares of the Templeton Growth Fund. It is a remarkably simple investment philosophy. John Templeton, now age seventy-six,

---

*Author's Note: The Templeton Growth Fund is being mentioned in this and subsequent Chapters only as a specific example of the successful implementation of an investment philosophy and plan over a long-term period. The author has no direct business involvement whatsoever with the Templeton family of mutual funds, and the laudatory mention of it in this book is in no way intended to serve as a current recommendation for purchase of shares in any Templeton-related investment. The author's wife and step-daughter do own shares in Templeton Growth Fund.

searches the world for what he considers to be investment bargains. His definition of a bargain is an investment whose price is cheap relative to its prospects. He is aware that markets are cyclical, that there will be bull markets and bear markets, that there will be inflation and disinflation, that there will be times when stocks are cheap versus bonds, and *vice versa*, and that value will ultimately be recognized by higher prices in the marketplace. He holds investments as long as he considers they are bargains, and when they are not bargains any longer (for whatever reason) he sells them and looks for other bargains. He tends to accumulate stocks of well chosen companies during bear markets when pessimism abounds, and phase out of them during bull markets, when optimism is unbridled.

He has a global perspective, in recent years favoring the U.S., Australia, Canada, and England. He cashed out of Japan several years ago. In recent years he has been invested from 65% to 90% in stocks and from 10% to 35% in bonds. His bonds are either country bonds, issued by sovereign governments, or highest-rated corporate and utility bonds. His investments are always extremely carefully researched by him and his staff, and selections are made from literally thousands of candidates (remember, he is looking at every marketplace worldwide). He is constantly reviewing and keeping track of things. He keeps his total operating expenses at about 0.75% of total assets every year.

Today there are 26 industry groups for 150 stocks from 18 countries, and 25 bonds issued in five countries. It all adds up to about $2.1 billion of investments. For the past five years the portfolio turnover rate has averaged about 13% per year.

We are told that there are several investors who purchased shares in Templeton Growth Fund on day one, November 29, 1954, and have never sold them, reinvesting all cash dividends and capital gains distributions in additional shares along the way. They paid a "full load" sales commission on their original purchase. There have been five years out of thirty-four when these investors have suffered their adjusted net asset values going down, with the decreases ranging from 1% to 14% in these years. During 1987, the year of the recent Crash, the net asset value was actually up 3% for the year, although there was a decrease of 31% from the August high to the October low.

The point of the above paragraph is to show that even the best investments are not one-way streets. In fact, the performance of the Templeton Growth Fund has never, in any single year, ranked it the Number One performer in its category. But it is usually in the top third, and when ranked over longer time frames, its relative peer group performance gets better and better.

Onward! To the bottom line on the Templeton story. We are not told the size of the original investments that the Templeton Growth Fund investors made who bought shares on November 29, 1954, and reinvested all cash distributions in additional shares, and still own all their shares today. But let us suppose that it was $10,000 (which meant that $9,225 went to work, because the investor paid a full-load 7.75% sales commission to his broker). If this investor decided on June 30, 1989, to call his broker and liquidate all his shares, *he would receive a check on settlement date for $1,170,091.10.*

Again, I think I've made my point. From November, 1954, to June, 1989, the DJIA went from 380 to 2440, up about 642%. John Templeton has dramatically proven that market averages, over a very long period of time, can be substantially improved upon. A well-researched, well-managed balanced portfolio of extremely diversified stocks and bonds, dedicated to growth of capital and total return as opposed to current income, and *patiently owned over a long period of time,* went up 11,700%.

This is about 15% per year, compounded annually. It is our Magic Number!

1980

The Seasoned Veteran remembers being glued to the TV the horrible weekend of November 22, 1963, when John F. Kennedy was shot. Henry Cabot Lodge was Ambassador to South Vietnam at the time, and on the

Sunday of that weekend he was interviewed at the Washington Airport as he arrived from his post to attend JFK's funeral. He told us something that I was only dimly aware of, that there was a civil war going on in Vietnam but that, thankfully, he thought it would soon be over. He was soon proven to be very wrong. Two days earlier Lyndon B. Johnson had become President, and within only a few months three things happened: (1) The Great Society, with massive and expensive social entitlements, was underway; (2) the escalation of U.S. military involvement in the Vietnamese civil war, leading to another massive federal expense, was underway; and (3) the Tax Reduction Act of 1964 was passed, which of course meant that our country was putting itself in the position of a dreamer. Annual federal budget deficits, which had previously in the postwar period been either non-existent or inconsequential, became accepted as night follows day. The federal budget deficit in 1968 was over $25 billion, compared to a small surplus in 1960.

Deficits must always be financed, one way or another, and in most cases this is done by borrowing. And one borrower must compete with the next borrower for the funds that are available, and with increased demand and constant or reduced supply, the price goes up: the price of a loan is its interest rate. The federal government thus became a big player contributing mightily to demand as a borrower in the marketplace.

Let's look at the New York Prime Rate as an index of how interest rates have behaved in our recent history.

From 1920 to 1929 there were nine changes in the Prime Rate, ranging between 3.75% and 6.00%.

From 1930 to 1939 there were three changes in the Prime Rate and it ranged between 1.50% and 3.50%. (It was constant at 1.50% from 1933 to 1947. The economic policies of the New Deal did not contribute to a free marketplace, and credit virtually dried up during the Depression.)

From 1940 to 1949 there were two changes in the Prime Rate and it ranged between 1.50% and 2.00%. (There were some federal controls on interest rates during this period in order to finance World War II and the subsequent readjustment from a wartime to a peacetime economy.)

From 1950 to 1959 there were sixteen changes in the Prime Rate and it ranged between 2.00% and 5.00%. (The Seasoned Veteran distinctly remembers when he was a stockbroker trainee in the summer of 1959 and the U.S. Treasury issued a Treasury Note, due in five years with a coupon interest rate at 5.00%. The Magic Fives, they were called! The seasoned veterans of that time, whom I regarded with some awe, felt that it was the arrival of the millennium. It was, in fact, a significant milestone.)

Then, in the period we have been looking at, from 1960 to 1969, there were nineteen changes in the Prime Rate and it ranged between 4.50% and 8.00%.

The Seasoned Veteran, as you have read, was a commercial banker during the period 1963 to 1982. The first 10 years were an extremely interesting time in banking, and for me to be in it.

I began to learn, for the first time, the real and tremendous power of compound interest, or better put, a compound rate of total return.

I began to learn about interest rate volatility, its challenges, pitfalls, and best of all, opportunities.

I learned for certain that a loan, or a bond (because a bond is nothing more than a loan obligation of its issuer), is not worth anything unless the borrower or issuer has the wherewithal to pay the interest along the way and then pay the principal in full at its maturity.

I saw the emergence of the small private investor as a player in the U.S. Treasury securities market, because as interest rates on these securities went above what bank deposits were allowed by law to pay, little old ladies came in from the street and asked me "How do I buy a Treasury?" Before, Treasury securities for almost all individuals meant either War Bonds or Series E and Series H Savings Bonds. (Savings Bonds in 1942-45 were called War Bonds. School children kept books of stamps, bought for dimes and quarters, and when $18.75 of stamps was accumulated, the book was exchanged for a $25 discounted Bond. This was my first exposure to the vast U.S. Treasuries market!) Only banks, institutions, and extremely wealthy individuals bought and traded Bills, Notes, and Bonds. A new word, financial 'disintermediation,' was coined.

I learned that there are only three ways a nongovernment loan can be paid: from income; from selling assets; or from financing elsewhere. A government has a fourth way to pay: it can print up new paper money, debasing the currency and creating inflation.

I served on Trust Investment Committees, and for the first time began to develop some theories, good and bad, on structuring and managing investment portfolios.

I saw what was happening to LBJ's "Guns and Butter" economic program, and our country as a result of it, and began to be aware that massive and frequent economic change was becoming the order of the day, and that one needed to adapt to it.

I saw the problems of the Penn Centrals, Lockheeds, and New York City, once proud and sound financial entities, and how isolated disasters could happen, and how they could possibly feed upon themselves, interrelate, and add up to total disaster.

But the most important thing I saw and learned about was inflation.

I certainly knew something was going on because in my career as a bank officer I was getting nice percentage salary increases each year, but these were not being reflected in my checkbook's ability to keep up with the cost of the goods and services that I and my family needed each month. The U.S. Bureau of Labor Statistics very accurately gives us some figures. Assuming that $1.00 in 1967 actually bought $1.00 worth of goods and services, the same $1.00 back in 1960 would have bought $1.13 of goods and services. But in 1970 the 1967 dollar only bought $0.86 of goods and services; by 1975 it bought only $0.62 of goods and services; and by the end of the decade in 1979 the 1967 dollar bought only $0.46 of goods and services. Then in 1980 the figure became $0.40, and in 1981 it was $0.37.

Expressed another way, inflation averaged 1.3% per year 1960-1965; it averaged 4.2% per year 1966-1970; it averaged 6.8% per year 1971-1975; and it averaged 8.9% per year 1976-1980. It hit 11.3% in 1979,

13.5% in 1980, and was 10.4% in 1981.

For all kinds of good reasons that professional economists love to pontificate about (for a primary reason that they get paid rather well for doing so!), it is very difficult for an economy to grow when inflation is dominant and rampant. Recovering from a recession in 1974-1975, the gross national product grew in inflation-adjusted terms about 5% in each of 1976, 1977 and 1978. But when inflation hit double digits in 1979-1982, the inflation adjusted GNP rate of growth was up only 2.8% in 1979, down 0.4% in 1980, and up only 1.9% in 1981. Unemployment as a percentage of the national workforce crossed over into double digits.

Dramatic changes were occurring, almost all of them bad.

Let's go back several pages and remember that the New York Prime Rate changed 19 times in the Sixties, ranging between 4.50% and 8.00%.

In the decade of the Seventies, the New York Prime Rate was changed *118 times*, and it ranged from 5.00% up to 15.75%.

Then in 1980 *alone* there were 38 changes and the Prime Rate was 11.00% at its lowest and *21.50%* at its highest.

In 1981 there were 25 changes and the range was 15.75% to 21.50%.

And in 1982 there were 14 changes, with a range from 11.00% to 17.00%.

By 1983, there were only three changes with a considerably less volatile range of 10.50% to 11.50%.

All of this interest rate volatility, and the alarming trend toward higher interest rates, was being largely caused by inflation, which was being caused by a lot of things.

In 1973 OPEC came onto the world scene with a well-organized and disciplined cartel that caused the price of oil, the world's primary source of energy, to increase in price nearly 925% from 1969 to 1982.

Productivity of the workforce, a key element in the equation, was stagnant, which caused all available dollars (which were too many dollars in this case) to chase too few goods and services, forcing prices higher.

The natural forces of the marketplace, which in time might have adjusted things to prevent the surging inflation, were being denied. As early as 1971, President Nixon had implemented an experiment with price and wage controls. They did not work; they were modified in 1973, and abandoned entirely in 1974. They were tried again under President Carter in 1978, but abolished entirely by President Reagan almost as he stepped off the platform after being inaugurated in 1981.

There was even a time under President Ford in 1975 when the battle for beating inflation would be won if all citizens would wear a large lapel badge which said WIN (an acronym for "Whip Inflation Now") - a futile attempt at moral suasion to get business to hold the line on prices, and to get labor to hold the line on wages.

The Seasoned Veteran believes that the most important of all factors in determining the level of inflation during the Seventies and very early Eighties was the *supply of money.*

Money can be printed up by the Treasury Department printing presses, but the most important way money is created in the economy is through the activity of the banking system.

I hope all of you might have taken a sophomore economics course in college and learned how money is created by Bank A making a loan to Customer A, who spends it with a Bank B customer who deposits it in Bank B which uses the deposit to make a loan to a Bank C customer, etc. In this way Bank A has actually started a process which creates money out of thin air! The theory always was that *the level of interest rates would control how much money was being created* - at low rates people would borrow, at high rates they would not borrow.

Since 1913, the nation's central bank has been the Federal Reserve System, which from now on I shall refer to as the Fed. The Fed is politically independent in theory and is charged with regulating the level of the money supply; conventional wisdom until nearly ten years ago was that as the Fed changed its discount rate - the interest rate at which it would itself make loans to the commercial banks of the nation - the money supply would decrease at high discount rates and it would go up at low discount rates.

Other credit regulating techniques were available to the Fed - regulating stock market margin requirements; performing "open market" operations whereby the Fed would itself buy U.S. Treasury securities from commercial banks, and by paying for them create "reserves" to the banking system; or by itself selling U.S. Treasury securities to the banking system, and in requiring the banks to pay for the securities, "reserves" could be temporarily or permanently withdrawn from the banking system. But these two techniques, margin requirement adjustments and open market operations, were thought to be not as effective in regulating the money supply as timely changes in the Fed's discount rate.

The Federal Reserve discount rate was 6.50% in January, 1978. There were six upward changes that year, to 10.00% in early 1979. That year there were three upward changes, to 13.00% in early 1980, followed by seven changes to 14.00% in May, 1981.

These changes were an attempt by the Fed to dissuade the nation's banks from themselves borrowing money, so that they would not be able to make loans to their customers. The creation of new money would be slowed, and there wouldn't be all those dollars chasing too few goods and services, and prices would therefore go down or at least not go up so much.

But it just plain did not work.

I will tell you why. The Seasoned Veteran was one of the culprits!

The commercial banks had borrowed themselves silly!

Commercial banks historically have made profits largely by taking in money in the form of deposits, which are *liabilities* to the bank, and then using these deposits to make investments, in the form of securities purchased from broker/dealers, and to make loans to individuals and businesses. These loans and investments are *assets* to the bank. The interest they receive on their investments and loans is hopefully more than the interest they pay for the deposits, creating the profit to the bank. The specific difference can be measured in dollars, but internally in a bank it is first measured as a percent, which is the "interest margin," or more commonly, the "spread." If the assets produce 8.00% interest, and the liabilities cost 5.00%, the "spread" is 3.00%. If the above asset and liability percentages were reversed, the bank would have a "negative spread" of 3.00% and this would create an operating deficit in this most important category of bank management, which is referred to within the bank as Asset/Liability, or "spread," management.

In order to better understand the nearly runaway inflation of the late Seventies and very early Eighties, the Seasoned Veteran wants to again be a history professor.

In 1950, the commercial banks had total loans and investments of $122 billion, of which 37% were loans and 63% were investments. These were funded by a liability structure which was 92% deposits, 7% stockholders' capital, and 1% "other liabilities," including borrowings by the banks from the Fed.

By 1960, loans and investments were $191 billion, with 61% in loans and 39% in securities. (Notice how these percentages reversed from ten years before.) These assets were funded by 88% deposits, 8% stockholders' capital, and 4% "other liabilities," including borrowings from the Fed.

In 1970, loans and investments had increased to $427 billion, of which 70% were loans and 30% were security investments. The funding of these was accomplished by 82% deposits, 8% stockholders' capital, and now, very importantly, 10% "other borrowings."

In 1978, with inflation now really taking hold, loans and investments were $1.109 trillion, 75% loans and 25% investments, funded by 81.8% deposits, only 5.8% stockholders' capital and 12.4% "other borrowings."

In 1980, inflation was 13.5%. The banking system had loans and investments of $1.340 trillion, 75% loans and 25% investments. Funding was only 79.8% deposits, only 5.7% stockholders' capital, and 14.5% "other borrowings."

So now, you rightly ask, what were these "other borrowings?" Were they conventional borrowings from the Fed, over which the Fed had control of the specific cost of the borrowing by virtue of its discount rate, and could therefore control the volume of the borrowing?

Absolutely not.

The banks were borrowing every day from their customers, paying interest at rates *above* the discount rate, on jumbo C.D.'s, on short-term commercial paper, and on repurchase agreements, where they actually pledged their securities as collateral. They were borrowing longer-term on subordinated notes and debentures. They were borrowing short-term from financial intermediaries outside the banking system, such as S&L's and credit unions, in daily purchases of so-called Federal Funds. And they were borrowing from other places as well.

The bottom line is that the banking system was no longer dependent on Federal Reserve Borrowings. They had found other sources - an "end-run" around the Fed - to fund the loans they wanted to make, so that they could create a favorable spread with additional loans. With the prime rate in 1980 averaging 15.42% every day all year, there was (believe the Seasoned Veteran!) plenty of room to enjoy a favorable spread. Banks were making record profits, returning 14.1% on stockholders' equity in 1980. The same figure for 1950, 1960, and 1970 was 8.2%, 10.2%, and 8.7%.

The money supply was up 9.6% in 1979, and despite the beginnings of constructive efforts to control it, it was still up 10.2% in 1980. And inflation, as we have seen, was 13.5%.

Things were, to put it mildly, not good. In fact, they were in a terrible mess.

Now we are at the point where you find out for certain why the Seasoned Veteran regards 1980 as such a significant year.

As you are probably by now aware, I am not a particular fan of the peanut farmer President, Jimmy Carter. His administration was January, 1977 to January, 1981; professional historians will certainly argue there were some beneficial accomplishments, notably the Begin-Sadat accord at Camp David in March, 1979 (although on this I say: "Peace! Peace! But there is no peace!"). In my view, the most beneficial accomplishment was Carter's appointment, in October, 1979, of Paul M. Volcker as Chairman of the Board of Governors of the Federal Reserve System.

Volcker was 52 years old, an imposing man of 6' 8" and a natural leader, a Princeton man with graduate training in Economics at Harvard and in England. He worked as an economist for a very large and prominent bank in New York, and then from 1961 to 1974 he was a senior official at the Treasury Department in Washington. He returned to New York in 1975 as President of the New York Federal Reserve Bank, and was serving there when he was made Chairman of the Board of Governors.

Paul Volcker seems to have been the only person in Washington, and maybe in the world, who was smart enough to see what was going on. He viewed the situation as a banking system totally out of control; he realized that the money supply increases created by the leveraged banking system were the culprit, and that the Fed could raise the discount rate to 50% and it still wouldn't do any good. He announced that henceforth the level of the discount rate would be of secondary importance. He was going to beat inflation by using *Federal Reserve open market operations* to regulate the money supply. He was going to, on balance, sell Treasury securities to the banking system and take bank lendable reserves away from them when they paid for the securities. He must have thought to himself "If interest rates in the money market go to 25%, so be it. If there is a severe recession, I hope it's a short one, but so be it. *I am going to beat inflation. It is killing us!"*

In 1980, Volcker went to work. He implemented his strategy. It took a while for it to "kick in." There was a time lag, but, very thankfully, it certainly did. And it was painful, very painful.

There was indeed a recession, the severest one in postwar history.

There was double digit unemployment, with eight million Americans suffering all the terribly painful things that entails.

Money market interest rates, which had averaged about 6.50% in the 1976-1978 period, averaged 11.38% in 1979, 13.25% in 1980, and 16.13% in 1981. But they were 12.54% in 1982, 9.32% in 1983, 8.33% in 1984, and have been mainly lower than that over the past five years.

And rampant, runaway inflation was throttled! The consumer price index, as we have seen, went up 11.3% in 1979, 13.5% in 1980, and 10.4% in 1981. But it was up only 6.1% in 1982, up only 3.2% in 1983, and the increases for the next five years through 1988 were an annual average of 3.5%, never higher than 4.4%.

Mr. Volcker, take a bow!

The other significant newcomer on the Washington scene in 1980 was a midwesterner by birth, who became a radio sportscaster and then a movie star. By the mid-Fifties his career had waned, and according to the Seasoned Veteran's uncle who was a member of the same Los Angeles area country club, he was seen playing a lot of golf and on some days had trouble finding a game. But California Republican politics is a strange animal, and by 1966 he was in the Sacramento Statehouse, elected by the largest plurality ever. He ran the state well, ascended to national prominence, and the peanut farmer was easy to beat. So the Gipper had become Governor and now he became, in 1980, the Great Communicator.

Ronald Reagan brought some interesting ideas with him to Washington. He believed in free markets. He did not like big government and governmental regulations. He professed not to like government deficits. He did not like income taxes. He did not like the weakness of the military posture he inherited. He did not object to bigness in business. And he believed in "supply-side" economics.

Supply-side economics was a theory that had its origins in 19th century France, and work on it in this country had recently been performed by a controversial economist named Arthur Laffer. It held that a supply of goods creates a demand for goods, and the creation of the supply of goods can be stimulated by the government's reducing taxes. Jobs will be created, and the reduction in the tax rates will not, in the long run, mean reduced governmental income because the larger economy will still produce enough income for the government. Savings and investment would be stimulated, and tax credits for capital expenditures would channel the savings and investment in the proper direction.

It is very apparent to the Seasoned Veteran that historians will be scratching their heads for many years as to what grade to award the eight years of Reagan's administration.

But I would, in the words of one of his predecessors, like to make several things perfectly clear:

We had, of course, the longest and best bull market in equities in our history. (But, as we know, we can't grow our capital in the future using markets that have existed in the past.) The "Volcker Recession" was over by late 1982, and the longest peacetime economic expansion is still intact seven years later. Supply side economics *has* worked. We can debate until doomsday about the deficits that have not gone away. But I argue with others that they are not caused by flaws in the economic theory but rather by a Congress that has total control of the purse strings. Because of its compulsion with elective self-perpetuation it does not properly exercise the required degree of spending discipline.

Inflation has been wrestled to the ground.

Interest rate volatility is in a manageable range.

We have had no major foreign military involvement to waste our manpower and our resources.

We have . . .

But wait! I find myself using words and making points intended for the next two chapters. So let's pause here and just say: "Gipper, thanks for the peace and prosperity!

6
1987 to 1989

On Friday evening, October 16, 1987, I sat down to watch *Wall Street Week with Louis Rukeyser*. It had been a very tough two weeks in the markets.

The DJIA had hit its record high of 2722 on August 25. What was thought to be normal profit-taking had caused it to go down to 2596 by the end of September. But the first week of October the DJIA went down another 115 points. The U.S. Treasury 30 Year Bond had been trading at an 8.75% yield basis at the end of June. By the end of August it was 9.10% and a month later 9.70%. On October 9 it was 9.95%, and it crossed over 10.00% on Monday, October 12. On this day the DJIA went down only 11 points and the next day it went up 37 points, with average volume. But Wednesday the DJIA went down 95 points as volume crossed over 200 million shares. On Thursday it was down 59 points on 263 million shares, and on Friday it was down 108 points on 338 million shares. The Treasury Long Bond was at 10.23%. The DJIA was now at 2246, down 17.5% from its recent high.

Mr. Rukeyser's panelists and guest were not their usual incisive selves. Nor was Mr. Rukeyser. They were clearly perplexed. They basically said the worst seemed to be over, but maybe not. There was a lot of uncertainty.

The "maybe not," of course, turned into a 508 point decline on the next

Monday, October 19, with 604 million shares changing hands. The DJIA was down 36% in less than eight weeks. The pundits and commentators began having field days with the 1929 comparisons, and forty miles from where I live a very distraught stock trader murdered one stockbroker and maimed another before turning his handgun upon himself.

The Seasoned Veteran cannot account for the violence in Miami, but I can account for the violence in the markets.

Let's look at some recent history.

The bull market of the Eighties began in August, 1982 from a level of DJIA 777. It closed the year at 1047, up 35% in five months. 1982 was the last year of the Volcker recession, with the GNP down 2.5% for the year but beginning to go up in November. Inflation was 6.1%, down from double digits the past three years. The U.S. Treasury 30 Year Bond was settling down from 15.00% plus into a yield basis range of 10.00% to 13.00%, where it would stay until the end of 1985. The DJIA closed 1982 at a P/E multiple of 14.4 times actual 1983 earnings.

The bull market continued in 1983, closing the year at DJIA 1259, up 20%. Inflation improved to 3.2%, the real GNP improved by 3.6%, but the federal budget deficit grew to $195 billion. At 1259 the DJIA was only nine times what it would actually earn in 1984.

1984 saw a bull market breathing spell at best, a correction at worst. Trading as low as DJIA 1100, it finished the year at 1212, down 3.7%. Inflation was 4.3%, the budget deficit was $175 million, and real GNP climbed 6.4%, fueled importantly by consumer spending. The DJIA closed the year at 12.6 times what it would actually earn in 1985.

Trading a bit on either side of 1300 for the first half of 1985, the bull market got its second wind in July and closed the year at DJIA 1547, up nearly 28%. Inflation was 3.6%, real GNP was up 2.7%, but the budget deficit showed no signs of succumbing to supply side economics, and grew to $212 billion. At year-end, the DJIA was 1547, 13.4 times what it would earn in 1986.

1986 was an interesting year. OPEC showed signs of falling apart; oil prices went below $15 and briefly down near $10 for a barrel. Inflation in the U.S. was only 1.1%, very close to being the best year in the post-war era. As a result, bond prices were on a bull market of their own, with the U.S. Treasury 30 Year Bond at a 7.75% yield basis by year-end, the lowest yield since 1977. Real GNP was up 2.1%, but the budget deficit was more than the previous year, an alarming $221 billion. And a new and very serious problem, which had really been incipient in 1980, began to get some serious attention. We were importing more than we were exporting, and the trend was alarming. From a merchandise trade surplus of $11 billion in 1975 we had a deficit of $24 billion in 1980, $57 billion by 1983, and $132 billion in 1985. For 1986 the figure was $141 billion, and showed no signs of reversing. Our dollars were depreciating in the foreign exchange markets as a result, and this at a time when we were increasingly dependent upon foreign investors to finance our budget deficits by buying our Treasury Bonds. But the main item for attention in the summer and fall of 1986 was domestic tax reform. Just as Ronald Reagan had made good on his 1980 campaign promise to reduce taxes, so he now made good on his 1984 promise to reform them. The Tax Reform Act of 1986 would largely become effective on January 1, 1987 - with generally lower and more equitable rates all around. The year ended with the DJIA at 1895, up 22.5% on the year. It was up 144% in four years. It was 14.2 times what it would earn in 1987.

The Seasoned Veteran believes that 1987 was entitled to an orderly market gain of about 15%. This would have put the DJIA at about 2180 at year-end. The bull market would be intact at about 12 times what it would probably earn in 1988. Against the background of actual inflation of 4.4% for the year, and an actual budget deficit that turned out to be a much lower $147 billion, and a concerted effort on the part of the entire world to help us with our foreign trade problem, this type of performance would have been in order.

But it was not to be.

Like a sprinter waiting in the starting blocks for a 100 yard dash on New

Year's Eve, and not paying any attention whatever to the revelation six weeks before that one of Wall Street's biggest heroes was in fact a cheat at best and a crook at worst, the market exploded on the upside. January 31: DJIA 2117, up 11.7% for the month. February 28: DJIA 2200, up 3.9% for the month. March 31: DJIA 2305, up 4.8%. A pause in April and May but a strong June, closing at 2419. July 31: DJIA 2580, up 6.7% for the month.

And then on August 25 the DJIA closed at its high for the year, 2722. Since January 1 it was up 43.6%. It was trading at 20.5 times what it was expected to earn in 1987. It was providing a dividend yield of 2.65%, down from 3.90% one year before. It was being fueled by the euphoria of fuzzy-cheeked Wall Street neophytes who were about to have their sophomore slump, in spades. They were seeing money pour into the stock market from all over the country and all over the world, and who thought it would never end. They were buoyed by the announcement of the Bureau of Labor Statistics at 8:30 A.M. on August 21 that the CPI for July was up only 0.2%, after having been up 0.4%, 0.3%, and 0.5% the three months previous. The U.S. Treasury 30 Year Bond had been trading at an 8.75% yield basis on June 30, and the present yield of 9.10% was well within the normal range of trading volatility.

Much has been written about the role of program trading, portfolio insurance, and the financial futures exchanges in the October debacle. Much has been written about the foreign central bankers who were giving our man, Treasury Secretary Baker, some problems in the foreign exchange markets at the time. Much has been written about the trade deficits and the budget deficits. All of these things were contributors. But I believe that more than any other single thing that caused the Crash was the September 23 announcement that the CPI for August was +0.6%, substantially reversing the trend and showing an alarming break-out on the upside. By September 30 the U.S. Treasury 30 Year Bond was at a 9.70% yield basis, up 60 basis points since the August 25 DJIA high. And on October 12 it hit 10.00%!

The stage was set for what happened in the four trading days October 14 to 19. It was bound to happen. The market had nearly quadrupled in five years. The economy was at the end of its fifth year of growth. Budget and trade deficits showed signs of going out of control. A managerial scandal had been exposed in the White House. Unseasoned people were rampant on Wall Street. Computers were furnishing technical mumbo jumbo. The consumer was possibly at the end of his credit card rope. Major money center banks were acknowledging uncollectible LDC debts in the billions. And the performance of the market since January 1 had been a classic, a prototype, the absolute epitome of a bull market blow-off, a bandwagon that everybody wanted to get on and everybody was afraid to get off. The rearing of inflation's ugly head was all that it took, and then everybody wanted to get off - *all at the same time.*

Alan Greenspan, who had replaced Paul Volcker as Chairman of the Fed in August, was getting his baptism under fire and he performed extremely well. Early in the day on Tuesday, October 20, he proclaimed that the Federal Reserve, in its role as lender of last resort, would supply all the credit needed to provide liquidity to a Wall Street whose collateral was all of a sudden depreciated by over 35%. The floor specialists rose from the dead. The bond markets quickly recovered. The U.S. Treasury 30 Year Bond yield went down over 100 basis points in a week, and was 8.95% at year's end. The CPI was +0.5% in September, +0.3% in October, +0.1% in November and unchanged in December. The index for the entire year was +4.4%. The DJIA went up 212 points Tuesday through Friday of Black Monday week, and another 42 points the next week. It closed October 30 at 1993.

For the next fourteen months it traded in a narrow range between 1767 and 2183. 1988 was a year dedicated to digesting the aftermath of the Crash, electing a new President, observing the incipient but amazing changes in major geopolitical relationships, and watching Alan Greenspan perform a tightrope walk worthy of Guinness.

This is being written in late Summer, 1989, several months short of the seventh anniversary of the current economic expansion. Seven years without a recession, as measured by history, is a very long time. To be sure, there have been several major sector dislocations, as steelworkers, farmers, and oil field workers would attest, but the overall domestic economy, and those of our trading partners, have continued to grow. Domestic consumption, capital spending, and export sales have combined to produce two years of nearly full employment and steady if unspectacular GNP increases. OPEC is behaving itself, Iran-Iraq hostilities have ceased (and the man who caused them is dead), *Perestroika*, *Glasnost*, and Solidarity are being given their main chances, disarmament is becoming more than a word, and the flicker of light in Tiananmen Square will someday soon be lit again. Our new President is proving his mettle and there are even a few people in Congress who seem to want fiscal sanity and logical prioritization.

All of this is not to say that there are not problems. The budget and trade deficits are still worrisome, the education offered in many schools is mostly a sorry story, and the drug problem is very real. Our ability to successfully compete in world markets is an area where the need for improvement is, and will be, a constant.

The bottom line, I believe, is that things are falling rather nicely into the scenario that will be described in the next Chapter. This is not to say that there will not be a recession. It will happen someday, hopefully short and shallow, and then it will again happen another day. And, too, there will someday again be bothersome inflation. The high wire that Alan Greenspan and the Fed have been walking has these two nemeses waiting below on either side, and the balancing act will not last forever. These things are ingredients of capitalism, facets of a market economy, part of freedom of enterprise. But the Seasoned Veteran believes the pains will be tolerable and the illnesses will be short; we must take the bad with the good, as we always have, particularly when the latter will dominate.

So far in 1989 the GNP has been growing at about 3%, unemployment has been around 5.25%, annualized inflation is 5% but showing signs of improvement, and the budget and trade deficits aren't getting any worse. The U.S. Treasury Thirty Year Bond yield has hiccupped each time Greenspan has appeared to lose his balance, going in 1989 from 9.00% to 9.44% to 7.76% to 8.20%. And the stock market, measured by the DJIA, has averaged a gain of nearly 85 points per month as it traveled from 2169 at year-end 1988 to an all-time high of 2752 in August. It has been fueled by earnings growth. Despite its year-to-date 27% gain, it is trading at less than 12 times trailing twelve month earnings and is yielding a respectable 3.75% on its dividends.

I am aware many of the readers of this book will be implementing their Investment Plan in 1990 and 1991. *It should be an excellent time to get started.* Lessons of the Eighties will have been learned and digested. Excellent values in financial instruments will be obtainable. There will be money to be made, capital to be compounded and grown.

Onward! This lesson in history is nearly complete. We will use it to embark on our investment strategy with the knowledge that our program is designed to succeed no matter the short-term scenario.

7
The Future: The Nineties and Beyond

The world is exploding with pure knowledge.

It has accurately been said that there has been more pure knowledge accumulated in the past seventy-five years than in all the previous history of mankind. It has been exactly twenty years since we proved we have the know-how to send men to the surface of the moon and bring them safely home. The babies who were born the day Neil Armstrong took "one small step" will be graduating from college in 1990 and 1991. Think about that.

And the volume of pure knowledge is growing exponentially. The amount accumulated in the past seventy-five years might well be duplicated in the next twenty-five or forty years.

The pure knowledge I am talking about is not all scientific or technical. Much of it lies in areas that embrace economic, educational, cultural, and philosophic disciplines. For certain, there will be breakthroughs in superconductivity and telecommunications, biochemistry and rocketry. But there will also be breakthroughs in educational techniques for grammar schools and high schools, labor and management relations, the management of geopolitical power, international debt management, including consortiums of private and quasi-governmental capital, and the regulation and efficiency of financial marketplaces.

Information is the communication of knowledge. As the knowledge has grown, so has the dissemination and sharing of it. As this is written, a tropical depression has become a hurricane in the Atlantic Ocean off the African Coast, near the Cape Verde Islands, heading my way. As it heads westward, we will know about its steering currents and exact wind strength, its barometric pressure to the hundredth of an inch, and the exact dimensions of its eye and its circumference. Late this afternoon we will see pictures of it in real time via satellite as we sit in our living rooms. We will have time to plan. We can take action if it threatens us. We can hopefully spare ourselves devastation. This was not possible fifty years ago, when two hours' warning was a lot. Fifty years from now, it may well be possible to destroy this storm or steer it harmlessly away via some technical means before it develops, before it threatens lives and property. Such a thing would seem to be a possibility.

Developments of this sort will benefit all of mankind. And money will be made in the process. Investors who own shares in companies that participate in these types of activities will be able to sell their shares at prices higher than they paid for them. Much higher.

In Chapter 5, I provided some long lists of events, both domestic and international, that were vicissitudes our country and markets have not only endured but prospered under since World War II. Now I am going to provide another list. It is a list I've compiled in about an hour of cogitation, without any research or investigation - just off the tip of my tongue, as it were. It is a list of new economic activities, each associated with a specific company or companies, that have come into full flower in the past forty years. In each instance it can be proven that investors benefited handsomely as owners of the companies that were involved. Here is the list:

Instant photography; cold tire recapping; xerographic copying; theme parks; recreational vehicles; jet air travel; cordless telephones; door-to-door cosmetic sales; birth control pills; TV and then color TV; bank credit cards; mainframe computers; discount retail stores; secondary markets for mortgages and other loans; nuclear power; generic drugs; disposable diapers; fuel injection; silicone lubricants; transistors and diodes; microwave cooking; health foods and supplements; plastic packaging; fast food restaurants; personal computers; touch-tone dialing; hydraulic dumpsters; frozen meals; store coupons; super-chip semiconductors; automatic teller machines; smokeless tobacco; health and fitness clubs; electronic toys; lasers and fiber optics; casino gambling; public lotteries; disposable razors; home equity loans; nuclear medicine; catamarans and windsurfing boards; mini-computers; designer clothing for the mass market; condominiums; video games; CB radios; specialized hospitals; industrial robotics; front wheel drive; cellular telephones; condoms as a disease preventative; VCR's; athletic footwear; cable TV with 24 hour programming; communications satellites and satellite dishes; computer software; disposable lighters; aluminum cans; tinted windows; supercomputers; microfilm and microfiche; polio vaccine; day care centers; transistor radios; video rentals; camcorders; magnetic ink and magnetic tape; desktop publishing; telephone answering machines; hospice care; condominium time sharing; environmental cleanup; doublewide mobile homes; portable computers; pocket calculators; direct dialing across oceans and continents; beepers; retirement villages; stereo cassettes; frost-free refrigerators and self-cleaning ovens; laptop computers; smoke detectors; non-wooden skis and tennis rackets; walkman stereos; overnight mail and package delivery; computer-driven home shopping; facsimile machines; WATS telephone service; snowblowers and power mowers; aerosol containers; and quartz wristwatches.

Given another hour to the task, I am sure I could significantly expand the list. The point is that someone will be able to sit down ten years from now, and twenty and thirty years from now, and compile such a list of things that we today do not know anything about, have probably never even *heard* of or are just beginning to learn about, where some very real money will have been made by the owners of the businesses that will be operating in the new areas.

And at the same time the basic industries, the ones that have been in business year after year doing essentially the same things in a more efficient manner, will continue to prosper - provided they continue to identify a need for their products and services and can deliver them competitively.

As the world has gotten much smaller with advances in transportation and communications, so have we learned how better to get along with our neighbors, and use their knowledge, skills, and aspirations to complement our own just as they use ours. Our products are their products, their technology is our technology. Our markets are theirs, and theirs ours. Protectionism is almost as dead as the proverbial duck, just as it should be. Western Europe essentially becomes one economic entity in 1992 and five years later China takes over the very large Hong Kong economy. We have much more to gain than to lose by going along with all this.

For over forty years the world has been divided generally into three parts: the western world, mostly democratic and capitalistic; the eastern world, mostly totalitarian and communistic; and the rest, the "third" world, mostly politically unstable and economically underdeveloped.

Now it is all changing.

History will probably give Richard Nixon a high grade for his 1972 overture to the government of mainland China, effectively starting the long, arduous, and frequently frustrating process of integrating that country into the world economy. There are over one billion people there, proven to be industrious and interested in improving their quality of life. We see the cool intensity of their youth on the TV screen under the five rings of the Olympic Games and eight months later, in Tiananmen Square; they look to the Seasoned Veteran to be the sort that would be good co-workers and a good market for many products. One billion people!

And what am I hearing about Mr. Gorbachev's country striking some agreements toward the use of VISA and MasterCard? Think of it! The restructuring of the Soviet political edifice as well as its society and its economy (and those of its satellites) is the subject of many books thicker than this one. I regard it all as very, very hopeful straws in the wind. It is being proven that Gorbachev would like to reduce his defense outlays - they simply take too high a percentage of his gross national product, and he has some very real economic problems which are a hangover from seventy years of Communism. Perhaps - just perhaps - if he really does reduce his, then we could reduce ours. And voilà, a one-third reduction on our part is more than $100 billion toward a balanced budget in Washington. And the Soviets as a market for consumer goods - well over one-quarter billion people who crave what we have taken for granted each day for years. Then one could add the 100 million people in the Soviet-dominated countries of Eastern Europe. It boggles the mind!

And Africa, over 500 million people. India, about 700 million people. Undereducated, underdeveloped, undernourished, undercapitalized, poorly governed. Large problems, but large opportunities. Very large opportunities.

We must always remember that the world's greatest engine for economic growth is a human being with two arms, two legs, and a brain. And there are literally billions of them out there who want to go to work to improve their lives. Instantaneous global communication has made them aware of what they are missing out on!

The ideas that were put forth by Jefferson and Adam Smith in 1776 are now closer than ever before to being implemented worldwide. Think what these ideas, put to practice, have done for us. Think what they can do for the rest of the world! And think of the money that will be made.

The past twenty years have been an educational and maturing period for a generation of business managers who are oriented to the idea of making money. Pure and simple. And the "bottom line" syndrome, the "lean and mean" attitude, will reflect itself in higher EPS, which will translate into higher share prices. The concept of speed is a factor in this. As research and technology germinate into a money-making idea, what formerly might have taken five years to find its way to the bottom line now takes three and soon will take one.

And all this will be happening in an era of smoother business cycles, low inflation, improved governmental efficiency, manageable interest rates, and relatively stable foreign exchange rates. The knowledge explosion has included lessons learned in these areas, too. The tuition charges for many of these courses were very expensive, but the Seasoned Veteran sees reasons to believe that, long-term, they were worth it.

And on the subject of tuition charges, as well as the industrious-looking Chinese young people, the Seasoned Veteran has seen his own two sons graduate over the past five years from two of our very fine universities. I have visited the campuses, eaten at the fraternity houses, and attended a few lectures. I have liked what I've seen. We take a backseat to no one in our own oncoming human raw material!

Against all these backgrounds, there will be a pool of capital from the citizens and institutions of the global village that will be totally sufficient to support the technology and the entrepreneurs and the managers. Free trade and economic consolidation in Europe, the China/Hong Kong merger, the industrialization of the third world, lower governmental and trade deficits, instantaneous communication and arithmetic, travel from New York to Tokyo in perhaps one afternoon - things of this sort augur for more and more investment dollars from more and more countries that will be searching worldwide for a home that promises relative safety and maximum return. These dollars will be looking for economies that are dynamic and financial marketplaces that can be trusted, that are intelligently and uniformly regulated, that provide liquidity for both buyers and sellers under all types of economic scenarios.

The Seasoned Veteran believes that our NYSE, ASE, and NASDAQ markets, as well as the primary and secondary dealer network for U.S. Treasury Securities, provide what is required, and a very large part of the money-making action will be taking place in this country. An increasing number of foreign companies will have their shares, or ADR's, listed on our markets. A corollary to this is the very large U.S. mutual fund industry, which is increasingly using its domestic base to search out international bargains and execute trades worldwide - often using the Tokyo or London branch of a New York-headquartered investment firm to handle the order. An interesting scene is already well underway. Until a few years ago, the

U.S. Treasury market was a New York market, with the securities trading 9 A.M. to 4 P.M. Eastern time. Now, when New York goes home Tokyo starts trading, and after their day ends, London picks up the action. The result is a 24-hour market, with New York often looking at a bewildering overnight price change at 9 A.M. Eastern time.

Within a few years there will probably be 24-hour trading in stocks as well; there already are evening trading hours on several of the commodity futures exchanges.

I believe that the Nineties will be characterized by equity bull markets. They will be very powerful bull markets, and they will be fueled by corporate earnings that will attract investment dollars like a magnet.

They will be augmented by a phenomenon of the past five years that has seen a very significant diminution in the absolute number of shares that are available for purchase in the equity markets of the NYSE, ASE, and NASDAQ. Stock "buy-back" programs have taken vast numbers of shares from the floating supply, and more than a few public companies have "gone private" in LBO's or have seen their equity replaced by debt courtesy of the various methods of corporate restructuring.

For the past twenty-five years the average net earnings of the DJIA have grown at 6.75% compounded annually. For the past ten years the average net earnings of the DJIA have grown at 7.90% compounded annually, and this includes a severe dip in the 1980-82 recession. The Seasoned Veteran believes that for the ten year period 1990 to 1999 it is entirely possible that net earnings of the DJIA can grow at an average 10.00% compounded annually.

As this is written in 1989, the trailing twelve month DJIA earnings are $227. Let's be conservative and presume a 1990 level of only $200 earnings for the DJIA. And then let's compound those earnings at 10.00% annually. The figure comes out at $322.20 in 1995 and $518.80 in 2000.

Nearly all bull markets get to DJIA at 20 times earnings at one point - usually near the end - just as all bear markets go under 10 times earnings, usually seven or eight times earnings at the bottom. Let's do some arithmetic for three different multiples that seem reasonable: 14, 16, and 18, and presume a DJIA level of 2000 as a starting point.

At 14 times earnings, the DJIA would be at 4511 in 1995. At 16 times the number is 5155 and at 18 times it is 5800.

For the year 2000, the DJIA at the three multiples comes to 7263, 8301, and 9338, respectively.

These are numbers which might seem difficult to fathom. You have just seen, though, that they were not plucked from thin air. They represent very good possibilities. Recent history tells us that from 1982 to 1987 the market went up 350% from 777 DJIA to 2722. A 2000 DJIA going up the same percentage in five years is at 7000 in 1995, and our highest projection was only 5800.

The problem, of course, is that an alarm clock does not ring at the instant a bull market or a bear market starts and stops. From 1953 to 1966 the DJIA went up 390%, from 255 to 995. During this period there were three declines, or corrections, or minor bear markets, of from 17% to 27% (lasting 14 months, 10 months, and 7 months). And the recent 1982-1987 bull market had an 11% correction from June, 1983 to August, 1984. There will always be corrections, dips, bear markets.

The Investment Plan that you are to embark on does not have any market timing features whatever. The strategies you will learn about in Sections V and VI will keep you fully invested at all times - not in the same individual issues, but in the same types of issues. You will not pay any attention to the direction of the market, except as you attempt to determine the perception that *others* will have as they focus on an individual equity. These other investors might be oriented toward market timing strategies which will possibly affect the share price. There will be periods when you are caught in a correction, or a bear market, and it will seem prudent to "bail out." *You must not succumb to this!* You have seen history, and you have seen a glimpse of the future as you have studied the past. And you have seen that there is reason for great optimism. The decades in front of us will have more bull than bear markets, stronger bull than bear markets, and higher highs on the bull markets and higher lows on the bear markets. You will be directed in Section V on a program of using your brain for individual investment selection rather than determining the short-term direction of the market.

The Seasoned Veteran is in camp with J. P. Morgan, who nearly 100 years ago was asked what he thought the market would do in the next six months. He said, "It will fluctuate."

I believe it will fluctuate in such a way that it will achieve DJIA 5000 by 1995 and DJIA 9000 by the year 2000. And maybe more!

In the periods when the fluctuations are on the downside, you will do well to remember the story about the King of Persia, in the days of Marco Polo. He summoned the seven wisest men in his kingdom, and sent them forth into the mountains. He instructed them not to return until they had unanimously determined a truism for all ages, the one supreme law of the universe that could always be depended upon. Months later, they came back and reported their conclusion. It was to always be aware that "This, too, shall pass."

As stressed in Chapter 2, you must learn patience. There are no shortcuts. Great things require time. Ivan Boesky attempted a shortcut, and he ended up writing a very unproductive $100 million personal check and is currently asking an eighth grade drop-out for permission to go to the bathroom.

This book's history lesson is complete. Hopefully you will, with me, always be a student.

Do you want to take the trip, learn the techniques and strategies of the Investment Plan? Believe me, it's worth it!

SECTION IV.
PACKING THE SUITCASES AND PREPARING THE VEHICLE

8
Publications and Public Libraries

The Seasoned Veteran strongly believes a successful investor is an informed investor.

The past ten years have seen an absolute avalanche of economic, business, financial, and investment market information disseminated by the media; daily newspapers have larger and better financial and business sections; radio and TV stations give business news and market updates throughout the day; the weekly newsmagazines have informative and well done stories in their business sections; the magazines devoted entirely to business and financial subjects are better than ever; there are cable TV companies that carry Financial News Network, which provides a barrage of market and business news throughout the day; there are specific radio and TV programs - talk shows and call-in shows - devoted to investment-related subjects; and in a lot of cities you could go to investment seminars morning, noon, and night six days a week and probably seven.

You are probably thinking "Wow! The Seasoned Veteran wants me to spend about 27 1/2 hours a week reading, watching, and listening."

Not so. Fortunately!

Here is how you should do it.

Subscribe to *The Wall Street Journal* and have it delivered at home. It is published five days a week and is a terrific newspaper. Home delivery is better than at your office because you'll be inclined to spend too much time there reading it; you might get fired from your job, and that would be very bad in most cases. To read the WSJ front to back can take about an hour; this is too much time and is unnecessary. Get in the habit of scanning the two "What's News" columns on the first page. The "Business and Finance" column on the left will give you a capsule on the important stories, and will refer you to the inside page if you want the details. Then scan the "Today's Contents" at the bottom of the first page to see if there are other articles of interest. If you are awaiting a specific earnings report or dividend announcement, look for the pages in the Contents under "Earnings Digest" and "Dividend News." Then go to the second page of the second section; in the upper left corner you will find an "Index to Businesses." Check it to see whether there are any stories on companies that you're interested in.

Then, if you have time, go to the second page of the third section and scan the "Abreast of the Market" column to quickly see what happened yesterday. While you're there, check the subject of the "Heard on the Street" column - usually it's a specific company, and you might get an investment idea. Then glance over at the right hand page to quickly look at the charts of the Dow Jones Averages, to get some perspective on where the market is now versus where it's been over the past six months. Lastly, go forward about 15 to 18 pages until you see the columns for "Treasury Bonds, Notes & Bills." Look at the yield for the last Treasury Bond in the column. It is a Bond with a maturity of about 30 years, and is called the Treasury Long Bond. You will see its importance later in this book. Make a mental note of the yield, which is the far right hand number in the column.

If you follow this procedure with *The Wall Street Journal* every day or evening, you will have gone a very long way toward being a well-informed investor. All for about 15 minutes a day! Try to do it every day; when you are traveling or on vacation, the paper is usually available at hotels, newsstands, or in coin-operated dispensers.

You will notice in the above paragraphs that the Seasoned Veteran did not mention anything about checking daily prices on specific stocks and bonds (except for the Treasury Long Bond yield). This is something you should try to avoid. I do this on most Sundays in my local paper, which has weekly range, volume, and closing prices. As a long-term investor, once a week is usually often enough. An exception might be if you want to see how your specific investment reacted to specific news related to it, or an earnings announcement, or a dramatic day in the overall market.

The other publication that the Seasoned Veteran would strongly recommend subscribing to is *Forbes,* published biweekly. It is an excellent magazine, with well written articles on a wide range of good subjects, usually oriented toward specific investments or categories of investments. The "Fact and Comment" section, featuring some insights of Mr. Forbes, is fun and stimulating.

If you feel you have time, the third publication you might consider is *Barron's.* It is published every Saturday, and includes detailed week-ending market data on every market from Wall Street to Singapore. The articles and interviews at the front of the publication are well written, intelligent, usually fun to read, and often contrarian.

The Seasoned Veteran's last suggestion in connection with keeping yourself informed on a weekly basis is to tune in for one-half hour to *Wall Street Week with Louis Rukeyser.* Mr. Rukeyser is an engaging, articulate host, his overview of the week's market activity is concise and to the point, and the panelists and guests are representative of current Wall Street thinking.

If you do the things advised in the above paragraphs, you will average spending two to three hours a week toward being an informed investor, and you will be a currently informed investor. You will get more insights on this in Chapter 21.

You will have probably noticed that the Seasoned Veteran has not mentioned anything about where to go to get "basic" information as opposed to "current" information. You are perhaps wondering "Do I have to communicate directly with every company whose securities I might want to buy to get their annual reports for the last ten years, or other documents, so that I can make some basic decisions?"

The Seasoned Veteran has good news for you. About 98% of the written information you are going to need on a continuing basis for your investment program is available at one single location, probably not more than a ten minute drive from your home.

I am referring to the Reference Room of your local Public Library.

In recent years the degree of interest in investment subjects, and the proliferation of published material, has not gone unnoticed by local librarians, library boards, and their purchasing departments. Usually the books and manuals I'm going to refer to are all located on the same book shelf, or at least within a few feet of each other.

Also available in the library will be certain newspapers and magazines such as *The Wall Street Journal, The New York Times, Barron's, Forbes, Fortune,* and *Business Week.*

Some of you living in very small towns or rural areas will not have a good public library within ten minutes, but I'll bet you do within no more than an hour's drive. Over a period of a month or two, keep a list of things and subjects you want to look up or check on. Then get in the car, take along a pad or notebook to write on, and spend a productive several hours at the library.

Once you get to the Reference Room, here are some of the things to look for:

Standard & Poor's Stock Reports. A total of twelve ring binders containing a separate page for each of about 4500 companies (four binders for NYSE companies; four binders for ASE companies, and four binders for actively traded OTC companies). There is only one page for each company, and the Seasoned Veteran has been amazed for 30 years as to how much information S&P is able to get on two sides of a 5 x 8 piece of paper. You must look for yourself. The reports are revised with current information every few months; the date of the report is always at the bottom center of the front page. These reports are indispensable for a quick review of an individual common stock. (Your broker will usually have these, too.) *Standard & Poor's Security Owner's Stock Guide.* A nearly pocket-sized booklet that is published monthly (usually available about the 15th of the month with figures as of the last day of the preceding month). There is one finely printed line for each company, stretching across both pages so that there is about 15 inches of data. (You will possibly need a magnifying glass for the footnotes.) Much of the same data as in the Stock Reports, but in even more concise form. One additional item is the trading volume of the stock during the preceding month. Your broker will have this publication, too, and if he really likes you he might give you his copy that is a month or two old.

Value Line, Inc. This company is both a statistical service and renderer of opinions on individual stocks. Your library might or might not subscribe to it, but it's the best of the increasingly large number of similar services.

You will probably notice that Moody's has similar publications to those of Standard & Poor's. I have always thought S&P's material on stocks is superior to Moody's, and Moody's has the edge on statistical material for fixed income securities. Your library should have these:

Moody's Manuals, published annually for these categories: Industrials - two thick manuals, red covers; Public Utilities - two thick manuals, brown covers; Bank and Finance - four manuals, black covers; Transportation - one manual, green cover; Municipal & Government - two manuals, blue covers; and International - two manuals, light blue covers. There are also color-coded loose-leaf binders with News Reports that give updates through the year. These manuals have statistical information on just about every corporation and political subdivision that has a bond currently outstanding. Further, and most important, there is detailed information on every single bond issue, including Moody rating, description, date of issue, maturity date, interest payment dates, denominations, paying agent, trustee, call provisions (in detail), collateral if any, sinking fund provisions, original underwriter and price at issue, and original purpose and use of proceeds. An investor should *never* buy a specific municipal or corporate bond without looking up the specific issue in the appropriate *Moody's Manual*.

Moody's Bond Record is a monthly publication with a bright red cover, issued about the 15th of each month with data as of the last day of the preceding month. It is to corporate bonds what the S&P Stock Guide is to stocks. The footnotes, particularly regarding call dates, are important. Information on municipal bonds is limited to an abbreviated name of the issuer and the current Moody rating. It is absolutely necessary to go to the *Moody Manual* for all detailed information on specific state and municipal issues.

So, between Standard & Poor's, Moody's and with maybe Value Line as a bonus, your public library gives you a good return on your tax dollar insofar as basic statistical information on individual stocks and bonds is required.

There is, as you shall see, a requirement to have available information of the same sort on mutual funds. As this part of the investment product spectrum has mushroomed in recent years, so have the number of publishers of mutual fund statistics. There is much to choose from, but none of us has time to read it all.

When I first became a stockbroker in 1959 I was introduced to *Wiesenberger Investment Company Service*. Chances are excellent that your library has it. It has been published each year since 1940, the year of the Investment Company Act of 1940, so it is the granddaddy of all the mutual fund services. The current manual is nearly 1000 pages. The first 85 pages are absolute *must* reading for every reader of this book; they provide general information about mutual funds - information you must have as background for the important specific decisions you are going to make when it comes time to select individual mutual funds for your portfolio. The remaining pages are given to information on specific mutual funds, including statistics and performance data. An added feature is a performance chart for each fund; the inside cover of the manual has a little envelope containing a clear plastic overlay which can be put over the individual fund chart to compare its performance with that of the DJIA and S&P 500 over the last ten year period. The manual also has a comprehensive Table of Contents and an Index, so even considering its bulk you'll be able to find what you're looking for.

You probably won't get the Wiesenberger Manual for the current year in your library until about October. This will have statistics, etc. as of the end of the preceding year. This timeliness disadvantage is overcome by Wiesenberger publishing a *Current Performance and Dividend Record* each month - it runs about 20 pages of statistics on individual funds - and is usually in the library about the 20th of the month, with figures as of the last day of the preceding month. Leaving no stone unturned, Wiesenberger also publishes in May of each year *Mutual Funds Panorama,* which is a compilation of pertinent individual fund statistics as of the preceding December 31. Your library should have this.

As a supplemental tool to studying and evaluating mutual funds, you should look forward to August or early September each year when *Forbes* includes as part of its regular issue a mutual funds survey, with lots of statistics, some ratings on performance, and an Honor Roll of the top-performing funds. There are good mutual fund articles. It's a fun issue to read, and you will learn more on how to use it in Chapter 13.

There are a lot of mutual fund newsletters, and even newsletters on newsletters. There is an independent publication that is a newsletter on what goes on within the Fidelity family of funds. Some of these are pretty good, others aren't. There is only so much reading time available, and to read too much from too many different viewpoints can often be mighty confusing. If you want to expand your reading in these directions, I don't seriously object. But the Seasoned Veteran tries to keep it simple. Such reading reaches the point of diminishing returns.

And diminishing returns are the opposite of what we are after!

9
Murphy & Carroll,
and the Customer's Person

A problem an author frequently has is structuring his book in a logical sequence. Often it happens that the outline of the Chapters, and the outline within a particular Chapter, is more difficult to accomplish than the writing itself. That is the case in this instance.

This Chapter must be integrated into Chapters which follow! It will be necessary for you to keep this in mind.

We are at a point where advice is to be given on choosing the guide for your journey. The guide will be a person who is employed by a business entity that is in the investment business.

You have seen that during the last thirty years I have been employed by three banking organizations and six investment organizations. I feel I know these two financial service industries very well. I certainly have seen a lot of changes! And I feel very strongly about the advice provided here.

This Chapter also includes a brief discussion of the types of investment organizations operating in these two industries. But we will first concentrate on describing the qualities and qualifications of the specific type of business organization, and a specific employee of that organization, that will be most important to *you*. This may seem to you like the proverbial putting of the cart in front of the horse, but you will see the reason.

It is *absolutely imperative that you select only one* business organization for the journey, for the help that you will need in implementing your Investment Plan. The reason for this will probably be clear to you only after you have read this entire book. And within that organization you will select only one (or maybe, for your use on *very* rare occasions, a second) employee who will be next to you on the front seat for the entire journey.

You will be selecting a member firm of the NYSE that is "full service" as opposed to a "discount" firm. The likelihood is that you will have your account at a branch office of this firm, as opposed to the headquarters office (although the latter is a possibility). The firm may be either a national firm or a regional firm. You will be selecting a certain employee of that firm who, for our purpose at this time, will be called a "broker." (We will be changing this word a little later, and have some fun doing it!)

The remainder of this Chapter will be structured as follows: (1) a description of the firm you select; (2) a description of the employee you select; (3) a brief description of some of the other types of business entities in the investment field, and (briefly) our reasons for not using these types of investment firms as the guide for the journey.

NATIONAL AND REGIONAL NYSE MEMBER FIRMS

I am well aware that your geographic location will play a large role in your selection of the NYSE member firm where your investment account will be domiciled. If you are in a large metropolitan area, you will have a very wide choice. If you are in a small or medium-sized city, you will have a much more limited choice. And if you are in a rural area, your choice might be extremely limited, and involve a distance between you and the firm's branch office. Your proximity to the office is not a large factor, because once your account is opened, the telephone can well serve as your principal means of communicating, just as it probably will if your home or place of employment is just one block from your investment firm.

Once the geographic situation is addressed, you must determine for certain that the firm's office is equipped to offer you certain specific services and has certain specific qualifications. I am now going to provide a list of these things. Be aware that (1) the list is not in any order of ranking as to importance - they are *all* important; and (2) the answer to whether or not the firm offers these things can be readily gotten by your interviewing the branch office manager, with whom you will (believe me on this!) very easily be able to secure an early appointment.

Here is the list:

(1)   The firm must have its own bond trading desk, which will probably be at the headquarters office (this is OK). The trading desk should deal in Treasuries, corporates, and municipals. The firm should have the ability to execute trades in the "bond room" of the NYSE.

(2)   The firm must offer margin accounts with competitive interest rates on debit balances, and loan values on both stocks and bonds that are at Regulation T maximums.

(3)   The firm should have a stock (equity) research department of which it is extremely *proud*. The research should be broadly based as to industries and geography, with emphasis on long-term capital appreciation using moderate risk equities. (Regional firms will tend to emphasize stocks of companies located in their region - this is satisfactory provided that the research is not *exclusively* geographically oriented.) You should ask to see, and then you should examine, at least six of the firm's equity research reports that were written *one or two years ago*. Examine these against the current market prices. (You will have better insights into this after reading Chapter 12.)

(4)   The firm should *not* have the policy of charging "full" commissions on every account. Your account's size and activity will justify a discount of from 10% to 50% off "full" commissions. Get a commitment that your account will be reviewed every six

months and a new commission discount level will then be negotiated for the next six months.

(5) The firm should do its own "clearing," which means that there will not be a second firm involved with the "back office" activity.

(6) It is preferable (but not absolutely necessary) that the office has its own "library" of the same Moody, S&P, and Wiesenberger manuals referred to in Chapter 8.

(7) The firm must have a "clean" audited balance sheet, with no irregularities mentioned in the footnotes.

(8) The firm must be a member of SIPC, and in addition it should have its own insurance, which covers securities in all its accounts up to at least $2,500,000, preferably higher. The "cash" insurance levels will not be important to you. You will see why in Chapter 10.

(9) The firm should have "sales agreements" with a very large number of the open-end *equity* and *balanced* mutual funds.

(10) The firm should have its own employees on the "floor" of the NYSE and ASE, and use "$2 brokers" only as supplemental help on the "floor."

(11) The firm should have Quotrons or similar machines on each broker's desk. It is very helpful if the terminals are programmed to "screen" a particular customer's account to determine holdings, interest and dividends received since the last statement, current credit or debit balance, current buying power, current loan value, etc.

(12) If the terminals do not give current margin account information as just described, the brokers should have a hard copy "money line" or similar report with this information on all margin accounts. This should be current each day.

(13) The firm should have the capability to execute trades on all the major *option* exchanges.

(14) The firm should have the capability to execute trades in the

commodities area, particularly precious metals, energy, and financial futures.

(15) The firm should be its own Custodian (in the legal and IRS sense) for IRA plans, and have the ability to administer Keogh plans if you are at all involved with them. "Self directed" IRA plans should be allowed.

(16) The firm should have sufficient telephone trunk lines coming into it such that the lines are not always busy. (This is more important than it might seem to be, if only to save you great personal frustration!)

(17) The branch office should have at least one "Monroe Bond Trader" or "Compucorp" machine in the office, and somebody who knows how to use it. It is also a plus, but not a necessity, if the office has a Telerate machine with all the U.S. Treasury pages.

(18) You should feel very "comfortable" with the firm. You will not be dealing much if at all with the manager, but you should know this person so that if there *is* a problem in your overall relationship with the firm, or with your broker, you can comfortably discuss it with him (or her). And the firm should enjoy a good national and local reputation, so that you can be "comfortable." It is very important to you that the firm not go bankrupt, or get into serious regulatory problems. You can usually depend on the news media to immediately "zero in" on these situations; if they should develop, you must monitor them closely.

So now that you have presumably selected the one and only investment firm that you will use as your guide's employer, now let's go about selecting the specific guide.

YOUR INVESTMENT BROKER

As you have seen, I have been employed as an investment broker at a

NYSE member firm nonconsecutively for a total of 7 1/2 years, over a period from 1959 to 1985. There have been three different firms; one was a large national firm, headquartered on Wall Street with offices coast to coast; one was a much smaller national firm, this one headquartered off of Park Avenue; and the third one was a regional firm where I was located in a branch 1000 miles from the headquarters office.

I have certainly seen a lot of brokers come and go!

When I first became a broker in 1959, the requirement was to spend six months employed by the firm as a trainee, working in all the "back office" departments; take a correspondence course offered by an adjunct of the NYSE; and then pass a test, which took about thirty minutes, with most scores in the 90's. Then you had your license, and became a Registered Representative.

Now and for about the past fifteen years, it is very much different. A trainee is hired by the branch office manager, with more emphasis placed on potential "salesmanship" qualities than anything else. The pre-test training period is usually about three months, during which time the trainee will largely listen while other recently licensed brokers in the office make dozens and dozens and dozens of "cold calls" each day on the telephone, trying to develop a clientele. After about six weeks of employment, the trainee is usually enrolled in an outside "cram course" which will take the trainee out of the branch office for two weeks to attend. This course will be designed to enable the trainee to pass the NASD Series 7 test. The course will probably be excellent, both in quality of instruction and quality and quantity of book-type study materials. At the conclusion of the course, for the next month the trainee will study full time - eight hours in the office, six or eight hours at home, and if it's a smart trainee, twelve hours each Saturday and Sunday. And then on a much anticipated Saturday morning the trainee will arise about 6 A.M., drive to a metropolitan auditorium, and begin a written test (with several hundred other very nervous people) at 9 A.M. that lasts until noon. Break until 1:30 P.M., come back and take another three hour written test in the afternoon. And then the following

Thursday the trainee's employer will be advised by the NASD whether the trainee has scored the necessary passing grade of 70. Only about 60% of the trainees in the investment brokerage industry pass the test the first time. So for 40% it's back to another month of intensive study, maybe even the "cram course" again, and then an attempt at the test a second time. I have worked with brokers who were ultimately extremely good and successful brokers who passed the test only on the *fifth* attempt. However, most branch office managers will, with varying degrees of gentleness, suggest another line of work after two or three failures.

The NASD Series 7 license that all brokers possess today almost insures that the broker has an excellent knowledge of things that are of the nature of the list of 100 that you scored yourself on back in Chapter 2. He or she will know the *mechanics* of the business very well.

But now the Seasoned Veteran will be heard from!

The Seasoned Veteran wishes to state that of all the licensed brokers working for NYSE member firms today, perhaps only 20%, probably closer to 10%, will have the qualities and qualifications that will best serve you. You are looking for a guide for *your* journey, a guide for helping *you* to implement *your* Investment Plan.

The Seasoned Veteran wishes to explain, and to do so will take more than a few words.

Investment firms are in business to make money. They make money from a variety of sources, but one of the principal ones is via the production of *sales commissions* generated by the productive activities of the salesmen they employ. The salesman is your broker, your guide for our journey. He or she works on *straight commission*. Of the commissions that he or she produces, the formulae for determining how much of it he or she gets to keep are very complicated, depending upon type of investments, levels of production, and lately even more. But as a rule of thumb the Seasoned Veteran will say that the salesman's "gross take-home" is about 35% of gross commissions produced. The other 65% goes to the firm. The investment firm's senior management spends a lot of time determining what types of investment products are good for the investor, but it also spends a lot of time determining what investment products are easiest to sell with the best gross commissions at the lowest cost. We cannot blame them for this - they are in business to make money. And so is the salesman - who is your broker - who is, my gosh, *your guide!*

Several pages ago I suggested you interview the branch office manager. In a few pages more I am going to suggest you interview your prospective broker *and* his manager, together. But let me first give you some "background" before the interview.

Your guide should be hired *only* for the purpose of helping you on the implementation of the Investment Plan that you are committing yourself to with this book.

In many ways you are, by adopting the Investment Plan as your primary means for growing capital, in a business of your own which has as its objective maximizing total return with minimum expense. And in this instance your expense is your broker's gross income. So you are at cross-purposes! Your broker's branch office manager will be reviewing daily, or in some extreme cases hourly, the gross sales commissions that your broker has produced month-to-date. Both the manager and the broker are *under extreme pressure* to produce sales commissions.

The senior management of the firm has equipped them with many more types of investment products to sell than you are going to want to buy.

The products today include publicly traded stocks, bonds, and mutual funds, which we will be using for well over 95% of our Investment Plan. But they also include puts; calls; index options; covered call writing; commodities; financial futures; limited partnerships of every conceivable description; life insurance products of all types; initial public offerings of the stock of unseasoned companies; proprietary and "outside" market timing strategies for which special fees are charged; asset allocation and financial planning strategies for which special fees are charged; portfolio review services for which special fees are charged; zero coupon bonds that are marked up drastically in price before the customer buys them; unit investment trusts that are really a long term "basket of bonds" that have about a 5.0% mark-up when the bonds themselves could individually be bought with about a 0.5% mark-up; mortgage-backed securities that neither your broker nor his manager will begin to understand the complexities and idiosyncrasies of and that you can't follow in the paper and that have high mark-ups; new issues of fixed income closed-end mutual funds that almost by definition must go down 8% to 10% in price the minute after you buy them; and I could go on but I'll stop.

I think you get the picture. For reasons that I will largely point out in the next Section of this book, almost all of the investments or services mentioned in the preceding paragraph are absolutely unsuitable for the Plan, and the few that will be used will be used very sparingly. If your broker, or guide, is under great pressure either from his manager or his own checkbook to sell them to you, it will not only be an unpleasant journey, but it will make the financial results of your Plan woefully short of what they should be.

It has the potential to be an extremely serious problem. Even a disaster!

But it need not be. You are in a position where you can, and your Plan can, be in total control!

The reason lies in the area of orientation, which then turns into motivation.

Many investors, perhaps most of them, buy investments because they are sold on buying them by a salesman. Frequently they make the decision out of ignorance and fear, sometimes because they are intimidated. Frequently they very reluctantly say to the salesman "yes, go ahead and buy it for me" and they are immediately and even permanently afraid they have made a wrong decision. And they probably have! They have no real knowledge of the investment, they have no plan into which they are fitting it, they are totally in the hands of and control of the salesman and the large inventory of investment products that his firm has provided him with. They cross their fingers and hope for the best.

You are not in that position. You know, or soon will know, exactly what you want! You have a Plan! You have very tight parameters on what fits the Plan and what doesn't. By the time you have read and digested the remaining chapters of this book, you will know *exactly* what investments you want to buy, and you will know exactly when they should be sold, when they no longer fit. You will *use your broker as a guide - you will do the driving!*

You are at a point now where you can establish some qualifications that your broker should have. Again, I am going to provide a list. All of the items are of equal importance. I am not going to give long reasons for these requirements - they will mostly be self-evident, particularly after you have completed this entire book.

Here is the list:

(1)   The broker can be of either gender. (But for ease of writing I will continue referring to this person as "he.")

(2)   The broker should have at least three years experience as a Series 7 licensed broker, and the last year should have been with the NYSE member firm that you have selected.

(3)   The *principal* area of the broker's activity will be helping clients who have a medium term or long term time frame with total-return-oriented common stocks and mutual funds.

(4)   The broker should have a "fundamental" approach to stock selection as opposed to a "technical" approach, although he should be knowledgeable on basic technical tools.

(5)   The broker should be extremely interested in and involved with the firm's stock research department. He should read and digest thoroughly *all* the reports that recommend stocks for maximum total return over the medium to long term.

(6)   The broker should be knowledgeable about how bonds are traded and have good communications with the bond trading desk. He should have access to the person who knows how to use the "Monroe Bond Trader" or "Compucorp" if he is not that person himself.

(7)   The broker should *not* be the largest producer of commissions in the office. (There are really good reasons for this. Trust the Seasoned Veteran!)

(8)   The broker should have a Sales Assistant (preferably also Series 7 licensed) who is always in the office to assist him with all his activities.

(9)   It will be helpful if the broker has a Series 3 license, which allows him to place orders on the commodities and financial futures exchanges. He probably will not have this. (In many firms these activities are in a separate department.) In this case, determine if there is someone else in the office who does, and determine that a "commission sharing" arrangement can be made. (Commodities and financial futures will be used only very rarely. This will be discussed in Chapter 12.)

(10)   The broker should have a thorough knowledge of margin accounts - loan values, buying power, maintenance requirements, etc. He should be familiar with how these accounts are administered within his firm.

(11)   The broker should have an unblemished "compliance" record with the NASD, NYSE, and SEC. This is a sensitive area, of course, but you have every right to inquire and get an honest answer.

(12)   The broker should have thorough knowledge of the mechanics of writing covered call options. He should also know about index options. He should be prepared to offer you a larger percentage commission discount on option trades than the discount on regular stock trades.

NOW you are at a point where you should arrange an appointment with both the branch office manager and the broker you have selected. Your presentation should go along these lines (Remember, some of these things will be clear to you only after you have read this entire book):

"I want to establish a margin account with your firm. I will also establish a cash account, but that account will be dormant most of the time. The chances are excellent these accounts will be with you for a very long time. The accounts will be the vehicle for a long-term Investment Plan I will be using. There are very tight parameters for the Plan. I will be depositing (here mention your dollar figure - at least $10,000) to establish the margin account. I will be buying a certain number of bonds that will be long in my account. They will probably be U.S. Treasuries, and I expect to pay no more than 8/32 commission above the true inside market, even for odd lots. With the rest of the cash I will be buying fifteen common stocks, no more and no less, that will be long in my account. I will use a part of the loan value of this portfolio to purchase for cash some open-end equity and balanced mutual funds, and when they are load or 12(b)1 funds I will buy them through my cash account and you will make a commission. The no-load funds will be purchased directly from the fund distributors. All mutual fund shares will be held outside your firm, by the custodian that the mutual fund employs.

There will be fairly frequent turnover on my fifteen common stocks, and I expect you will give me commission discounts that will be fair to me and still profitable to you. Occasionally, I will write some covered calls. Very occasionally, I might buy some calls on individual stocks and I might do some index options. Once or twice every ten years or so I might want to buy some commodity contracts, perhaps energy, precious metal, or financial futures. I will be very interested in the output of your equity research department; I will always be looking for bargains in certain categories, and my holding period will almost always be from six months to two years. My fixed income strategy will be very inflexible, and it will require good executions in U.S. Treasuries. There will be periods of weeks and sometimes months when you will not hear from me, but when you do I will want your very best service.

And lastly, let me tell you something that is very important to me. As I said, the investment parameters and strategies of my Plan are very inflexible. Many, many of your investment products will absolutely and positively not fit my Plan. I will use my broker primarily for help and advice on my stock and mutual fund selections, and possibly some covered call writing suggestions. I will depend upon him for good executions and accurate and timely "money line" information on my account. But when I want some advice from him on any matter whatsoever, I will ask him for it and I will tell him specifically what I want. So now you completely know what my Plan is, and your role in it. If my phone ever rings with any type of suggestion to buy something that is outside the parameters of the Plan, I will close my accounts here faster than the market crashed on October 19, 1987."

The Seasoned Veteran believes you should now be all set with an account relationship at a full service national or regional NYSE member firm, and ready for the journey with a qualified guide.

Let me now give you several bits of advice on how you should relate to your guide, your broker. First, he is a busy person, attempting to give maximum good service to many clients. He is extremely busy during "market hours." That is how he makes a living. When you have something you wish to discuss with him, and you anticipate the discussion might take 15 minutes or longer, arrange an appointment for one-half hour after the market closes. You will have a better meeting; he will have fewer distractions and interruptions. Or take him to breakfast before "market hours" (and I hope you will pick up the check! The poor soul probably does not have an expense account). And use his Sales Assistant to get quotes, check on your account balances, etc. Also, do not get in the habit of heavy socializing with your broker. It is certainly OK to play golf, go to a football game, or enjoy a nice dinner. But you must avoid a situation where some wonderful time at 2 A.M. you discover you have agreed to place a major portion of your assets in some absolutely dreadful open-end mutual fund that you have never heard of and that charges an 8.50% sales commission!

OTHER INVESTMENT FIRMS

I earlier promised that reasons would be given for choosing a full-service NYSE member firm over the many other types of business enterprises that are active in the investment industry. I will now do this, at the risk of seeming to disparage them. I do not have this as an intention, for many of them are excellent at what they do. But your Investment Plan will *not* be served by them as well as by the selection you've made.

Investment Banking Firms. Large and small, they are primarily concerned with underwritings, mergers and acquisitions, corporate finance "deals" of all types, institutional broker/dealer activities, sales of securities to large institutions, computer-driven short-term strategies and long, very good, research reports on industries and companies that they charge large amounts for, one way or another. (Some of these will find their way to your member firm.)

Discount Brokerages (NYSE members). Quality of brokers is generally inferior. No research departments and impersonal service. Your full service firm will give you discounts, too, perhaps not as large, but you will get research and service that is much more suited to your purpose.

Discount Brokerages (at banks). No research department. Quality of brokers is generally inferior. They use an outside firm for clearing trades and domiciling accounts. Emphasis on full-load fixed income mutual fund sales, which have no role in your Plan.

Bank Trust Departments. For most banks, the investment function performed here has improved greatly in recent years, with much more flexibility and creativity. However, the concepts, techniques and strategies that your Plan utilizes will largely be contrary to theirs. Again, I believe I could write a separate book on this subject. In one sentence, the Seasoned Veteran believes that Trust Departments are so anxious to 'protect' capital and produce a 'return' on it that they significantly lose the ability to grow it. Further, a Trust Department will not have a margin account capability, will not normally use mutual funds (rightly so: you would then be paying double management fees), and you will tend to get placed into a commingled fund of some sort.

Investment Counselors/Investment Management Companies. Many of the preceding paragraph's comments can be repeated here. On balance, these firms usually do have a better record for growing capital. They will have some concepts, techniques, and strategies which are at variance with your Plan. One very important "plus": Many of the best of these firms offer publicly traded no-load or low-load equity and balanced mutual funds, which might be selected by you within the parameters of Chapter 13.

Financial Planners. They are not brokers. Any brokerage activities require an outside firm. Some of their investment advice might be good, but most of what I have seen is awful. They are very fee and/or commission oriented. There are a lot of unethical "bad guys" in the business, which is largely unregulated. If you have any involvement with these people, your Plan should simply be regarded as a separate asset which you are controlling in its entirety. In short, I feel the Plan is way too good to let it get adulterated by the financial planners that I have seen.

"Door to Door" Mutual Fund Salesman. There might be some very nice person who is a friend of yours who is involved, probably part time, as a salesman of mutual funds, quite possibly for a company that has some life insurance/mutual fund strategies. He will have a Series 6 license (which is fairly easy to get) and you would like to help him earn a commission by buying his full-load product, which *might* be qualified for your Plan. Don't do it. You owe your business to your guide, your broker.

"Research Boutique." This is a specialized brokerage firm that may or may not be a NYSE member. They will have a good or excellent stock research department, but it will specialize in only one or two investment areas. There is a good chance that there is also a large underwriting activity that springs from the research activity, so the sales force concentrates on selling the stocks and bonds that are underwritten. Your only involvement might be to "pick their brains" for equity research without opening an account. The Seasoned Veteran knows that this can be done!

NASDAQ OTC Firms and "Penny Stock" Firms. Some of my best friends have worked at these places. They are not NYSE member firms. They deal in OTC NASDAQ and "pink sheet" stocks that are almost always small and unseasoned companies, priced well under $10. The salesmen/brokers are very persuasive in painting a picture that XYZ stock will be the next GM, IBM, or Xerox. Sales commissions are inordinately high because of the large percentage bid and ask spreads. The stocks are usually very illiquid. There is a good story in the industry:

Salesman: "The stock is 50¢ and is headed for the moon. Let me buy 10,000 shares."

Customer: "OK."

Three weeks later.

Salesman: "The stock is now $1.00 and is definitely headed for Jupiter. Let me buy another 10,000 shares."

Customer: "OK."

Three weeks later.

Salesman: "The stock is now $1.50 and is absolutely headed beyond the solar system. Let me buy another 10,000 shares."

Customer: "Not so fast. I think now I'll *sell* my 20,000 shares."

Salesman: "Fine. To whom?"

I hope that little story has set you up into a mood to have a little fun. We are now nearly at the half-way point in the Seasoned Veteran's lessons to you, so I think we're entitled to a little break. This will be fun for me, and I hope it will be for you. It is largely personal, but it will serve a purpose for the rest of the journey. You will see!

So far we have referred to the NYSE member firm that you have selected as simply that: "The NYSE member firm." But that simply won't do. It is too impersonal. It has no style. It lacks flair. We must come up with something better to call it. But we can't use the name of a real-life, actual firm. That would give the impression of playing favorites, which the Seasoned Veteran definitely does not want to do. So we must come up with an imaginary name, a hypothetical name that has no connection with an actual firm. We can still take the name of some real-life people if we want, like Able and Baker. I don't think there is any real-life, actual firm named Able & Baker. But we can do better than that.

Please go back and read the Acknowledgments at the very beginning of this book. You have seen that my boss when I first got into business in 1959 after serving in the Air Force was named Jim Murphy. He was Resident Partner in the San Francisco office of a large, national NYSE member firm. He took a special interest in me. He was quite a guy. In 1956 he had been national chairman of Citizens for Eisenhower. He knew Ike well. He knew everybody on the highest level of San Francisco business and society. He was a member of every Club in town. He always wore a vest, a homburg hat, and carried a furled black umbrella. The firm's membership in the Pacific Coast Stock Exchange was in his name. This was a very quiet, even sleepy, exchange in those days. One day Jim Murphy took me to the "floor." Once there, he loudly announced that he had 80,000 shares of Kern County Land Co. (subsequently a part of Tenneco, then sold to Atlantic Richfield) for sale. There was silence. The specialist in the stock was aghast - his book showed buy orders for only 200 shares. The price would either plummet or the specialist would have a horrible personal financial problem. Jim Murphy put his hand on the specialist's shoulder, smiled his wonderful smile, and said "Not to worry! I also have a buy order for 80,000 shares of Kern County Land." So, in those days of no "off-floor" trading, he "crossed" the orders at the last, unchanged price. The commissions on the two orders added up, as I recall, to about $90,000 in those days of pre-inflation and fixed, non-negotiated commission schedules.

In 1963 I went back to Wisconsin and took up my banking career. Jim Murphy stayed on until about 1980, when I learned he had retired and then soon passed away.

In 1982, I decided to leave my banking career and return to investment sales. My boss, as you saw in the Acknowledgments, was Andy Carroll. I met him for the first time in 1980 in Fort Lauderdale. I worked for him in two member firms, for three years. Again, I could write a separate book about Andy Carroll. He is one of those people who puts about fifty hours into every day, with large quantities of work, a devoted family, and play. He has been a stockbroker in the same city for thirty years, and he has earned magnificently and invested wisely. I see Andy Carroll frequently these days, and it is always a treat.

But here is the twist!

In the late Sixties, the investment firm that Andy Carroll worked with in Fort Lauderdale was acquired by the same firm that Jim Murphy was Resident Partner of in San Francisco, and pretty soon, in the early Seventies, Andy Carroll became Resident Partner for Florida.

So Jim Murphy and Andy Carroll were in business together (while I was a banker) and became good friends!

This has been not only a story which demonstrates how small a world it is, but it gives us a name for our imaginary, hypothetical NYSE member firm.

Your account, for the balance of the journey that this book provides, is now domiciled at the imaginary investment firm of Murphy & Carroll.

Now what about your "broker?" He deserves a better name than that. I have heard him called a registered executive, an account executive, a floor man, a sponsor, and other names. (Some of them are absolutely unfit for these pages, those that disgruntled customers are wont to use.) But again, these names are mundane, they are trite, they are hackneyed, and they are stale. We can do better.

In Chapter 13, the Seasoned Veteran will tell you about the mutual fund that was my first financial investment, purchased in 1950 when I was 17 years old. But let me now tell you the circumstances of the transaction.

I had saved up about $400, and upon urging and recommendation mostly from my mother, I determined to invest it in the stock market via a certain equity mutual fund. The only stockbroker I knew was a very good friend of my parents, about ten years older than they, and his name was

"Beanie" Shepherd - Mr. Shepherd, to me. He was located at the local office of a Chicago-headquartered NYSE member firm, a very good firm that is still in business today under the management of the founder's sons. I made an appointment to see Mr. Shepherd. On his desk when I got there was one of those old-fashioned glass contraptions that had an actual ticker tape coming out of it, falling into a wastebasket. "Beanie" Shepherd had been a stockbroker since the Twenties. He was Ivy League educated. He had married well. He bought his clothes in New York City, which was then the only city where Brooks Brothers had a store. He had a very patrician bearing. He lived in a big house on the lake.

He treated me very well on this occasion - like an adult capitalist should be treated. He opened an account for me. I gave him my order. He explained how it would be executed. He gave me a prospectus and other literature. He explained I would receive quarterly and annual reports. He explained why he thought it was a good investment for an investor in my circumstance. I thanked him and went home.

Soon my father got home from work. He inquired how my appointment with "Beanie" Shepherd had gone. I told him I thought it had gone very well. He said, "Fine. I think 'Beanie' will be an excellent *customer's man* for you." I looked at him, and inquired what a customer's man was. I had never before heard those words used. He explained it was what one called his own stockbroker.

The term has largely gone out of use. It had its vogue in the Twenties and Thirties. It is old-fashioned, but it is in the large current dictionaries and it is not denoted there as being *archaic.* And the Seasoned Veteran thinks it's wonderful!

But today, being mindful of the age and times, and because a large percentage of the people who should use this Investment Plan would rightfully and strongly object if we used the words Customer's Man, we must modify them somewhat.

From now on, your broker and your guide will be a Customer's Person at the NYSE member firm of Murphy & Carroll!

By now we have done a lot of preparation. Our bags are packed! We know generally how the journey is going to unfold. Let's now make sure our vehicle is ready to help us to its allowable maximum!

10
Your Margin Account:
A Slightly Faster Trip

The Seasoned Veteran is now going to do something I reluctantly did in the last chapter. I am again going to "put the cart before the horse." I am going to tell you the bottom line of what your Plan calls for in terms of structure. You will find out the exact details of this structure in the next two sections of this book, beginning in the next Chapter.

We are dealing in this Chapter with the specifics of your relationship at Murphy & Carroll.

Your primary account at Murphy & Carroll will be a margin account. The Seasoned Veteran's margin strategy, as you will see, is a conservative one and is designed to take advantage of the economic and market scenarios forecast in Chapter 7. I am well aware that leverage is a two-edged sword; in our Plan we are using the proper side of the blade.

You will also have a cash account, but it will be secondary in importance and absolutely dormant most of the time.

Your accounts will be titled in the name of whatever entity owns your capital. The Seasoned Veteran is not going to give you any advice on the subject, as to whether it should be in your name, joint with your wife or other family member, a trust, a personal holding company, or whatever.

This is a matter totally up to you, your attorney, your accountant, or some other expert in this field. I do not mean to downgrade the importance of this; it is simply out of my area of expertise and outside the scope of this book and the Investment Plan it represents.

When you open your margin account, you will be asked to sign the firm's Margin Agreement. There will be a lot of fine print. I have read through these forms at several firms, and I strongly believe you're not placing yourself at risk at any NYSE member firm if you go ahead and sign these forms without consulting your attorney. They are required by the Federal Reserve Board, which is the federal entity with the power to regulate margin accounts. You may wonder about this; remember, a margin account is going to enable you to borrow from your broker by pledging the securities you own as collateral. In a major way, your broker is in the banking business by performing this function.

All of the securities you buy in your margin account will be held "in street name" by Murphy & Carroll. This means that you will never have in your physical possession a bond or stock certificate. (U.S. Treasury securities will be held by Murphy & Carroll as a "book entry," which for your purpose is the same as "street name.") This means, among other things, that the individual companies you are an owner of, or a creditor of, do not know you at all! You will not be on their books as a stockholder or bondholder—Murphy & Carroll will be on their books. Murphy & Carroll will make an effort to forward to you the regular stockholder and bond- holder written communications that the specific companies publish and mail, as well as proxies and other voting material. My experience is you will get these most of the time, but not always. You may wish to separately contact the company to be placed on their mailing list—this will give you everything but voting proxies, which legally must go through Murphy & Carroll.

Your Customer's Person will be invaluable to you in explaining the details of how your margin account operates.

You will use your intitial capital, which was discussed way back in

Chapter 2, to establish your margin account. Once deposited to the account, it will be used to purchase and pay the full price for the fixed income securities described in Chapter 11, the next chapter, and the equity securities described in Chapter 12. The allocation of your capital between these categories will be discussed in Section VI, which will give you specific advice on portfolio management.

Once your fixed income securities and equity securities are "long" in your margin account, you will have a certain borrowing power. This will be determined by the specific loan value on the individual securities. The loan values are established and defined by Regulation T of the Federal Reserve Board. They can be changed at any time, but most of the maximum loan values have been unchanged since the mid-seventies. They range from 50% of market value on common stocks up to 92% on short term U.S. Treasury securities.

When you have securities "long" in your account, and use your borrowing power to get a loan against them, the amount of the loan is the "debit balance." You are charged interest on the debit balance, usually at an increment above the prime rate, with the increment dependent upon size of debit balance: the higher the debit balance, the lower the interest rate. You do not have to write a check for the interest; it is simply added to the debit balance, usually on the last day of the monthly statement period.

All income generated by your long securities, interest and dividends, will be received by Murphy & Carroll and credited against your debit balance. Our Plan has an objective that the income will largely offset the debit balance interest on a before-tax basis.

The loan that you take from Murphy & Carroll via the margin account will have its proceeds deposited to your cash account. This cash amount will be used to purchase open-end mutual funds. These will be discussed in Chapter 13. Open-end mutual funds cannot be purchased on margin, or in a margin account. They must be paid for in cash. Once they have been paid for in cash and held for 30 days, they may be deposited to a margin account and borrowed against up to 50% of market value. You will not normally be doing this. You will not normally be borrowing even up to the maximum loan value of the fixed income and equity securities in your margin account. You will, as you will see in the remainder of this book, always be in excellent position to maintain your margin account without having to bring in your open-end mutual fund shares to meet a margin call if there should be one. You will never be leveraged anywhere near the absolute maximum. Your open-end mutual fund shares will always be maintained in an account at the mutual fund company or its custodian bank, for the purpose of having all cash distributions, usually dividends or realized capital gains distributions, credited to your account in the form of additional shares. These should compound nicely. And the open-end mutual fund shares are available if needed for margin maintenance purposes, which can be reassuring.

The profits from sales of fixed income and equity securities in your margin account will be used to reduce your debit balance. The losses will, of course, increase your debit balance. Once a year, on January 1, you will totally review your portfolio and make adjustments on category allocations. This will be explained fully in Section VI.

Now you have been exposed to the Seasoned Veteran's basic strategy.!

Your margin account will, through its fixed income and individual equity holdings, be a vehicle for capital gains and for moderate leverage. Most importantly, it will be a vehicle for *compounding total return!* The income it generates through interest and dividends will be used to offset the cost of the leverage, which is the interest charged on your debit balance. The leverage, which is the borrowing against fixed income and equity securities, will come from the permanent "sub-portfolio" of open-end mutual fund shares that the borrowed funds will purchase.

This is what I'm talking about when I mention a slightly faster trip!

All new cash that you consider as new permanent capital will simply be deposited to the margin account, which in most cases will just reduce the debit balance. If the new capital is large enough to pay the debit balance in full and create a credit balance, it will occasion a January 1 type review and allocation changes. This will be discussed in detail in Section VI.

All withdrawals of any sort, be they for a major one-time personal expense, or be they regular monthly withdrawals for retirement type living expense, will simply be loans from Murphy & Carroll against your borrowing power. Again, Section VI will discuss this. But I will again "put the cart before the horse" and say that to grow at 15% and withdraw at 8%, or even 10%, in retirement years isn't a bad scenario at all!

There are additional major benefits that your margin account at Murphy & Carroll will provide.

One has already been alluded to, in the discussion of securities long in the account, in street name and book entry. This totally takes you out of the business of being your own custodian. You have no worries about bearer bonds or lost certificates. You will never need to visit a safe deposit box or deliver on or before the settlement date. You will never concern yourself with a delayed dividend check. Your securities will be covered by SIPC insurance as well as the larger, supplemental policy that Murphy & Carroll told you about when you qualified them as your NYSE member firm. And there is not one penny of additional cost to you for the custodian service they provide.

Of equal importance and value is the bookkeeping service that Murphy & Carroll furnishes at no extra cost. In this age of computers it is literally fantastic! Every month, usually the last business day of the month, Murphy & Carroll's computers will print up and mail to you a statement that has even more bells and whistles than your bank statements. You will get a current market price and total market value on every individual fixed income and equity security. The sum of these valuations will be provided. All activity during the month will be itemized: purchases, sales, income received, interest charged, etc. You will be given year-to-date totals of sale proceeds. You will be given your total current debit balance and your total net equity. You will be given the name of your Customer's Person and his or her phone number, including toll free numbers if needed. These statements should definitely be retained by you over all the years. They will be invaluable to your tax accountant. And they will be invaluable to you in your overall portfolio management. You will learn more about how to use them in Sections VI and VII.

Onward! We shall now get into the real nitty-gritty of the Investment Plan.

SECTION V.
THE INVESTMENTS
AND THE STRATEGIES

11
Fixed Income Securities: UST and FIPS

The Seasoned Veteran has been involved with the bond markets every working day for twenty-five years and at least weekly for five years before the twenty-five.

All through my nearly twenty years in banking, to 1982, the successful management of my employer bank's bond portfolio was a key ingredient in the success I attained on my career path. The securities involved were U.S. Treasuries; U.S. Agencies; commercial paper; bankers' acceptances; C.D.'s of other banks; "Yankee" C.D.'s; G.O. municipals; revenue municipals; insured municipals; and investment grade corporates.

Following that, I was a stockbroker for two NYSE member firms for three years. For a portion of every day I was involved with U.S. Treasuries; U.S. Agencies; fixed rate C.D.'s; floating rate C.D.'s; zero coupon Treasuries; zero coupon municipals; G.O. municipals; revenue municipals; insured municipals; unit investment trusts - short-term and long-term, insured and uninsured, national pools and state pools; corporates of all ratings, including "junk;" mortgage-backed securities of all three major agencies - GNMA, FNMA, and Freddie Mac; and all the fixed income mutual funds, open-end and closed-end, non-hedged and hedged.

For the past three years I have been an institutional bond salesman, selling fixed income securities in large volume to portfolio managers at banks, S&L's, credit unions, insurance companies, pension funds, mutual funds, and others. I have dealt exclusively with all of the types of investments mentioned in the preceding two paragraphs for three years. For one six-month period I dealt only with mortgage-backed securities. For one two-month period I dealt only with Treasury zero coupon securities. For a four-month period I dealt only with C.D.'s.

The point I am attempting to establish is that I really know fixed income securities and the markets in which they trade. An analogy might be that the bond markets are like a wonderful wife to me - I have a long-term, very comfortable relationship with them; the stock market might be compared to an exciting mistress; and mutual funds might be compared to a long-term friend, dependable and engaging for a lifetime. To take the metaphors one step further, I believe the relationship with my wife - the bond markets - can be made, from time to time, as exciting as though with a mistress and always dependable as though with a long-time friend.

U.S. TREASURY SECURITIES

The recommendation the Seasoned Veteran is going to make to you is the result of a lifetime of experience and cogitation. And the wonderful thing about it is that it is unbelievably simple.

Your Investment Plan calls for owning in the fixed income section of your portfolio *only* those securities issued directly by the Treasury Department of the United States. We will be calling these securities simply "UST."

I am not going to give you lengthy explanations on why I believe this is an excellent recommendation. Certainly all of the other types of fixed income securities mentioned in the earlier paragraphs have attributes that make them suitable for some investors. Someday I might well write a separate book, as lengthy and as detailed as this one, on the pluses and minuses of the plethora of fixed income investment products that the investment banking community has designed and helped borrowers issue to investors of all types.

But the attributes we are looking for are totally to be found in UST. No other fixed income investment can match them in these important categories: creditworthiness; liquidity; absolute and pure price sensitivity to the money market; wide selection of maturity dates; virtual absence of call features; and high margin loan value in your account at Murphy & Carroll.

Let us examine each of these features in turn. The Seasoned Veteran will resist the temptation to bring into this discussion all of the other specific types of fixed income securities, and the reasons why they do not measure up. Suffice to say that for our purpose - which is to maximize total return and compound it over periods of years and decades - the other types of fixed income securities have drawbacks and risks which disqualify them. (And we *will* discuss some of them further in Chapter 14.)

Creditworthiness. A bond is simply a promissory note. The domestic issuer promises to pay the owner of the note a certain number of U.S. dollars at some definite date in the future, with interest, at a specified percentage of the total, to be paid - also in U.S. dollars - along the way.

I can remember my grandmother during World War II saying that it would be amazing to her if "the government" could ever pay off the debts that it was incurring with the War Bonds issued in those years; the bonds would probably default. She was a wonderful lady, but in this instance she totally missed the point. The only "person" who can print up the dollars required to pay any debt is the Treasurer of the United States, and that "person" is, in the case of UST, the issuer! He (or she) alone has the franchise, the printing press! The State of California issues bonds. General Motors issues bonds. Those bonds are very "creditworthy," rated very highly by Moody. But neither the Governor of California nor the Chairman of GM (and certainly not the Mayor of Podunk nor the CEO of Junkcorp) has the franchise to print up U.S. dollars. That is what makes UST the only fixed income securities that are absolutely and positively creditworthy. It follows, therefore, that there is no ultimate dollar risk in owning them. The par value will be paid at maturity, and the interest will be paid exactly on the dates specified. This fact alone qualifies UST as the bedrock of your portfolio. Remember: we must *protect* capital in order to *grow* capital.

Liquidity. The issuance of UST is simply the Government's method of financing the annual budget deficits which over many, many years have added up to a national debt of close to three trillion dollars. U.S. Treasury Bills are short-term obligations (maturing less than one year from date of issue); U.S. Treasury Notes are medium-term obligations (maturing from one to ten years from date of issue); and U.S. Treasury Bonds are long-term obligations (maturing beyond ten years, to a current maximum of thirty years, from the date of issue). There are, in total, about 230 issues presently outstanding. Over 95% of the issues have *billions* outstanding in each issue; the few other issues are outstanding in the hundreds of millions in each issue. The largest banks and investment firms are the approximately 40 *primary* dealers in making markets and assisting the Fed with its open market operations. There are literally hundreds of other smaller banks and investment firms making up the rest of the market. The 'inside' market, the primary dealers' spread between bid and asked, is usually less than $1.00, and frequently less than $0.50, per $1,000 par value (although the daily press, including the *Wall Street Journal,* usually quotes about a $2.50 spread). There is *always* a highly liquid market in UST. This can be taken for granted. If ever there should be a total financial calamity in this world, the liquidity provided in the UST marketplace would be of tremendous value to those owning them.

Absolute and pure price sensitivity to the money market. To a large extent, the UST market *is* the money market. This has been more apparent than ever in the Eighties, due to larger Fed open market operations and massive foreign investing in U.S. markets, among other reasons. The interest rates on all other money market and longer-term fixed income securities are set at premiums to, and trade at increments above, the yields presently available on UST of the same maturity. Changing credit situations, changing investor appetites and perceptions, changing tax laws, etc. all have the possibility of influencing the prices and yields of other fixed income securities. These outside factors are not applicable to UST. A corporation with a AA credit rating may be subject to a LBO financed by massive debt. The already outstanding AA bonds are downgraded to Ba or worse overnight, and the market price of the bonds can go down precipitously as a result. This will not happen with UST. Or a pool of GNMA's with 30 year mortgages is expected to pay off in 12 years, which is the *average* time a single family residential mortgage is outstanding. The individual mortgages in this pool, however, are in the depressed "oil patch," there are massive foreclosures, the government makes good on any shortfalls or deficiencies, and the GNMA's pay off at par in three years. The maturity has changed, and if you paid a premium above par for the GNMA's, you are stuck with a problem known as a quick loss. The yield increments over UST that other riskier securities possess is not enough to compensate. Fifty basis points on our Plan's grand scheme means very little. Five hundred basis points is simply not worth the associated credit risk. I could give dozens or even hundreds of other insights and examples. The pure price sensitivity to the money market makes UST eminently suitable for the specific strategy for owning them that I will outline for you very shortly. No other type of fixed income security qualifies.

Wide selection of maturity dates. The same specific strategy that I just referred to mandates that exact maturities be available over a long period of time.

As this is written, there are 232 issues of UST in total. Twenty-seven issues of Bills come due within six months; eight issues mature from six months to one year. There are 115 issues of Notes and Bonds maturing within five years (Remember: a Bond, long-term when issued, can mature next week!); there are 35 issues maturing in from five to ten years; and 47 issues maturing in from ten to thirty years.

There is just no way any other type of fixed income security provides this maturity spectrum. The use of corporates or municipals would involve many different issuers. U.S. Agencies come close in the early years, and they do carry small yield advantages, but they lack the overall liquidity and have considerably higher bid and asked spreads, particularly for small blocks.

Virtual absence of call features. For me to use the term "virtual absence" might be a bit of an overstatement. There are presently seven issues that are callable through 1995, but three of these have coupon interest rates below 5.00% and almost certainly they won't be called. There are 19 issues that are callable after 1995, of which 16 are callable after 2002. Everything is relative; so the point is that there is a wide selection of UST issues that are totally non-callable, and of those that are, the call dates are far enough out that they are not a big factor. Most corporates, and many municipals, are callable. All mortgage-backed securities are, in effect, callable at any time because of unpredictable mortgage prepayments. For the purpose of the fixed income positioning strategy that the Seasoned Veteran will soon explain, the absence of a call feature is a decided plus.

Marginability. Your UST securities will be "long" in your margin account at Murphy & Carroll. The loan value will be in a range of 85% to 92% of market value, depending on maturity. For our calculations later, we will use 90% as the UST loan value. The loan value of corporates or municipals would be in a range of 65% to 75%. This will be an important factor when we discuss portfolio strategies in Section VI.

Now that we have addressed and explained the six attributes that make UST so suitable for our purpose, let us again remind ourselves of what our purpose is!

Our purpose is to grow capital by maximizing total return and compounding it over a period of years and decades.

FIXED INCOME POSITIONING STRATEGY

Stereotyped thinking for many years held that bonds were a safe investment to buy and hold for the income produced. In historic periods of low interest rate volatility and low inflation, this was good thinking. Interest rate volatility, however, causes price volatility. You have all learned that as interest rates go up, bond prices go down. And vice versa. And the longer the maturity on the bond, the more price volatility there is. This is called "market risk," as opposed to "credit risk."

Let me tell a story that will dramatize market risk.

I was in banking in 1981 when a very nice elderly couple came to my office. (We will give them anonymity by changing their name very slightly.) They were Mr. and Mrs. Goldstein. They had large checking and savings accounts at my bank and several C.D.'s. I had met them once before. They wished to borrow $50,000 for the purpose of investing in their son's entrepreneurial venture on Long Island. I told them that the easiest way to make the loan would be for them to post collateral. They agreed. They said they owned large amounts of utility bonds. I said we would need $75,000 in market value of utility bonds to support a $50,000 loan. Mr. Goldstein asked his wife to go to their safe deposit box and bring back $75,000 in utility bonds. She was gone about twenty minutes, during which time Mr. Goldstein reminisced about his days in the garment district in New York City, where he had made his fortune. Mrs. Goldstein returned to my office with a veritable armload of bonds. She put them on my desk. There were seventy-five $1,000 par value bearer bonds of Boston Edison Co., a highly rated utility. They had been issued in 1965, when the Goldsteins had bought them at 100. The coupon interest rate was 4.75% and they were due on November 1, 1995. In other words, the bonds had been 30 year bonds at issue and in 1981 they were about half way along.

I could immediately see there was a problem, but to make the point with the Goldsteins, I called a brokerage firm and asked *my* Customer's Person what the current market price on the bonds was. He came back in a minute or two and said it was 37.

I said, "Mr. and Mrs. Goldstein, because of the historic high interest rates in today's money market, with the prime rate at 20% and U.S. Treasury Long-Term Bonds at 15%, your 4.75% bonds here, which have 14 years to go before they mature, are only worth today 37 cents on the dollar. They will be worth 100 cents when they mature, providing Boston

Edison is still solvent, but today the $75,000 par value is only worth $27,750. We will need much more collateral."

The Goldsteins, fortunately, understood; Mrs. Goldstein was dispatched to the safe deposit box a second time, bringing back not an armload, but a shopping cart full of additional utility bonds. The loan was made!

The wonderful thing about market risk is that it creates magnificent opportunity.

The Seasoned Veteran is going to outline a strategy for owning UST that will protect you in terms of market risk and aid you greatly in terms of market opportunity.

I believe that over any ten year period in the future, an excellent total return can be attained. The strategy is 100% dictated by the movement of the market.

You will use the yield to maturity of the current 30 year U.S. Treasury Bond as your benchmark, and "trigger for action." This Bond is called in the trade the "Long Bond."

Before explaining the strategy, let's examine where the Long Bond yield to maturities have been, and make a forecast as to where they might go.

During the Fifties, the Long Bond yields ranged between 2.00% and 4.00%.

During the Sixties, the Long Bond yields ranged between 4.00% and 7.00%.

During the Seventies, the Long Bond yields ranged between 5.50% and 11.00%.

During the period 1980-1984, the Long Bond ranged between 9.75% and 15.00%, with several back-and-forth gyrations from 10.00% in early 1980 to 15.00% in late 1981 to 10.50% in late 1982 to 13.30% in mid-1984.

During the period 1985 to mid-1989, the Long Bond has gone from 12.00% to 7.50% to 10.25% to 8.50% to 9.40% to 7.65% to 8.15% as this is being written.

The Seasoned Veteran will now make a bold prognostication. For the next ten years the Long Bond yield will range from 7.00% to 15.00%, with most of the time spent between 8.00% and 10.00%. The surges toward 15.00% will be swift and sudden. A corollary forecast is that yield spreads vs. the Long Bond for other UST maturities will *average* as follows: 20 year - 20 basis points; 10 year - 40 basis points; 7 year - 60 basis points; 5 year - 75 basis points; 3 year- 100 basis points; 2 year - 125 basis points; 1 year - 140 basis points; 6 months - 190 basis points; and 3 months - 225 basis points. (Please remember the word average; flat or inverted yield curves will continue to be the exception to the rule.)

Now the Seasoned Veteran will explain the detail of the UST Fixed Income Positioning Strategy, which we will call "FIPS."

The benchmark that will trigger action is the present yield to maturity on the 30 Year UST Long Bond. You must *always* keep yourself informed of what this yield is.

When the Long Bond is less than 7.00%, the investment is 100% UST Bills of 90 day maturity.

When the Long Bond crosses over 7.00% on the upside, the UST-Bills are rolled over as they mature into UST Bills with maturity of 180 days. As these mature, they are rolled over into 180 day Bills if the Long Bond yield is between 7.00% and 7.99%. If the Long Bond has gone down below 7.00%, the rollovers are into 90 day Bills.

On the day after the Long Bond crosses over 8.00% on the upside, all UST-Bills are sold and full proceeds are invested in UST Two Year Notes (or Bonds). These are held either (1) until maturity, when they are rolled into 90 day Bills if the Long Bond is then below 7.00%, or 180 day Bills if the Long Bond is 7.00% to 7.99%, or UST Two Year Notes (or Bonds) if the Long Bond is 8.00% to 8.99%, or (2) on the day after the Long Bond crosses over 9.00%, *all* the UST Two Year Notes (or Bonds) are sold at the market (producing a small loss) and replaced by UST Three Year Notes (or Bonds).

The UST Three Year Notes (or Bonds) are held either (1) until maturity, when they are rolled over into the maturity categories outlined above depending on the Long Bond yields at that time, or (2) until the Long Bond Yield crosses over 10.00%. On the next day, 50% of the UST Three Year Notes (or Bonds) are sold at the market (producing a small loss) and replaced by UST Five Year Notes (or Bonds).

The Long Bond Yield has now hit a benchmark, of sorts, by breaking out of the 8.00% to 9.99% parameters that the Seasoned Veteran believes will be the normal range. You have 50% in UST Three Year and 50% in UST Five Year maturities, and have taken some small losses to get there. You have also improved your cash "throw-off" by about 400 basis points over where you were when you were in UST-Bills (about 275 basis points attributed to change in the absolute yield curve and about 125 basis points attributed to the narrower yield spread because of longer maturities).

You will stay in this 50% Three Year and 50% Five Year position until (1) they mature, when they should be replaced with UST maturities as outlined in the 8.00% to 10.99% brackets above; or (2) the UST Long Bond goes down to a 7.99% yield, when on the next day they are sold at the market (producing very nice capital gains) and proceeds go to 180 day UST Bills; or (3) the UST Long Bond yield goes to 11.00%, when all the UST Three Year Notes (or Bonds) are sold at the market (producing a small loss) and proceeds are reinvested in UST-Notes (or Bonds) with a Seven Year maturity.

Now you have 50% Five Year and 50% Seven Year positions, and these are held either until (1) they mature, to be replaced in the maturity brackets previously given for 8.00% to 11.99% Long Bond scenarios; or (2) the UST Long Bond goes down to a 7.99% yield, when on the next day they are sold at the market (producing, again, some very nice gains) and proceeds go to 180 day UST-Bills; or (3) the UST Long Bond goes to 12.00% when on the next day all the Five Year Notes (or Bonds) are sold at the market (producing a moderate loss) and proceeds go to a UST Ten Year Note (or Bond).

You are now in a 50% Seven Year and 50% Ten Year position, and it is apparent to you, with the Long Bond Yield at 12.00%, that you are in an interest rate climate that has existed only in a few very highly "reaction to inflation" years in the early Eighties. If Long Bond yields do not get to 13.00%, you will follow the holding or selling strategy that has been outlined in the preceding paragraph.

If the Long Bond Yield *does* get to 13.00%, you will sell all your UST Seven Year holdings (not paying any attention to the loss!) and replace them with a Twenty Year UST-Bond.

Now you are in a very high (historically) interest rate scenario, and you will enjoy the very nice cash "throw-offs" of your Ten Year and Twenty Year UST until either (1) maturities, as outlined above (changing 11.99% to 12.99%), or (2) sales at a 7.99% Long Bond Yield, where you will have some *really* nice capital gains. Or, and this now is very possible because inflation seems to be in a 'runaway' phase (which the Seasoned Veteran believes will be quite temporary) the Long Bond yield goes to 14.00%. If this happens you will sell 50% of your Ten Year UST (again ignoring the loss) and invest the proceeds in the Long Bond itself.

Now you will be 25% Ten Year, 50% Twenty Year, and 25% Thirty Year. Your weighted averaged current yield as well as yield to maturity on this UST portfolio will be on the order of 12.80% (11.60% on the Ten Year, 12.80% on the Twenty Year, and 14.00% on the Thirty Year) and this is where you will stay under ALL interest rate scenarios until the Long Bond yield hits 7.99% on the downside. On the next day ALL the UST Notes (and Bonds) are sold with proceeds going to 180 day UST-Bills. The capital gains will be enormous!

You will then stay in UST-Bills until the Long Bond yield crosses back over 8.00% (and in this instance stays there for ten trading days) when the FIPS is implemented again by selling the Bills and buying the Two Year Note (or Bond).

The purchases of the Notes and Bonds will always be made by selecting the designated maturity as closely as possible from the date of purchase, and by selecting a coupon interest rate that makes the Note or Bond as close to par or 100 (a "current coupon" security) as is possible in the market as it exists on the date of purchase. If the Note or Bond selected is callable, you will need to make a judgment as to whether or not it will be called, based on the coupon interest rate. You do not want it to be called (unless you are able to purchase it at a discount, which the Seasoned Veteran would say should be a price of 96 or lower, and this would be very unlikely for a current coupon security).

I am aware that the preceding paragraphs were "heavy going" for some of you. I would suggest re-reading them, and I'll bet it becomes clearer. To help you further, I am going to recap the FIPS in columnar fashion:

Designation	Long Bond "Trigger"	UST holding/action
A	Less than 7.00%	90 day Bills
B	7.00% (to 7.99%)	180 day Bills
C	8.00% (to 8.99%)	Two Year UST
D	9.00% (to 9.99%)	Three Year UST
E	10.00% (to 10.99%)	Sell 50% of D To Five Year UST
F	11.00% (to 11.99%)	Sell 50% of D To Seven Year UST
G	12.00% (to 12.99%)	Sell 100% of E To Ten Year UST
H	13.00% (to 13.99%)	Sell 100% of F To Twenty Year UST
I	14.00%	Sell 50% of G To Long Bond
	14.01% plus	No change
	14.00% to 8.00%	No change
	7.99% minus	Sell G, H, I To B

Based on a ten year scenario of Long Bond Yields going from 7.00% to 14.00% over the first five years, and then back below 8.00% in the second five years, there would be an average annual total return, including interest and net capital gains, of about 14%, with 10% coming from interest and 4% from net capital gains.

If the scenario were changed to a five year round-trip on the Long Bond from 7.00% to 14.00% and back again to 7.99%, the average annual total return would be about 19%, with 11% coming from interest and 8% coming from net capital gains.

Let's take a look at a really fast scenario (and the Seasoned Veteran says it could happen!). Suppose the 7.00% to 14.00% round-trip is made in two and one-half years. The average annualized total return would be about 23%, with 11% attributable to interest and 12% to net capital gains.

The best thing is that you are protected, by being short in maturity unless yields are historically high, from the sort of market depreciation that the Goldsteins experienced and endured. If Long Bond yields should go into historically *new* high ground above 15%, I doubt they will stay there for long, and your purchase yields of nearly 13% are something that you can live with.

Some of you may say: "I can improve my return with corporates." "My tax bracket dictates only municipals." "I will buy fast paying GNMA's at a discount." "I will buy zero coupons to lock in the reinvestment rate." "I will *really* improve my return with junk." "I will *never* sell a bond that is paying me 14%." "I will buy fixed income mutual funds to take advantage of hedging strategies involving financial futures." "I will speculate in the T-Bond contract on the Chicago Board of Trade." "I can't bear to sit with 6% T-Bills."

To you the Seasoned Veteran says three things: (1) I will discuss some of these investments in Chapter 14; (2) I have thought of all your arguments and rejected them; and (3) Trust me!

12
Equity Securities: FFF, ESG and SSS

In Chapter 9 and Chapter 10 the Seasoned Veteran gave away the fact that your portfolio power will be largely, but not exclusively, attained by using three categories of securities. Fixed income and equity instruments will be the margin account vehicle serving as collateral for borrowing from Murphy & Carroll for the purpose of purchasing mutual funds. It was further stated there would always be fifteen individually selected common stocks (equities) long in the margin account. It is this Chapter's objective to assist you in this extremely important area. This portion of our overall portfolio will be the most significant in terms of possibly *exceeding* the underlying objective of compounding annually at 15.00% total return. It will be the most aggressive part of the Investment Plan. It is important to do well, not only because of the absolute contribution that the fifteen stocks will make, but also the leverage they will contribute to the mutual fund portion of the plan.

In Chapter 7 I made a case for the decade of the Nineties, and probably beyond, being on balance an excellent time to be alive. I made a case for consistently rising stock markets. I said there would be both bull and bear markets, but the bull markets would have much higher highs and the bear markets would have much higher lows. And I said the Dow Jones Industrial Average would exceed 5000 by 1995 and go through 9000 at some point

before the Twenty-First Century began. I said maybe these prognostica-
tions were on the conservative side.

This Chapter will tell you how to take advantage of this situation!

The balance of this Chapter is divided into four parts. The first two parts
will give you detailed instructions on how you should go about selecting
the fifteen stocks that will be part of *all* portfolios that will be discussed in
Section VI. The third part will give you detailed instructions on what you
should do with the fifteen stocks once you own them. And the final section
will give you some ideas of how you can enhance your total return in certain
specific economic and market conditions.

THE FUNDAMENTALLY FAVORED FIFTEEN

In Chapter 5 you learned quite a bit about John M. Templeton and his
initial mutual fund, the Templeton Growth Fund. You saw the record it has
compiled in its 35-year history. You became aware that over all the
domestic and global problems of the post-war years, the dedication to a
consistent investment philosophy of diversification and bargain hunting
allowed the attainment of a 15% compounded total return, whereby
$10,000 initially invested had a present market value just a bit over
$1,170,000.

For nearly eleven years, at least one member of my immediate family
has owned shares in the Templeton Growth Fund. This has meant all the
quarterly and annual reports have been delivered to my house, as well as
reports of the annual meetings and sometimes even copies of speeches that
Mr. Templeton has made. I have taken time to read all these mailings. And
I have several times seen Mr. Templeton interviewed on *Wall Street Week
with Louis Rukeyser*. Although I have never met Mr. Templeton, I feel I
know him well. He is a very well-spoken person but he does have a habit
that a high school English teacher would find fault with. She would say it
is a bad habit. The Seasoned Veteran says it's an excellent habit. Mr.
Templeton tends to overuse two words in his writings, speeches and

conversations. The two words are "bargain" and "diversify."

We shall use those two words as our watchwords for the pages immediately following. I will take care of the diversification and I will tell you how to look for bargains. *You* will find them.

The Seasoned Veteran's parameters for the selection of fifteen stocks are again both inflexible and flexible. I am going to tell you exactly what to look for, but you will have wide latitude in the actual selection.

First of all, fifteen stocks will *always* be a part of your portfolio, but over a period of years and decades you will be selecting and owning many, many more than fifteen stocks. You will be buying *and selling*, but you will only own fifteen at any given time. These will be called the Fundamentally Favored Fifteen, and we will simply call them the "FFF" from this point on in our journey. The reasons for your selections will be based on fundamental analysis as opposed to technical analysis.

You will be looking for bargains. They're easy to find if you know where to look.

You will be working closely with your Customer's Person, and you will be diligently reading many of the reports on industry groups and individual stocks that Murphy & Carroll's research department publishes. You will be getting investment ideas from *Forbes*, maybe *Barron's* and *Value Line*, maybe your daily newspaper readings. You will be getting investment ideas from real life trips to such as the drug store, supermarket, clothing stores, auto dealers, liquor stores, shopping malls, book stores, and fast food emporiums. You will be looking at companies that are successful. Or companies which are not successful now but for which you think a strong case can be made that they will rather quickly become successful. You will know a bit about mundane products like aspirin tablets, and you will know a bit about superconductivity, molecular biology, and telecommunications. You will always be on the prowl for investment ideas. There are always a lot of good investment ideas around.

And once you have an investment idea, you will make a determination on whether the stock involved is a bargain in today's market and in today's economy. *It must be a bargain.* You must take a look at the stock's recent history. The front side of a Standard & Poor's Stock Report, the section called "Per Share Data," is an invaluable tool. You get a ten-year per-share history of book value, earnings, dividends, price ranges, and P/E ratios. On the same page you get a six year price bar chart with monthly ranges and monthly volume. You, and your Customer's Person, must be absolutely and totally convinced that the stock is a bargain on the basis of all the fundamental yardsticks, which will involve the total economy, the industry, the company, and its standing in the current marketplace. Very important is the EPS growth and the P/E ratio. What you want is a low P/E and the chance of an EPS explosion! But then it gets more complicated than that. You, and your Customer's Person, must make a determination that thousands and millions of other investors will *also* perceive it is a bargain. Because if they, too, think it's a bargain they will buy it. And they will be buying it from reluctant sellers. And that is what makes prices go higher! You want a situation where *you* will soon become a reluctant seller to somebody who thinks it's a bargain, a bargain at a significantly higher price.

But then it gets still more challenging. Because you must determine that the price has an excellent chance of going higher by *at least 60%* within two years.

Because you will never own stock in the FFF for longer than two years.

But that's again putting the cart in front of the horse. That is talk about selling. We will do that in a bit. We must first talk some more about buying.

You will buy within certain categories. This will give you diversification. Your FFF will be divided, really, into *seven categories*. Is is *not* complicated:

Category I. Two stocks selected from the thirty stocks that comprise the Dow Jones Industrial Average. This list is found every day in the *Wall Street Journal*'s last section, where the DJIA charts are. They are household names. They are large capitalization stocks and most of them have extensive multinational operations. The vast majority pay a dividend.

They are marginable and have listed puts and calls. Your objective will be at all times to own the two of these stocks that have the best chance of going up in price by 60% in the two year period from the date of purchase. (This will be your objective for *all* categories of the FFF.)

Category II. One Stock selected from the twenty stocks that make up the Dow Jones Transportation Average. The same comments made for Category I are applicable, except that multinational activities are in most cases not as much a factor.

Category III. Two stocks from the universe of NYSE, ASE, and NASDAQ that are companies operating in *your own life specialty*. If you are a banker, choose from banks, S&L's, finance companies, etc. If you are a physician, choose from ethical drugs, medical equipment, specialized hospitals, health insurance, etc. If you are a rocket scientist, choose from aerospace, specialty metals, exotic fuels, etc. If you are a pro athlete, choose from sports equipment, artificial turf manufacturers, TV networks, etc. If you are a computer "hacker," your choices are obvious. If you are a housewife, choose from food, soap, cable TV, etc. If you are an attorney, choose from legal publishers, ambulance manufacturers, personal computers, menswear, etc. If you are a beach bum, choose from frisbee manufacturers, swimwear, yachts, athletic footwear, etc. If you are a librarian, choose from publishers, printers, etc.

Work with your Customer's Person. Put your brain to work. The stocks must meet these parameters: They must be marginable, they must have a trading history of three or more years since their IPO, and they must have a current market capitalization of at least $50 million. It will be helpful if there are listed options. Again, your objective is 60% appreciation within two years.

Category IV. Two stocks that have *major operations in your specific geographic region*. They can be from any industry group, but the same parameters just given in Category III do apply. These stocks might be local banks, utilities, department stores, manufacturers, restaurant chains, transportation companies, etc. You will see a lot and read a lot on these companies. You will be able to have a personal "feel" for these companies, which usually is an advantage. Nevertheless, do not sacrifice diligent fundamental "bargain hunting" research to your personal "feel." And do not feel that you for sure have the inside track on some unseasoned company that is barely out of the "entrepreneur in the garage" stage, that it is certainly a better bet toward your objective than the local electric utility or phone company. Maybe, but maybe not. Probably not.

Category V. One stock from the list of *"Closed-End Diversified Common Stock"* funds that are listed every Monday in the Wall *Street Journal,* usually on the page with the mutual fund prices, in a table called "Publicly Traded Funds." These are closed-end investment companies, with professional investment management, whose shares are traded, at either premiums or discounts to net asset value, on the NYSE or ASE. There are about twenty stocks to choose from, and you will choose only one. Work with your Customer's Person. Detailed statistics on all of them are to be found in Wiesenberger, as well as Standard & Poor's. This holding will give you diversification and professional investment management, and it is marginable. The Seasoned Veteran likes the idea of buying things at a discount, and the large majority of these lately have been trading at discounts to asset value ranging from 3% to 30%. In true bull markets, these discounts usually become premiums. So there is leverage in this situation. You, and your Customer's Person, should use all of your fundamental analysis tools to determine the best bargain on this list of about twenty.

Category VI. Two stocks from the section of the same Publicly Traded Funds list that is labeled *"Specialty Equity and Convertible Funds."* There are about 50 stocks on this list, of which five or so are "convertible" funds. You don't want any of these, so cross them off. That leaves about forty-five. Of these about twenty five are funds specializing in utilities, precious metals, etc. Cross these off. That leaves about twenty which are "foreign" or "world" funds. It is from these twenty that you will select two. These twenty are broken down into about fifteen that specialize in specific countries or regions of the world, and about five that go to any place in the world for investment bargains. They are usually named descriptively. They trade at both discounts and premiums to net asset value. Again, you must work with your Customer's Person to decide which are the best bargains for you. These two holdings will give you diversified and professionally managed exposure to global equities. This will be enhanced by your mutual fund ownership, to be discussed in the next Chapter. These two holdings are marginable, there is ample statistical data on them in Wiesenberger and, since they are exchange-listed, the data is also found in Standard & Poor's Stock Reports. But do not *ever* buy a closed-end fund as a new issue, an IPO. The underwriting commission is usually about 8%, and for that reason the share price inevitably and quickly goes down by at least that amount (because fund managers have only 92% to invest) after the underwriting is completed.

Category VII. The remaining five stocks of the FFF will be *any* stocks you wish to choose from the NYSE, ASE, or NASDAQ universe— provided they meet the same basic requirements mentioned in Category III: they must be marginable; they must be seasoned in the investment market-place at least three years; they must have a current market capitalization of at least $50 million; and it is helpful if options are listed. Again, try to diversify, try to find bargains, and try to find bargains that other investors will recognize over the next two years as bargains at successively higher prices, prices at least 60% higher! That is the name of your game!

EQUITY SELECTION GUIDELINES

Now that the game has been very specifically defined, let's spend some time determining how to play it, how to go about finding bargains in the stock market.

Long and very good books are written nearly every year that deal exclusively with this subject*, and it is not my intention to duplicate their detail here. Nonetheless, the Seasoned Veteran has accumulated some very definite ideas over the years and I feel they are well worth sharing with you. I am going to call them the Equity Selection Guidelines (ESG). They can be applied to growth stocks, both mature and emerging; cyclical stocks, companies that see their fortunes fluctuate with changes in the overall economy and its subsectors; and turnaround situations, which involve exercises in corporate problem solving.

You may ask, "Why not potential takeover stocks, stocks with undervalued assets or hidden sources of cash flow that will suddenly be bid to huge premiums by the growing number of takeover tycoons?" The answer is simple and twofold: (1) I believe there is too much difficulty for the individual investor in analyzing these factors ahead of the professionals; and (2) the tools I am going to give you will by themselves win the game for you. However, further on in this Chapter a separate technique will be provided that will help you, on occasion, successfully play on the takeover turf if you so choose.

EARNINGS, EARNINGS AND MORE EARNINGS

Companies are in business to use their land, buildings, machines, and most importantly, their people, to produce goods and provide services that can be sold for money. They take this money, pay the costs of the land, buildings, machines, and people, pay their various governments the taxes that are due, and provide for the replacement of worn-out buildings and machines. What is (hopefully) left over is profit, or net income, or earnings. These earnings belong to the owners of the business, each of whom owns a specific number of the finite amount of shares that the company has outstanding.

---

*Two of them are *The Intelligent Investor* (4th revised edition, 1986) by Benjamin Graham, and the recent *One Up on Wall Street* (1989) by Peter Lynch.

The earnings per share are, I believe, by far the most important and significant determinant of what the shares are worth. What they are worth to their owners today is what a buyer will pay for them in money today. What a buyer will pay is based, more than anything else, on what the shares have recently earned and what the buyer expects they might earn in the future. Predicting what they might earn in the future is, unfortunately, not an exact science. It is based on a world (not a local) marketplace where the company's goods or services must successfully compete to be bought by those who can use the goods and services and pay money for them—money sufficient to generate coverage of costs and provide a leftover profit. It is the job of the company's management to direct the land, buildings, machines, and employees in such a way that profits next year are larger than they were this year. Each entity in the marketplace wants to make more money next year than it (or he or she) made this year. A share that is considered likely to earn considerably more money next year is determined, by the buyer, to be worth considerably more today than a share that is forecast to earn less money next year.

Ever since ownership and creditor instruments have existed they have been traded on a daily basis between buyers and sellers, for money, at prices which are based almost entirely on supply and demand. Representative instruments are selected by companies like Dow Jones and Standard & Poor's to create Indexes, so that the general price movements of the ownership and creditor instruments can be followed and tracked. In the case of ownership instruments like stock shares, the earnings of the Index components are likewise followed and tracked. Thus it is possible to determine the valuations the financial marketplace places on the shares in relation to their earnings. When, for example, the Index stands at a price of 2000 and the earnings per share of its component companies are $200, the Index is at 10 times earnings, or price/earnings ratio (PER) of 10, or a multiple of 10. This is said to be a "market multiple" because the stocks in the Index are representative of the overall market.

The same arithmetic exercise, of course, is performed for the shares and earnings of individual companies. The PER of the individual company can be compared to the PER of the Index, and a judgment can be made as to whether the company's share is cheap or dear in comparison with the Index. Further, and very importantly, a judgment can be made, after analysis, on what the earnings per share (EPS) might be next year, and what a prospective buyer might want to pay for these earnings next year versus what a current owner might give up his share of the earnings for by selling.

Expressed very simply, if a share purchased today earns more money in the future, it should be worth more to a buyer in the future. If the earnings grow faster than the average company (measured by the Index), the price can increase faster than the Index increases. Further, hundreds of years of experience tells us that a buyer will pay a higher multiple if he firmly believes the earnings will continue their increase (this is called multiple expansion). At the same time, particularly with cyclical companies, good share price increases can occur based purely on EPS gains, even if the multiple is contracting.

Let's look at four examples to make these facts clearer for you:

Example 1: A mature growth stock is priced at 10 when the latest twelve month EPS is $1.00. The multiple is 10. At the end of the first year, EPS is $1.20 and the stock is $12.00. All of the gain has come from the EPS increase; the multiple is still 10. At the end of the second year, the latest twelve month EPS is $1.40 and the stock is at $16. Now an expansion of the multiple has occurred - it is 11.43 ($16 divided by $1.40).

Example 2: An emerging growth stock is trading at $10 when EPS is $0.75, up from $0.40 and $0.60 the two previous years. The current multiple is 13.33 ($10 divided by $0.75). After one year EPS is $1.00, and the next year EPS is $1.50. The stock is now $30, so the increase over the two years is attributed $10 to the EPS increase and $10 to the multiple expansion. The multiple is now 20.

Example 3: A turnaround stock is priced at $10, down from $25 two years ago. EPS for the latest twelve months is $0.50, down from $2.00 two years ago. The stock is trading at a multiple of 20, but you make a strong case that EPS will rebound in two years to the previous $2.00 level. This indeed happens, and at the end of two years the stock is $30. The multiple has contracted from 20 to 15 but the EPS has driven the stock to an excellent gain. The reason for the multiple contraction is related to the stock changing from a turnaround environment to its previous context as a mature growth company.

Example 4: A cyclical stock is priced at $10 when latest twelve month EPS is $1.00. The multiple is 10. At the end of the first year, EPS is $1.20 and the stock is at $13. Both the EPS increase and the multiple increase (to 10.83) have contributed to the 30% price increase. At the end of the second year, the EPS for the latest 12 months is $2.00 and the stock is $18. All of this year's price increase is attributed to the EPS increase. The multiple has contracted to 9. The marketplace fears, on this cyclical stock, that "the party will soon be over."

OTHER ANALYTICAL TOOLS

Now let's look at eighteen other items, not directly related to earnings and EPS, that are popularly-used measures of a stock share's worth.

Stock buyback programs. These are very constructive for the stockholder. They do three things: (1) they prove that management agrees the stock is a bargain; (2) they create additional demand in the marketplace; and (3) by reducing the number of shares, EPS improves because of simple arithmetic (the divisor is a smaller number). An important caveat: companies frequently authorize a buyback program, but they don't execute it. This aspect can be monitored by a close examination of quarterly reports.

Additional issues of new common stock. Be mindful of dilution. The new shares must earn their keep. A negative example is Navistar International, which has earned magnificently the last few years. EPS has not significantly improved because the number of shares outstanding has quadrupled.

Cash dividends. The Seasoned Veteran pays very little attention to the current yield (if any) when selecting an FFF stock. At this time, the Dow Jones Industrial Stocks average a yield of 3.7% and the Dow Jones Utilities provide 6.9%. To attain the total returns we are looking for, price appreciation will be a far larger component of the equation than will dividends. It frequently happens that management can do a larger total return favor for stockholders if they use cash from earnings for capital improvements, stock buybacks, acquisitions, or debt payments as opposed to paying cash dividends.

Cash flow per share. We hear more and more about this item as an analytical tool. The concept rightfully has been expanded to a definition of "free" cash flow (net income plus non-cash expenses minus capital expenditures and dividend requirements). In certain industries (primarily those with large amounts invested in fixed assets - the hotel industry would be an example), it is a meaningful measure. Nonetheless, most of your FFF successes will be driven by EPS, pure and simple.

Management ownership. I find it very reassuring to see that officers and directors own at least 10% of a company (in very large companies the ownership level could be 3% to 5%). Expressed another way, is the total market value of an insider's stock ownership likely to be a significant percentage of his net worth? If these people own only token amounts, they obviously do not agree with you that the stock is a bargain.

Insider buying. Recent purchases by officers and directors are significant, particularly if they are open-market purchases as opposed to the exercise of stock options. A vice president investing $50,000 is more of a plus than the founder/CEO adding to his already large holdings by the same $50,000 amount.

Insider selling. Unless there is a significant story accompanying the sale, I do not pay much attention to these reports. They are frequently carried out for purely personal reasons (diversification, loan payments, estate planning, new home, college tuition, divorce) and are not directly related to the insider's view of his company's prospects.

Institutional ownership. Many investors find it reassuring to note that institutions own 80% of a company's stock. Two important observations: (1) the professionals are frequently wrong, and you can do better than they can; and (2) if every institution already owns the stock, who is there left to buy it?

Wall Street coverage. Your Customer's Person might tell you that he cannot find any firms that are recommending or have published reports on a particular stock. This is not necessarily a negative (the two best stocks I have owned over my lifetime were virtually unknown to Wall Street). Remember again, if every analyst has successfully recommended the stock to every investor, who is there left to buy it?

Stock splits and stock dividends. All these do is carve up a same-sized pie into smaller pieces. The company has not changed at all. I do not regard the possibility or actuality of a stock split or stock dividend as a reason to buy a stock. Management's reason for doing this is frequently to put the price of the stock into more of a "buyable" range. Stocks such as Capital Cities/ABC, Teledyne, American Home Products, Warner Lambert, Loew's, and Berkshire Hathaway have proven conclusively that a three-digit or even a four-digit price is not a hindrance to good performance (more on this in a few more pages).

Cash as a balance sheet item. Sometimes one hears that a $20 stock is a bargain because there is $8 per share in cash on the balance sheet. This is nonsense. The only reason for hoarding cash is to do something with it that can provide a better return to stockholders than the 8% to 10% return that cash might be worth. (It's worth only this level of return both to the company and to you if you held it, as cash, yourself.) The cash should be employed for acquisitions, stock buyback programs, new productive facilities, research and development, etc. that will return more than the 8% to 10%. If this can't be achieved, it should be paid out as a cash dividend to stockholders, so *they* can use it to try for more than the 8% to 10%.

Return On Equity (ROE). An important measure to determine overall profitability. Most of your FFF selections should show ROE of at least 15%, with 20% or more a definite plus. Be particularly mindful of the degree of debt leverage that's involved; if equity is very small relative to debt, ROE might look very good. However, if earnings stumble the opposite will occur and the debt level will present a servicing problem.

Working Capital. Early in my career, a ratio of current assets to current liabilities of less than 2 to 1 caused one to think Chapter 11 might be right around the corner. Now, chief financial officers and management in general are much more skillful in matching current sources of funds, inventories, and receivables with current needs. A ratio of 1.2 to 1 is frequently very sound, and public utilities can operate very well with less than 1 to 1.

Long term debt. A company that is debt-free will not go bankrupt. Still, a moderate degree of leverage can be very helpful in enhancing ROE. The Seasoned Veteran believes that if the ratio of long term debt to total capital exceeds 35% (50% for a public utility), you should consult the current monthly edition of Moody's Bond Record to determine the current Moody rating on the bonds that make up the long term debt. If the rating is investment grade (AAA down to Baa3) there is a level of comfort. If the bonds are rated below investment grade (Ba1 or lower), I would need a very compelling and extenuating circumstance to consider the stock.

Book value per share. This area gets very tricky. Carrying values for assets can be understated and they can be overstated relative to market and/ or replacement values. Different industries have widely different norms. I do not dispute that many takeover situations, at wonderful premiums, come about because of book value analysis, but I believe these exercises are better left to the professionals. You will do far better to spend your time analyzing the company and its stock from an earnings perspective.

Introduction of new products. IBM can introduce a wonderful new product that does $100 million in sales its first year, but it will be a nearly meaningless input on that company's bottom line. Conversely, a smaller company with $500 million in present sales can introduce the same product and it might be a bottom line bonanza. Be mindful of relative size on announcements of this sort.

Start-up and development stage companies. You are an investor, not a venture capitalist. The FFF requirement that you not buy a stock within three years of its IPO will keep you away from these situations. The rewards might be terrific, but the risk is inordinate. One-product experiments, new fast-food concepts, and direct investment in geopolitical high-risk areas are best left to those who can accept that they might lose every penny of the capital committed.

High profile CEO's. For a CEO or other prominent insider to be favorably mentioned in *Forbes* or *Barron's* is usually a plus for the stock. On the other hand, if a cover story appears in *Time* or *Newsweek* heralding the same person as the greatest business genius since Henry Ford, it is probably a better time to sell the stock than it is to buy it.

THE LIST OF TWENTY FIVE

Let's examine where we were on Friday, February 26, 1988.

The Dow Jones Industrial Average closed at 2023, up 285 points or 16.4%, from its October 19, 1987 Crash low of 1738. It had successfully tested the low when it went to 1767 in early December, 1987. At 2023 it was 699 points, or 25.6%, below the August, 1987, bull market high. Corporate earnings for 1987 had nearly all been reported; the DJIA EPS came in at $133.05, up from $115.59 in 1986, and provided a market multiple of 15.2. Monthly economic reports released over the four post-Crash months had mostly been favorable, including inflation-related announcements, beginning to silence the pundits who regarded the Crash as a harbinger of a Thirties-type Depression. A federal Budget Summit had been held in Washington and the politicians came up with a more-than-nominal but less-than-substantial deficit reduction. The presidential primaries were beginning, but neither party had a true frontrunner and the election forecasts were very cloudy. It had become clear that individual investors had fled the stock market in droves, and the banking system was awash with liquidity. The Long Bond yield stood at 8.45%, and the U.S. dollar was in a bear market on all foreign exchange desks. The Wall Street-inspired takeover movement was taking a nap and the IPO market was in a deep sleep. Memories of the Crash were causing nightmares.

It might have appeared to you that *any* FFF stock selection would have an absolute zero chance of achieving a +60% move in two years.

You would have been wrong.

THE LIST OF TWENTY FIVE

	February 26, 1988		August 31, 1989		
Stock	Price	Yield	Price	Increase	Category
Blockbuster Ent.	4*	None	15 3/4	294%	EG
Bank America	8 1/2	None	33	288%	TA
MCI Comm.	11 3/8	None	38 5/8	240%	EG
Home Depot	14 5/8*	0.3%	35 5/8	143%	EG
Long Island Lighting	8	None	18 1/2	131%	TA
Phelps Dodge	35 5/8	0.4%	74 7/8	110%	C
Circuit City Stores	11 7/8*	0.5%	24	102%	EG
Disney (Walt)	60	0.5%	117 1/2	96%	MG
Phillips Petroleum	14 1/4	4.2%	27 7/8	96%	TA
The Gap	26 5/8	1.9%	52 1/4	96%	EG
Mexico Fund	6	2.5%	11 5/8	94%	TA
Compaq Computer	48 1/4	None	91	89%	EG
Schwab (Charles)	8 1/2	None	15 3/4	85%	TA
American Bldg. Main.	20	4.5%	36 3/8	83%	TA
Coca Cola	36 7/8	3.0%	66 1/2	80%	MG
Boeing	31 5/8*	2.9%	54 3/4	73%	C
Alcoa	45 1/2	2.6%	77	69%	C
Delta Airlines	47 3/8	2.1%	79 7/8	69%	C
Sanford Corp.	14 1/8*	None	23 1/2	66%	EG
Flightsafety Int'l.	27*	0.7%	42 5/8	58%	EG
Templeton Emerging Mkts.	7 5/8	None	12 1/8	58%	EG
Mfgrs. Hanover	25 3/8	12.9%	40	58%	TA
Polaroid	30 1/4	2.0%	47 1/8	56%	TA
Schafer Value Trust	6 7/8	4.5%	10 1/2	53%	MG
Capital Cities/ABC	341 3/4	0.1%	513	50%	MG

*Adjusted for splits since February 26, 1988

Stock	February 26, 1988 Price	Yield	August 31, 1989 Price	Increase
DJIA	2023.21	3.42%	2737.27	35%
DJTA	826.36	2.63%	1509.42	82%**
DJUA	182.61	8.61%	217.30	19%
S&P 500	262.46	3.55%	351.45	34%

**Several takeover stocks in this Index were important factors in the 82% increase.

The above is a List of Twenty Five Stocks that improved in market price by at least 50% in the eighteen months from February 26, 1988 to August 31, 1989. Seven of them better than doubled, and another eight of them increased over 75%. You will see very shortly that every one of the 25 stocks *achieved its gain entirely by changes in EPS* and changes in investors' (both buyers and sellers) perceptions on what the EPS was worth, in money, 18 months later.

During this 18 month period inflation hit 7.4% annualized, the Long Bond yield got to 9.44%, recession forecasts were abundant, a man long perceived as a wimp was elected President, and the King of the Takeover Financing Industry was indicted on criminal charges.

Please spend some time examining The List of Twenty Five. You will immediately note they are almost entirely well-known market names, and none of them are esoteric OTC and pink sheet issues. Indeed, 22 of them trade on the NYSE and four of those are component stocks of the Dow Jones Averages (FFF Categories I and II). Also, three of them are closed end mutual funds that might have been selected for FFF Categories V and VI. A broad gamut of industries is represented. Over half of the companies have revenues in the billions. Every one of them could have been well analyzed just prior to February 26, 1988, from the S&P Stock Reports described fully in Chapter 8.

I have included in The List of Twenty-Five a column showing, for each stock, the dividend yield that existed on February 26, 1988. Let's suppose an investor insisted on a dividend yield of a minimum of 3.42% that existed then for the DJIA. This would have eliminated 21 of the stocks! Indeed, eight of them paid no dividend whatsoever, and another six carried a nominal yield of less than 1.00%.

I have denoted specific categories for each stock: EG for emerging growth, MG for mature growth, TA for turnaround, and C for cyclical. Nine of the stocks are EG, eight are TA, and four each are MG and C. Very importantly, *not a single one of The List of Twenty-Five was a stock whose appreciation resulted from a takeover* (one of them, Polaroid, successfully resisted a takeover during the period).

Every one of The List of Twenty-Five enjoyed its significantly above average price increase from positive changes in EPS. It's just that simple!

In the following capsule comments on each of The List of Twenty-Five, I have attempted to look at the stock as it existed and could have been analyzed on February 26, 1988. I have, incidentally, chosen this date as a starting point for the List of Twenty-Five for two main reasons: (1) the dust had well settled after the Crash, and it was evident that Armageddon was not going to happen tomorrow or next month; in fact, there were those in early 1988 who were beginning to project that the DJIA might earn close to $200 for 1988. (The actual DJIA EPS came in at $223.08, so at DJIA 2023 it was a very cheap 9.1 multiple of immediately forward earnings.) And (2) it sets up a neat 18 month period to the time this is being written (three-quarters of our two year FFF holding period) which makes statistical measurement easier and more meaningful.

Blockbuster Entertainment (BV on NYSE). At year end 1986, this company had 19 videocassette retail and rental stores, $8 million in sales, and an operating loss. In 1987, new management with a good track record in another industry came on, made a 15% investment, and began a very ambitious expansion and horizontal acquisition program. EPS in 1987 was $0.14, so to buy the PER of 28.6 was a speculative play on a new industry that hinged on the shopping demands of the rapidly expanding number of

VCR owners. At the close of the period, latest twelve month EPS had increased nearly 200% to $0.40 and the multiple had expanded to 39.4.

Bank America Corp. (BAC on NYSE). The third largest banking company in the U.S. suffered monstrous losses during 1985-1987, primarily due to bad loans. Still, the price at 8 1/2 was covered nearly two-fold by tangible book value. If earnings could recover to a very reasonable 0.50% of total assets, EPS would be nearly $2.50 per share. This indeed happened in 1988 (EPS was $2.77, with $4.70 forecast for 1989).

MCI Communications (MCIC on NASDAQ). The U.S.'s second largest long distance telecommunications company is capital intensive and highly leveraged. EPS and the stock price were in the doldrums 1984 through 1987 as expanding revenues were offset by expanding costs. There was an important, long-anticipated, and noticeable EPS breakout in 4Q 1987 when $0.14 was reported vs $0.06, $0.02, and $0.07 for the three preceding quarters. This breakout was confirmed in 1Q 1988 with $0.19 EPS. At the end of our period, latest 12 month EPS of $1.96 gives us a multiple of 19.7.

Home Depot (HD on NYSE). A fast grower in the early Eighties, this operator of do-it-yourself home improvement warehouse-type stores stumbled in (FY January) 1986 when EPS dropped 40%. This caused previous astronomical multiples to come down to market levels. In FY 1987 EPS recovered, and FY 1988 EPS was up 87% vs. 1987. The stock at 14 5/8 was 18.9 times earnings, a modest premium to the market multiple. At the end of our period, the latest 12 month EPS had increased 44% and the multiple had nearly doubled to 33.

Long Island Lighting (LIL on NYSE). Provides electric and gas service to nearly three million people. Since 1983, the stock has been a play on the political and economic ramifications of the $1 billion-plus Shoreham nuclear plant, which was never allowed to come onstream. By early 1988, an intelligent judgment could have been made that a political settlement of the matter would be forthcoming to allow the company to stay in business, and there were very viable earnings (average $2.74 EPS for five years 1983-1987) from non-nuclear operations. In February, 1989 the matter was resolved and the write-off of the nuclear plant is on manageable terms.

Phelps Dodge (PD on NYSE). The largest U.S. copper producer is importantly affected by the price of copper as a commodity on worldwide markets. After weathering dismal prices 1982-1985, the company presented a very sound balance sheet (current ratio 1.9 to 1; debt 25% of total capital) as prices began improving in 1987. At the beginning of our period, the stock at 35 5/8 was 7.7 times earnings and equal to tangible book value per share. 1988 EPS nearly tripled as copper prices doubled. At the end of our period, the stock is only 4.8 times trailing 12 month EPS, so the 110% gain in the stock price was accomplished in spite of a significant multiple contraction. This is an example of a cyclical stock where the marketplace now expects a downward cycle.

Circuit City Stores (CC on NYSE). The Japanese may manufacture most of our consumer electronics, but this company surely knows how to sell them. When the stock was 11 7/8, EPS had averaged 13% increases for eight years and nearly 50% increases for the past two years. Yet it was available at 11 times current earnings and its Superstore marketing concept had proven effective. At the end of our period the latest 12 month EPS had increased 37% and the multiple had expanded to 15.

Disney (Walt) DIS on NYSE). Aggressive new management came on in 1984. Theme park expansion and hit movies brought EPS from a (FY September) 1979-1983 average of $0.86 to $1.29 in 1985, $1.82 in 1986, and $2.85 in 1987. For the 12 months ending December, 1987, EPS was $3.05, so the stock at $60 was 20 times earnings, a modest premium to the market multiple considering such fast growth. Since then the latest 12 month EPS has gone to $4.55 and the multiple has expanded to nearly 26. A classic turnaround that is now again a growth stock.

Phillips Petroleum (P on NYSE). A very large integrated oil company whose EPS fell out of bed in 1986-1987 because of low oil prices. Nonetheless, only the first two quarters of 1987 showed (modest) red ink. By the last half of 1987 profits were restored, and in February, 1988, the investor could build a strong case that well-publicized cost cutting measures would significantly provide operating leverage at a time when OPEC was trying to restore oil price integrity. First quarter 1988 EPS was $0.55 vs. $0.12, $0.11, ($0.01), and ($0.16) the four previous quarters. Full year 1988 EPS came to $2.72, a record for the company, even though sales were about 30% below 1981 levels.

The Gap (GPS on NYSE). A specialty apparel retailer with upwards of 1000 stores, insiders owning 40%, and debt-free. After extraordinarily fast EPS growth 1982-1986, FY ending January, 1988 showed no growth and the stock at 26 5/8 was at a market multiple of 13.6. Eighteen months later, the EPS for the trailing 12 months had increased 21%. The market sees resumption of earlier growth rates because the multiple has expanded to 22.1.

Mexico Fund (MXF on NYSE). A closed end "country" fund that fits into FFF Category VI. Virtually all investments are directly related to the debt-ridden Mexican economy, with heavy emphasis on common stocks traded on the volatile Bolsa. At the beginning of our period, the price at 6 was a 21.7% discount to net asset value of $7.68. At the end of our period, Mexican debt restructuring and optimism regarding the new Mexican political administration had caused prices on the Bolsa to rise. Net asset value was up 48% to $11.39, and very importantly, the discount on the MXF shares had been eliminated.

Compaq Computer (CPQ on NYSE). A start-up in 1982 financed by venture capitalists with an excellent track record. Continuous introductions of new and more powerful IBM-PC compatible portable and desktop computers 1983-1987 had fueled sales growth from $111 million to $2 billion and EPS from $0.13 to $3.59. At 48 1/4, the stock was 13.3 times 1987 EPS and (unbelievably) at a market multiple. Finances were strong with a 2.0 to 1 current ratio and 27% debt to total capital. ROE had increased to 43%. In its five-year history management had never made a mistake, insiders owned 10%, growth prospects for the product were excellent, and the stock was cheap. At the end of our period, EPS has increased 110% and the multiple of 12 is still the market multiple. This is an excellent example of an earnings-driven stock that has not benefitted from multiple expansion.

Schwab (Charles) (SCH on NYSE). The largest discount brokerage firm in the U.S. suffered dramatically as individual investor market participation evaporated after the Crash. At the beginning of our period, the investor could look at the four quarter pre-Crash period EPS of $1.40 and realize that if only half of that level could be re-attained, the present price of 8 1/2 would be a market multiple. If $1.40 EPS could be re-attained the stock would probably expand the multiple. At the end of our period, trailing 12 month EPS of $0.42 seems to be just the beginning as individual investors come back into the market.

American Building Maintenance (ABM on NYSE). Janitors for hire, with 30% of the stock owned by insiders and solid finances. Growth slowed 1985-1987, and EPS settled on a plateau nearly 50% lower than 1981-1984. The stock at 20 was 13.5 times latest 12 month earnings but only 9.6 times average 1981-1984 EPS. Now the EPS growth rate has re-attained the 1981-1984 level and the multiple has expanded to 18.

Coca Cola (KO on NYSE). A DJIA component stock (FFF Category I) with magnificent earnings quality, increases averaging 16% every year since 1979. The company has re-purchased 10% of its own shares; it has a very strong balance sheet; and it has displayed management expertise in several very tough situations. At 36 7/8 the stock was at a market multiple of 15, current yield was 3.0%, and the global market shares for all soda products were improving. ROE has consistently been over 20%, now over 30%, without significant leverage. At the end of our period, the latest 12 month EPS had increased 30% and the multiple had expanded to 21.

Boeing (BA on NYSE). Another DJIA component stock and the world's leading producer of commercial jets. Airline deregulation has stimulated worldwide demand. The company has superb quality of earnings in a very competitive and cyclical industry. The stock at 31 5/8 was 15 times earnings at a time when backlogs were escalating and operating margins were improving. Debt/capital was only 4.7% and there was 2.9% current yield. At the end of our period, the latest 12 month EPS had increased 42% and the multiple had expanded to nearly 19.

Alcoa (AA on NYSE). Still another DJIA component stock and the leading U.S. producer of aluminum. The company has been working on improving its operating profit margin. When the stock was 45 1/2 it was 18 times earnings, slightly more than a market multiple, with operating profit margins up from 14.3% to 20.6%, year-to-year 1986 vs. 1987. Margins further expanded to 25.6% in 1988, and latest 12 month EPS are up 350% from 18 months ago. Because of the industry's cyclicality and fear of a recession, the multiple has substantially decreased from 18 to 7.

Delta Airlines (DAL on NYSE). A component stock in the Dow Jones Transportation Average (FFF Category II), earnings have been characterized by cyclicality. Route and fleet expansions have been accomplished without increasing debt to capital ratios (historically in the 20% to 30% range). When the stock was 47 3/8, PER was 9.9, moderately lower than a market multiple. At the end of our period, latest 12 month EPS has exactly doubled and the multiple (discounting a possible recession) has contracted to 8.5.

Sanford Corporation (SANF on NASDAQ). A small but well established manufacturer of marking pens, other writing instruments, and office supplies. EPS nearly doubled to $0.57 in the Fiscal Year ending November, 1987. The balance sheet was strong (current ratio 2.3 to 1, debt 14% of total capital) and insiders own 12%. The stock at a PER of 24.7 was not cheap but a case could be made for it. By the end of our period, latest twelve month EPS had again doubled to $1.25 and the multiple has contracted to 19.

Flight Safety International (FSI on NYSE). This provider of high-tech training programs to the aviation industry averaged consistent 21% EPS growth over eight years 1980-1987. Balance sheet was very strong, insiders owned over 30%, and the stock at 27 was at 21.6 times 1987 EPS. At the end of our period, EPS for the latest 12 months is up 33% and the multiple has expanded to 25.7.

Templeton Emerging Markets Fund (EMF on ASE). This is a relatively new closed end mutual fund that fits into FFF Category VI. It is managed by the John Templeton organization and seeks long term capital appreciation via equities in low and middle income world economies with 75 emerging countries to choose from. At the beginning of our period, NAV was $7.79, down from $10.32 pre-Crash and the stock at 7 5/8 was at a 2.1% discount to NAV. At the end of our period NAV had increased 67%, but the discount also increased to 6.6%.

Manufacturers Hanover Trust Co. (MHT on NYSE). The fourth largest banking company in New York City; from 1979 through 1986 high quality EPS ranged from $6.42 to $8.80 and the stock traded as high as 57. Then in 1987 the company took a gigantic charge-off on its LDC loans, causing a loss of over $27 per share. Still, when the stock was available at 25 3/8, tangible book value was over $30 per share, management seemed dedicated to maintaining the dividend, capital ratios were satisfactory (particularly considering the possibility of asset sales), and if earnings could be restored to 0.50% of total assets, EPS of more than $7.00 could be achieved. This has happened, with $7.50 EPS for 1989 a good possibility.

Polaroid (PRD on NYSE). This well-established photography company had shown an EPS break-out in 1986 with the debut of several new camera lines. 1987 EPS was $1.88, so the stock at 30 1/4 was at a market multiple of 16.1. The company was debt-free, and every year since 1981 had enjoyed a multiple of at least 22. Then a hostile takeover attempt (ultimately unsuccessful) prompted a massive stock repurchase and other productive restructuring; victory in a patent infringement lawsuit provided a kicker. At the close of our period, the latest 1989 EPS estimate is $2.10, so the stock is back up to its historic multiple of 22.

Schafer Value Trust (SAT on NYSE). A diversified closed end mutual fund that is an FFF Category V stock. To achieve the objective of long-term capital appreciation, management selects equity securities that have below-market multiples, good prospects for EPS growth, and (usually) market capitalizations of at least $300 million. At the beginning of our period, shares traded at a discount of 19% to NAV. At the end of our period, NAV had increased 51% and the discount to NAV had decreased to 14%.

Capital Cities/ABC (CCB on NYSE). This company was formed by a well publicized merger in January, 1986. Two years later the entities had meshed, with EPS up 51% from the pro-forma pre-merger level. At 341 3/4 the stock was 20.7 times 1987 EPS, reflecting consistent 18% average earnings growth for the past eight years, 17% ownership by the legendary Warren Buffet, proven management, and excellent communications properties. At the end of our period, latest 12 month EPS had increased 44% and the multiple had moderately expanded to 22.

TWO ADDITIONAL SUGGESTIONS

Before moving on to a discussion and specific instructions on stock selling strategy, the Seasoned Veteran wants to pass on two strongly held feelings that you should also share.

One has to do with the price of a stock in absolute dollars. There is a widely held perception, even among otherwise astute investors, that the lower a stock is priced, the better a bargain it is. This might be true when talking about onions or dry goods, but it is absolute and total poppycock when talking about stocks. A stock share priced at $100 might be a much better bargain than one priced at $10. And the chances are good that a share priced at 50¢ or $1 is no bargain at all. A $100 stock can go to $160 just as easily as a $10 stock can go to $16. To own 10 shares of the former might be much better than to own 100 shares of the latter.

The other strongly held view is in the area of prices on your buy and sell orders. In an earlier Chapter, the Seasoned Veteran stated that it is much easier to predict the price of a stock for next year than for tomorrow or next week. When you determine to buy a certain stock because it is a bargain, it will be as much of a bargain for the purpose of your Plan whether it is priced at 31 1/2 or 31 3/8 or 31 1/4. Of course, if it's priced at 35 or 36, or even 33, it might not be a bargain. But to try to squeeze the last 1/2, 1/4, or even 1/8 out of a transaction will not usually be productive, and further, you will tend to drive your Customer's Person to the nearest watering hole the minute the market closes for the day. Over 90% of your orders to buy and sell individual stock shares should acknowledge the good liquidity in the NYSE, ASE, and NASDAQ marketplaces. They should be placed with your Customer's Person "at the market."

STOCK SELLING STRATEGY

As the 19th Century progressed, the Rothschild family became the richest family in Europe. The founder of the dynasty had his business beginnings in Germany in the 1760's; his five sons expanded the family's interests and fortunes - which were mostly in banking and personal investments - throughout all the major countries of Europe. By 1875, the founder's grandsons were in their prime, and one of them, Lionel Rothschild, lent the British government the money needed to buy control of the Suez Canal. On that occasion, he was interviewed by the *Times*. The reporter asked him, "Sir, how has it happened that you and your family have, through your investments, grown so unbelievably wealthy? What is your secret?" Rothschild replied: "It is very simple, really. We always, and I repeat always, sell too soon."

Much more recently, a friend of a friend of the Seasoned Veteran was on his deathbed. He was 95 years old, and had lived a good life. For seventy years he had made his living in the stock market, as a speculator, trader, and finally and more successfully, an investor. On this occasion, both a doctor and a nurse were in attendance, and his children and several grandchildren were gathered around. The end was near. The man was absolutely comatose, and had been for several days. Finally a fever overtook him. The doctor asked the nurse to call out his temperature at one minute intervals. "101," said the nurse. The old man's breathing quickened slightly. "102," said the nurse. The old man moved one finger. "103," said the nurse. The old man tried to sit up. "105," said the nurse. The old man's eyes opened wide, and he looked at his oldest son. He said in a clear voice: "I'm glad I held on. Sell me out at the market, and do it now!" Thirty seconds later he expired, with a wonderful smile on his face.

For most of my career, I have believed that it is the easier decision to make as to when to buy a stock as opposed to when to sell a stock. The stories about Rothschild and the old man dramatize the two extreme positions. Every day for years I have wrestled with the question as to which selling position is the correct one: to sell too soon, or to hold on.

Now, with the extreme volatility of the recent markets as both an inspiration and an intellectual guide, I have developed a strategy that I have tested just as though I were a chemist in a laboratory.

I have worked with monthly bar charts of the Dow Jones Industrial Average and I have worked with monthly bar charts of dozens of individual stocks. I have set up real recent past situations of both bull markets and bear markets, and began concentrating on time frames - five years, one year, three years, etc. How has the DJIA performed within these time frames? How have the individual stocks, that looked fundamentally like bargains at the beginning of each time frame, performed not only in absolute terms but also in comparison with the DJIA during the same time frame? At what point going down does the stock no longer look like a bargain? Must a fundamental perspective be used to correlate to the price, or a technical perspective, or both? Can a strategy be developed that is absolutely price, or performance, dictated? Is volume truly a factor? How can profits be maximized? How can "losers" be weeded out early? How far and how fast must a good stock go up before it is absolutely not any longer a bargain? Is there a negative correlation between turnover rates and overall portfolio performance? How can capital be employed most productively at all times? How can a formula be developed that considers a scenario of higher highs on bull markets and higher lows on bear markets, with lots of volatility in both? And many other similar questions.

A lot of my work was trial and error. But as my testing progressed, I began to focus on the at-first-cloudy-and-then-wonderfully-clear fact that a selling strategy can be developed that is absolutely and totally price directed. What a Godsend! No longer would an owner of shares need to follow and interpret fundamentals during the holding period. What a timesaver! And better yet the strategy removes subjectivity from the selling decision. The owner can make his selling decision based on the calendar and arithmetic. Seventh grade arithmetic!

So the Seasoned Veteran presents to you a Stock Selling Strategy which will be called "SSS." It will be used to dictate the exact circumstance when a stock in the FFF is to be sold. It is to be used with great discipline and without exceptions.

Before presenting it, I strongly urge you to know how to use your pocket calculator to figure a percentage. When something goes from 100 to 120, it has gone up 20.0%. When something goes from 2138 to 2387, it has gone up 11.6%. When something goes from 31 3/8 to 26 7/8, it has gone down 14.3%. And then it is necessary to figure a percentage of a percentage. When the DJIA goes down 10%, how much is 20% worse than that? It is down 12%. When the DJIA goes up 17%, how much is 30% better than that? It is up 22.1%.

Now, here finally is the SSS:

You will *never* own a stock longer than exactly two years from date of purchase. And once you own it, you will buy no more shares; you will never average up or average down.

Whenever a stock goes up 60.0% from the price paid (forget about commissions) it will be sold immediately; the holding period can be any number of days from 1 to 730. It is good practice to enter a GTC sell order with your Customer's Person at the target sell price of +60%.

The SSS dictates that if the stock is not sold at +60%, it will be reviewed at six months from date of purchase, one year from date of purchase, and 18 months from date of purchase. These three reviews will compare the stock's price percentage performance against the percentage performance of the DJIA over the same time period.

At the six month review, the stock will be sold *if it has done 20% or more worse* than the DJIA during the six month period. One example only: Stock purchased at 20. DJIA then was 2000. At six months, DJIA is 1900 (down 5%). 20% worse than down 5% is down 6%. Stock price at six months is 18, which is down 10%. Stock is sold (at a 10% loss, which is only 5% annualized).

At the one year review, the stock will be sold *if it has not done better* than the DJIA during the one year period. One example only: Same stock purchased at 20. DJIA then was 2000. At one year, DJIA is 2400 (up 20%). Stock is 23 1/2, which is up 17.5%. Stock is sold (for a 17.5% per annum gain). If the stock were 24 1/2, it would be held because it is up 22.5% vs. up 20% on the DJIA.

At the 18 month review, the stock will be sold *if it has not done at least 30% better* than the DJIA during the 18 month period. One example only: Same stock purchased at 20 when the DJIA was 2000. At 18 months, DJIA is 2913 (up 45.6%). 30% better than up 45.6% is up 59.3%. Stock price at 18 months is 31 1/8, which is up 55.6% from purchase. Stock is sold because it is not up at least 59.3%. This sale produces an annualized before tax gain of 55.6% ÷ 1.5 = 37.1%. If the stock price was 32 or above, it would be sold under any time frame, because it would be up 60% from date of purchase.

At the end of two years, the stock is sold at the market if it has not earlier been sold as a result of being up 60%, or if it has not earlier been sold at the three review dates.

So that is the Stock Selling Strategy, the SSS. It is wonderfully simple! And it will produce excellent total returns in the markets the Seasoned Veteran anticipates.

Now let me make some comments and further directives.

When a stock is sold, it should be replaced immediately by another stock in the same FFF Category. The amount committed to the replacement will be the full proceeds of the sale if the sale was made at a loss. If there was a profit, the amount committed to the replacement will be the amount originally paid for the sold stock, with the before-tax profit going to reduce the Murphy & Carroll debit balance. You can anticipate the possibility of a sale because of price movement, so there should be plenty of time for you and your Customer's Person to have a replacement bargain stock from the same FFF Category in mind and in position. You will always own 15 stocks. Do not attempt to outsmart the market.

As to cash dividends, they are simply a bonus, or a kicker, or gravy. They will be credited to your margin account and have the effect of reducing your debit balance. Do not give any credit for dividends to your calculations; do not pay any attention whatever to ex-dividend dates. Your selling strategy is pure. It is based only on the market price of the stock in comparison to the DJIA at the exact six month, one year, and 18 month review dates, or on the "up 60% at any time" provision. (You will, of course, need to make arithmetic adjustments for stock splits and stock dividends.)

Commissions are not a factor. Your calculations are based simply on the market price per share. I do not dispute that commissions invade the total return, but not significantly enough to be a factor.

As this is written, the capital gains tax laws do not differentiate any holding period. All capital gains are taxed without regard to the period of time the asset is owned. It may be that this will be changed. One cannot be sure on these matters, but the Seasoned Veteran is inclined to say that any foreseeable change would not be so drastic as to change the SSS one bit.

The proceeds of all sales will, of course, be credited to the margin account, reducing the debit balance. The replacement purchases will, of course, be charged to the margin account, increasing the debit balance. In Section VI, there will be a more detailed discussion on proper allocation of the absolute dollars involved.

To conclude the specifics on the SSS, I am sure many of you are playing the Devil's Advocate: "I'd sell at too many six month losses." "Two years isn't long enough." "Dividends should not be disregarded." "A stock can still be a bargain after it has gone up 60%." "I am not protected in the event of a Crash." "I can't bring myself to sell a stock I like that is acting well." And many more similar comments. To you the Seasoned Veteran says two things: "I have thought the same thoughts, and rejected them" and "Try it. You'll like it!"

Before picking up with some promised concepts, techniques, and strategies that can improve total return in the equities area, let me provide the design of a form you can use in your implementation of the SSS. You can put it on one legal size piece of paper, reproduce it in quantity, and have one form for each FFF stock you own. You will always have 15 forms working. Save the forms that are "history" for leisurely review and learning.

STOCK SELLING STRATEGY (SSS) REVIEW

Name of stock_____

FFF Category _____

Date of purchase _____ DJIA _____

No. of shares _____

Price at purchase _____

+60% would be _____ target price.

GTC Sell Order entered_____

Target date _____ (Two years from now)

If sold at target price sooner than target date:

Date _____   Price _____

SIX MONTH REVIEW

Date _____   DJIA _____

Price _____

% change since purchase_____

% change in DJIA since purchase _____

20% worse than DJIA would be _____% which equals _____ price on stock. Stock is held _____ or stock is sold _____ at price _____ on _____. If stock is held, is it a candidate for call writing? _____

ONE YEAR REVIEW

Date _____   DJIA _____

Price _____

% change since purchase _____

% change in DJIA since purchase _____

Equal performance to DJIA would be _____% which equals _____ price on stock. Stock is held _____ or stock is sold _____ at price _____ on _____. If stock is held, is it a candidate for call writing? _____

EIGHTEEN MONTH REVIEW

Date _____   DJIA _____

Price _____

% change since purchase _____

% change in DJIA since purchase _____

30% better than DJIA would be _____% which equals _____ price on stock. Stock is held _____ or stock is sold _____ at price _____ on _____. If stock is held, is it a candidate for call writing? _____

TWO YEAR REVIEW (TARGET DATE)

Date _____

Price _____

Stock has not reached original target price of _____. Stock is sold for _____ on _____.

RECAP OF STOCK HISTORY

(1) Date purchased _____

(2) Total cost (incl. comm.) $ _____

(3) Date sold _____

(4) Net proceeds (incl. comm.) $ _____

(5) Profit or (Loss) $ _____
                                                        (Taxable)

(6) Add total dividends $ _____
                                                        (Taxable)

(7) Total return $ _____

(8) Number of days owned _____

$\underline{(7)} = \$$_____ x 365 = \$_____ (9) Before tax total return per year
(8)

$\underline{(9)} = $ _____ % = (10) Before tax total return per year
(2)

COVERED CALL OPTION WRITING

There will certainly be periods of two or three months, or longer, when the price action of markets and your FFF is sideways at best or downward at worst. A decision as to whether this scenario exists is subjective, but it frequently can be made with intelligence and a degree of conviction. These times provide the opportunity to write call options on your FFF holdings. This is a technique, or strategy, that can moderately enhance your total return. If you are unsure how it works, your Customer's Person can show you the detailed concept, the arithmetic involved, and the mechanics of the transaction.

The Seasoned Veteran believes your covered call writing should strictly adhere to the following parameters: (1) Concentrate on calls that will expire in the 45 day to 75 day time frame; (2) Make sure there is a good market with adequate volume and open interest in the call you select. Your Customer's Person can get this information on the Quotron. (Even if this parameter is met, you should use "limit" orders" on these trades.); (3) Deal in "in the money" or "just barely out of the money" calls; (4) Do not cry over spilled milk if you were wrong and a stock you like is called away; (5) Do not ever have more than five stocks of your FFF involved simultaneously in call writing; (6) Do not ever write an uncovered call; (7) Negotiate with your Customer's Person a higher commission discount percentage on all option trades - the published commission schedules on options are much higher than they should be!; and (8) Be certainly aware that covered call writing has no place whatever in a bull market or even an extremely volatile sideways market.

When you are involved with writing covered calls, the form just provided for the Stock Selling Strategy Review can be modified to include data for stock sales as a result of calls sold being exercised. Premiums received should be included in a new caption under (6) in the Recap of Stock History section.

TAKEOVER STOCKS

In recent months and years, the overall world economy has learned more and more about "value" investing. Businessmen and financiers are much more intelligent and creative than they were twenty or even ten years ago. Computer programs and screens, and recent MBA's, are put to work analyzing long lists that themselves derive from annual reports, 10-K's, and all the rest: share of market analyses, plant and equipment analyses, management capability analyses, natural resource analyses, manufacturing productivity analyses, analyses on everything right down to the quality of labor negotiations. And then the Icahns, Bass Brothers, Bilzerians, Trumps, and Goldsmiths of the world decide that a certain stock is, by their measure, undervalued. And then the lawyers and investment bankers on

Wall Street are told to fall in and pretty soon (happily for them!) they are called to attention, and the fun begins.

XYZ stock closes in quiet trading at 20 on Monday. Rumors on Tuesday, stock at 22. Announcement on Wednesday before the market opens that I. Beliv Gredisoka is going to take the company private and will pay all stockholders 28, providing they tender their shares by a week from Friday. Stock closes at 26 1/2. Thursday the rumors are that Kani Platu is going to offer 30. Stock closes at 29. And on and on, frequently for months.

How wonderful it would be if you and your Customer's Person had decided on Monday at 10:30 A.M. that XYZ was a bargain under the selection parameters of the FFF, and had placed a market order to buy when the stock was 20. Unfortunately, that did not happen. In fact, it was 10:30 A.M. on Wednesday before you first heard of XYZ, and the stock was then trading at 25 3/4. But there was something about the situation you liked. You did some research, and concluded the deal might finally be done at 35. You decided you wanted to play, too.

Here is what you do. You total up the full value of your FFF stocks at today's market prices. You figure what 0.5% (one-half of one percent) of the total is. You take this amount of money from your unused buying power and buy 60-day call options. With the stock at 25 3/4 or thereabouts, a 60-day call with a 25 strike price would hopefully cost no more than 5. If you are right and XYZ is finally taken out at 35, you have a nice quick double, albeit on a small investment. If you are wrong, try to sell your calls at a point where no more than 50% of your purchase price is lost.

That is the only way to play a takeover. And the Seasoned Veteran is going to impose some fairly harsh corollary restrictions: (1) Never have more than one call option takeover situation in play at one time; (2) Never change the number of calls you initially buy; (3) Never be tempted to buy the *shares* of the company once a takeover rumor or offer is in the marketplace - it will not qualify as an FFF stock; (4) Do not feel you need to play every takeover stock - only play those that you feel *very* good about and where the 60-day calls are not astronomically priced; (5) Set a price objective on the upside and stick to it - same for a stop on the downside; and (6) Make sure you get a good commission discount on your option trades.

A MARKET CRASH SCENARIO

Let us suppose that you are frightened almost to death. You are a student of what happened October 14 to October 23, 1987. You feel it "deep in your bones" that the same thing is going to happen again. You are absolutely convinced that the market has an excellent chance of quickly going down 25%, or 30%, or even 40%. You feel you should sell all your FFF, even though the SSS has not dictated this. You feel you should sell stocks short. You feel you should buy puts on individual stocks. Or you don't know what to do, except possibly check your balcony as to how a dry dive might work. You are nearly in a state of panic.

Here is the only strategy the Seasoned Veteran will permit you to attempt. Again, total your FFF at present market. Determine what 1.00% (that is one point zero percent) of the total is. Take this amount of money from your unused buying power and buy S&P 100 index put options on the Chicago Board. Buy puts with the lowest available strike price (this will usually be about 15% lower than the present index) with an expiration date of 20 to 40 days from now. These puts are so far "out of the money" that they will usually be available at prices of 1/4 to 1/2 or lower, so you will be able to buy many puts. If you are right, and the market crashes more than 15%, you will make a great deal of money on the transaction very quickly. (If you are wrong, you will lose your entire cost.) Do not be greedy. Sell your puts at the *first* significant market uptick. (Remember Rothschild.) And do not think that this is an employable technique every year. You *must* think a precipitous crash is going to occur. (The Seasoned Veteran knows one man who made about $200,000 in October, 1987, with a $7,000 purchase of these "deepest out of the money" index put options.)

A RUNAWAY INFLATION SCENARIO

In an earlier Chapter the Seasoned Veteran wrote many words on the general subject of inflation. To attempt to synopsize these words is difficult, but on balance a strong case was made that the lessons of the Sixties and particularly the Seventies were learned well, and the overall techniques and strategies of the Volckers, Bakers, and Greenspans in the Eighties have wrestled inflation to the ground.

Nonetheless, we know from watching the likes of Hulk Hogan on TV that a muscular opponent on the mat can sometimes break the best holds.

The Seasoned Veteran believes that in every ten year period for the foreseeable future there will be at least one time when inflation breaks the body press that keeps it on the mat. It will rise from the mat, flex its muscles, and be heard from, probably rather briefly.

In this scenario, the cost of living index increases will break their present and past five year range of 3% to 5% and head towards 10%. Interest rates will go up, and stock prices probably will go down.

The Seasoned Veteran believes that, with a higher than normal degree of risk, this scenario presents an opportunity to make a great deal of money very quickly, an amount greater than the realized and computational losses you will simultaneously be having on the FFF portion of your total portfolio.

The strategy I am about to give you should *only* be employed at a time when the annualized CPI has gone up *at least* 2.00% from what it was six months ago and the economists are almost unanimous in their convictions that it is headed *at least* 3.00% higher. You may think this point of entry is too late, but it won't be.

Here is the specific strategy.

Take the entire current net worth of your margin account at Murphy & Carroll (UST plus FFF minus debit balance) and figure what 3.00% of it is. (This will be less than 3.00% of your total Investment Plan, because the mutual funds which will be discussed in the next Chapter are not included.)

Talk to your Customer's Person and get in position to do commodities trading. (This requires a broker with a Series 3 license, as explained and discussed in Chapter 9.) Divide the 3.00% of money into three equal parts, and arrange to use this amount of unused buying power from your margin account.

Use one part (1.00% of Murphy & Carroll margin account net worth) as the initial margin to *buy* futures contracts in Gold on the New York Commodity Exchange, establishing a *long* position in the contract that expires four months from now. Establish a GTC stop loss order at a price where your loss is 50% of the original margin money. Establish a GTC sell order at a price where you have *tripled* your original margin money.

Use the second part (1.00% of Murphy & Carroll margin account net worth) as the initial margin to *buy* futures contracts in Crude Oil on the New York Mercantile Exchange, establishing a *long* position in the contract that expires four months from now. Establish the same 50% GTC stop loss order, and the same GTC sell order at a triple.

Use the third part (1.00% of Murphy & Carroll margin account net worth) as the initial margin to *sell short* futures contracts in Treasury Bonds on the Chicago Board of Trade, establishing a *short* position in the contract that expires six months from now. Establish the same GTC 50% stop loss *buy* order (remember: you have sold short) and the same GTC buy order to close out your position at a triple.

These trades have a satisfactory risk/reward ratio, they employ a conservative amount of money, and if the inflation scenario unfolds, they will work. One caveat: after each trade is completed, go home! Do not *under any circumstance* think that you are now a veteran commodities trader and "Where has this been all my life?!" That type of thinking will prove very hurtful.

The Seasoned Veteran has now given you his detailed thinking on the most aggressive part of your Investment Plan. Over time you will grow your capital very, very considerably by the use of the concepts, techniques, and strategies you have learned about in this Chapter. And you will be able to purchase more and more mutual funds, which await us in the next Chapter.

13
Mutual Funds: MFLS

The Seasoned Veteran now will hazard the educated guess that over the period of years and decades that your Investment Plan will be in existence, you will grow more dollars of capital with open-end mutual funds than you will with UST/FIPS and FFF/SSS.

You will always own UST and FFF for two purposes. They will themselves provide a total return. Marching hand-in-glove with the total return they will provide a leverage strategy that allows the accumulation of open-end mutual funds. This is simply called the Mutual Fund Leverage System, or "MFLS."

The better the annual total return that UST and FFF provides, the more leverage there will be for purchase of the mutual funds.

You will learn the specifics of how this works in Section VI, which is now right around the corner. Nonetheless, you already know that your UST and FFF will create a loan value in your Murphy & Carroll margin account, and you will borrow a part of this loan value to purchase the mutual funds. In a general way, let me say now that your loan value will always be in a range of 60% to 70% of UST and FFF total market values. In Section VI, you will see that your maximum loan against this will be 50% of the total market values, which is in a range of 71% to 83% of the *maximum* you could borrow. The reason for not borrowing 100% of maximum is in the prudence and conservatism, with the specific wish to protect you and your Plan from a margin call in a worst-case market scenario.

The objective of this Chapter is to furnish you some basic thinking on the mutual fund industry and provide you the hows, whys, and wherefores for the individual mutual fund selections you will make in accord with MFLS.

THE MUTUAL FUND UNIVERSE

At this time there are something on the order of 2000 mutual funds in the United States, not including money market funds.

This compares with about 450 ten years ago and about 250 twenty years ago. Total assets under management are just over $800 billion, compared with $100 billion ten years ago. The number of shareholder accounts today is in excess of 35 million, up from the 8 to 10 million level both ten and twenty years ago. It is indeed a growth industry!

The Seasoned Veteran ascribes this significant growth over the past ten years mainly to two things: (1) the generally higher level of interest rates available in the fixed income product spectrum has served as a catalyst in the creation and distribution of a wide range of fixed income mutual funds, and this has been where most of the growth has occurred; and (2) the overall complexity of the world's economy and financial markets has caused individual investors to acknowledge the need for and to cry out for the continuous professional investment management that mutual funds provide.

The approximate breakdown among the 2000 mutual funds is 800 investing exclusively in common stock and derivative products, 100 balanced funds investing in both stocks and bonds, and over 1000 operating in the fixed income area.

Fortunately, your Plan will not be faced with the selection of a few mutual funds from a universe where there are 2000 to choose from. In our quest for total return, we can eliminate quickly several large and specific categories.

We can eliminate *all* mutual funds that are invested exclusively in fixed income securities, as well as those that invest in a combination of fixed income securities and preferred stocks. The reason is very simple: the performance levels have not been there in the past, and in the economic and market scenarios that the Seasoned Veteran expects for 1990 and beyond, they will not be there in the future. According to Wiesenberger, an unweighted average of 110 fixed income funds had a total return of 78.0% for the 5 1/2 year period ending June, 1989 and a total return of 211.2% for the 10 1/2 year period also ending June, 1989. During the same two time frames, an unweighted average of 381 common stock funds and balanced funds had total returns of 91.1% and 402.9%, respectively. As to the future, please reflect back to Chapter 7 for my thinking on why equities will outperform debt in the years ahead.

So we are now down to approximately 900 mutual funds that are either stock funds or balanced funds. From these we can totally cross off the 65 closed-end funds that were just discussed in Chapter 12. As we saw then, many of these are candidates for FFF in two Categories, and your ownership options on these have already been explained. They do not play any role in MFLS (except as a leverage contributor through FFF).

We are now down to about 835 open-end mutual funds, of which around 665 can be called domestic stock funds, about 80 are foreign stock funds, and about 90 are balanced funds.

Let's take a look at the 665 domestic stock funds. Within this number are certain categories that can be eliminated.

There are about 15 funds that have as their primary objective the enhancement of total return by writing covered call options against their portfolio; inasmuch as we include this as an occasional FFF strategy, we will not be including these funds in MFLS.

There are about 10 funds that are called exchange funds. Simply put, these funds will issue shares in exchange for payment in stock that an investor already holds, which then becomes an asset of the exchange fund. These funds are not candidates for MFLS.

Within the past several years approximately 20 mutual funds have come into existence that are generically called index funds. They will invest in the component stocks of a particular index, and will therefore have performance identical to that of the index. Inasmuch as a large percentage of mutual funds do not perform as well as the major indexes, this is not a bad way to invest for those who want at least average performance. Our Plan strives for, and will attain, *above* average performance. These mutual funds are not to be included in MFLS.

There are a handful of stock mutual funds that invest exclusively in companies that have "socially responsible" or "environmentally responsible" products or objectives. Our business is to go for maximum total return, and these few mutual funds can be eliminated from our potential MFLS roster. Of course, if you are willing to forego some return, you may wish to consider these funds.

The Seasoned Veteran has long had mixed feelings about the 90 or so stock mutual funds that are called sector funds. These are funds that (usually with broad definitions) invest in a particular industry or product line. The Fidelity Family of funds alone has 33 of these funds. Most investors believe this type of mutual fund investing is relatively new; this is not so, although there are now many more funds to choose from. In Chapter 9, I told you about my first investment in financial assets in 1950 through my customer's man, "Beanie" Shepherd. As it happened, this was an investment in Chemical Fund, a mutual fund started in 1938 that invested in a portfolio of chemical manufacturers and chemical process industries. Believe it or not, I still have a personal ledger that gives my total experience with this investment. I bought it on September 12, 1950 for $399.60 and sold it on August 28, 1955 for $552.48. During this five year period, I received cash distributions (dividends and realized capital gains payments) of $138.90. So my noncompounded average annual total return for the period was 14.60%. Notwithstanding this example of youthful success, the Seasoned Veteran has elected to recommend *not* including sector funds as a part of MFLS. You will have ample opportunity to "pick a sector" with your FFF Categories, even to the point of moderate concentration, and your MFLS should embrace the principal of diversification. It is interesting to make an analysis of the total returns of the 33 Fidelity Select sector funds for the year ended June 30, 1988. This, of course, was the period of the Crash. The S&P 500 stock average was down 6.9% for the period and the Forbes stock fund composite Index was down 5.6%. Six of the Select funds were up, from 0.7% to 7.0%. Twelve of them were down less than 10.0%. Eleven of them were down from 10.1% to 20.0%. Three of them were down in a range from 20.1% to 30.0%. And one of them was down 37.0%. The Seasoned Veteran believes that by applying the criterion of diversification, the possibility of being in a mutual fund that does dramatically poorer than the broad averages will be just about totally eliminated.

That leaves a list of about 525 domestic stock funds, about 80 foreign stock funds, and about 90 balanced funds, a total of nearly 700 mutual funds.

Of this number, nearly 650 are members of so-called "families" of funds. This comes about when a particular investment management company or investment brokerage firm manages two or more funds, each with different investment objectives, possibly different fee structures, and so forth. There are about 125 mutual fund families, with more than a dozen management companies or brokerage firms offering ten or more mutual funds; the Fidelity company alone has over 70 funds in its family. There are obvious economies of scale in these endeavors, not the least of which is the sharing of common research by the individual fund portfolio managers. This does not mean that all funds within a family, even those funds with very similar investment objectives, will have identical total return performance. The individual fund portfolio managers are usually given fairly wide latitude, and this manifests itself in moderate to more-than-moderate performance disparities within the family. In our continuing desire to broadly diversify our pursuit of the best total return on all components of our Plan, we will be selecting our MFLS with a strict rule that each individual mutual fund will be from a different management group. This dramatically narrows our selection list down to about 175 mutual fund "groups" of one or more funds. There are still about 700 individual funds to choose from, but the selection process is much easier when looked at in terms of "one to a family."

Before providing some tools that can be used in the selection of the individual mutual funds, let's take a look at what it costs to own a mutual fund.

MUTUAL FUND PRICING

When you buy and sell UST, your round-trip commission will consist of a mark-up on the inside market that will total less than 1.00%, with no cost of maintaining ownership. When you buy and sell FFF, your round-trip commission to Murphy & Carroll will be (depending upon the commission discount you negotiate with your Customer's Person) somewhere in a range of 1.00% to 2.00%, and again there is no cost of maintaining ownership.

Your ownership of MFLS will cost you more than UST and FFF. It will consist of at least several parts.

Many mutual funds charge a *front-end load,* or initial sales commission, at the time the fund is purchased. This can range from 1.0% to 8.5%, and most of it will go to Murphy & Carroll and your Customer's Person. Frequently there are "break points," whereby larger dollar investments can be made with a lower percentage commission. It is very apparent that the longer you hold the mutual fund, the more the commission can be amortized against the average annual total return. A mutual fund with an 8.5% front-end load that is held for one year will obviously have its annual total return invaded by the full 8.50% cost. If the same fund is held five years, the annual average cost is 1.70%; on a twenty year holding, it is only 0.43% per year on an amortized basis.

Many mutual funds, particularly those that have commenced operations in the Eighties, do not have an initial sales commission to be paid by the investor. Instead they have a *back-end load,* or a contingent deferred sales charge. This is usually about 5.00% if the shares are sold, or redeemed, during the first year of ownership, decreasing by 1.00% each year until there is a zero sales charge if the shares are sold after five years of ownership. Again, this type of charge will invade your total return rather significantly if you redeem your shares in the early years.

In 1980, the SEC issued *Rule 12B-1* (pertaining to the Investment Company Act of 1940) which allows a mutual fund to recover certain of its marketing and distribution costs by an annual assessment against the net assets of the fund. Among other things, this can mean your Customer's Person will usually receive a commission paid by the mutual fund when you buy a back-end load mutual fund. Your net asset value will be invaded every year by the management company as they in effect reimburse themselves for this initial expense and the similar expense that is incurred on behalf of other investors. This charge continues *every year,* so that if you hold the fund for ten or twenty years you are continuously paying your capital to the mutual fund to allow it to attract new investors. The percentage is usually something less than 1.25% per year, but it will add up over time. Some front-end load funds, usually those with relatively low percentage sales charges, also have Rule 12b-1 costs.

Some mutual funds are pure no-loads, having neither front-end nor back-end loads nor Rule 12b-1 plans. These are the exception rather than the rule, but they do exist.

Every mutual fund will have *annual operating expenses.* This will result in a charge against your capital to compensate the management company so that it can pay expenses ranging from salaries to professional fees to postage. It will usually range from 0.50% to 2.00%, with 1.50% being about average for a stock fund and 1.25% for a balanced fund.

A last cost that the mutual fund investor bears is absolutely hidden. It relates to *commissions paid by the mutual fund on its own portfolio transactions.* Even though the mutual fund will negotiate much lower per share commissions with its brokers than you will be able to negotiate with Murphy & Carroll, these too are ultimately borne by the shareholder. A mutual fund portfolio that has an annual turnover of 10% will obviously be paying far fewer of your capital dollars in commissions than will a portfolio turning over at 300% annually.

From the above, it is obvious that a pure no-load without 12b-1 costs and with low operating expenses and portfolio turnover is ideal. Conversely, an 8.50% front-end load with additional 12b-1 costs, high operating expenses, and high portfolio turnover is not ideal. It will be up to you to analyze these factors *before* you make your purchase decision.

CHOOSING YOUR MUTUAL FUNDS

You will always own *five mutual funds* in the MFLS section of your Investment Plan. These mutual funds will be owned under plans you set up where all cash distributions are automatically reinvested in additional shares of the fund.

You will make your purchase decisions with the objective of maximizing total return. The cost structure of the mutual fund will be a secondary consideration. It is again obvious that a full-load 8.50% fund, with 2.00% operating expenses and 300% portfolio turnover, is a better fund to own if it provides 30% total return each year than is a pure no-load that has good annual cost figures but provides only 3% total return each year.

Your objective will be to choose five mutual funds that you *hope* to own indefinitely. You are looking for the same sort of long-term performance that the Templeton Growth Fund has provided for thirty-five years. You are looking for five mutual funds that will do well in both bull markets and bear markets. You are looking for five mutual funds that are not necessarily last month's or last year's best performers, but five that have shown UP-market and DOWN-market consistency of performance over, say, the past ten years, funds where you believe there is a much better than even chance the same favorable consistency can be maintained for the next ten years.

In Chapter 8, I mentioned that every year, usually in August, *Forbes* publishes its annual Mutual Funds Ratings issue. In 1989 it happens that the issue is dated September 4. It is always an excellent issue.

They give all domestic stock funds, all balanced funds, and all foreign stock funds that have been operating at least six years a rating, from A to F, based on how the funds have performed in terms of total return in recent UP markets and the same ratings on how they have performed in DOWN markets. In the current Ratings, *Forbes* has identified three UP markets since July, 1982 and three DOWN markets since November, 1980. For the UP and DOWN markets, the top 20% of the peer group gets an A, the next 25% a B, the next 25% a C, the next 25% a D, and 5% get F. There are mutual funds that get a D in UP markets and an A in DOWN markets, and vice versa. There are quite a few mutual funds that get a C in both UP and DOWN markets. The trick is to get an A in both.

Every year, in the Mutual Funds Ratings edition, *Forbes* provides an Honor Roll. The Honor Roll consists of mutual funds that have scored at least a B in DOWN markets, achieved an average annual total return of at least 15.0%, and have had the same portfolio manager for at least two of the three market cycles. In 1989 there are 20 such mutual funds. The mutual funds range in size from $31 million to nearly $11 billion. Twelve have front-end loads ranging from 2.00% to 8.50%, two have Rule 12(b)1 expenses and back-end loads, and three are pure no-loads. Two are closed-end funds and one offers shares only on a contractual plan requiring monthly investments (this is a very rare type of mutual fund). Average annual expenses are under 1.00% in nine of the funds; the highest is 1.52%. Portfolio turnover is under 50% in twelve funds, and over 100% in four funds. Most importantly, the average annual total return for the 8.6 year period from November, 1980 was in every case higher than the 14.8% provided by the S&P 500 Index; the range for all 20 mutual funds is from 15.0% to 23.9%, and this is after operating expenses. Also significantly, there is a consistency: five of the funds have been on the Honor Roll for at least five consecutive years. Fidelity Magellan Fund, with a 23.9% average annual total return, has been on for eight consecutive years.

These are the sort of mutual funds that you should attempt to choose for your MFLS. The problem, of course, is that past performance is no guarantee of future performance. But it is a very good tool. The Honor Roll provides the names of the individual portfolio managers and the number of years they have been on the job. This information, too, is an excellent input for you, but it does not make for a sure thing. You should work toward selecting the five mutual funds that in your judgment will tend to be on the *Forbes* Honor Roll each year *in the future*.

The Seasoned Veteran believes that your selections should include *three* domestic stock funds, *one* balanced fund, and *one* foreign stock fund. These should be from five different mutual fund families. You should always select from mutual funds that have been operating, hopefully with the same portfolio manager, for at least five years. You should be mindful of purchase costs, sales costs, and annual costs.

In Chapter 16 you will learn about your Plan's January Review. You will review your five mutual funds' performance in terms of total return at each January Review. At the time of your first Review for the mutual funds, they must have a total return performance at least equal to the DJIA performance since date of purchase. At the second Review, one year later, they must have a total return performance at least 15% better than the DJIA performance since date of purchase. If they fail to meet these standards of performance at the first two Reviews, they will be sold and replaced by a mutual fund of the same category: domestic stock, balanced, or foreign stock. That is one of the reasons to think twice or three times about buying high-load mutual funds; you will be penalized if you make a mistake. Nonetheless, the Seasoned Veteran believes this is a bullet that must be bitten in the overall effort to maximize consistent total return. After the second Review, a surviving mutual fund will be left to your own decision-making as to whether it should be held or sold. My feeling is that if a fund outperforms the averages in its first two years of your ownership it will probably be a keeper as long as management does not change. Be particularly mindful of changes in this area. Since your shares are held by the mutual funds' custodians, you will be on the mailing list for all communications from the fund including annual reports. These can be particularly helpful in developing a feel for the management, its philosophies and its outlooks. Also, you can frequently find FFF ideas from the mutual fund portfolios that will be revealed to you with these mailings.

I have mentioned the Fidelity group as well as Fidelity Magellan Fund. In the same spirit as I have earlier mentioned Templeton Growth Fund (without implying a current recommendation) let's take a close look at this Fund. Fidelity Magellan Fund has been managed for twelve years, since 1977, by Peter Lynch. Although started in 1962, it was closed to new investors for many years until 1982, when its total assets exceeded $100 million for the first time. Spectacular total return results for each year 1976 to 1983 (annual figures each year ranged from 14.5% to 69.9%) caused new investors to come running, with over $7 billion under management by 1986 and over $11 billion just before the Crash. The front-end load is 3.00% regardless of the amount, and the annual operating expense for the past five years ranges from 0.85% to 1.12%. During the same period the portfolio turnover ratio has ranged from 85% to 126%. There are presently about 1400 stocks in portfolio, with all but a handful accounting for less than 0.50% of assets (the vast majority are less than 0.20% of assets). Every year except two since 1976 Fidelity Magellan Fund has substantially outperformed the market averages. *Forbes* has done some arithmetic for us. In addition to telling us that the average total return since November, 1980 is 23.9%, they have given us a figure on what a $10,000 investment made on November 30, 1980, would be worth on June 30, 1989, after allowing for the initial sales load *and* income taxes (at the highest possible then-applicable tax bracket) on all cash distributions that were reinvested.

The figure is $47,871.

Many of you are probably saying "Wow! If John Templeton can

produce 15% per year on the average over thirty-five years, and Peter Lynch can produce 24% per year on the average for nearly nine years, why not just go with these two guys and forget about the Plan?" The answer to this question is "things change." John Templeton is seventy-six years old. Peter Lynch has been operating in a daily pressure-cooker every day for many years and he may decide to retire early. He can certainly afford to! Nothing is for certain. The most expensive words in the investment business are "it won't be much different this time."

Diversification is the key. Your five MFLS and your hold or sell strategies will help you avoid the situation that an investor might have gotten into in 1980 when he might have put all his capital into the 44 Wall Street Fund. During the period that Peter Lynch was achieving an annual average 23.9%, the 44 Wall Street Fund, a no-load fund with "aggressive growth of capital" as its objective since its organization in 1968, was achieving a *negative* average annual total return of 16.7%. That's *minus* 16.7%!

14
Other Types of Investments

    This Chapter will address various types of investments that will *not* be suitable investments in your Investment Plan.

    You must constantly remember that you have adopted your Plan for one reason only: to grow capital.

    The investment categories discussed in this Chapter simply do not meet the Seasoned Veteran's specifications for long term return opportunity.

    I am aware that many of you own investments in the categories we will briefly discuss here. There are certainly situations where these securities *are* suitable for some people. Many people have no need to grow capital, for various good reasons. There are, for example, many people whose sole investment objective is to protect capital and live off its return. These are primarily people who are in their retirement years. Chapter 20 will discuss this subject in detail and recommend a manner in which investors participating in our Plan will be able to handsomely meet their living expenses in retirement. This is done with a portfolio of securities that are purchased, and held, solely for their *total* return and without any regard whatever to current return. For people at or close to retirement, the choice is theirs. Other people, and I will mention one man as an example, have the ability and good fortune to grow their capital very significantly by their own labor, and for them our Plan may not fit.

So, with the above paragraph as background, and with your developing awareness that all of these categories may provide a source of capital for your Plan, let us proceed.

MONEY MARKET FUNDS

There is absolutely nothing wrong with money market funds. Almost all of them are well managed. The money market fund industry began only fifteen years ago, and today the total assets under management are more than three hundred billion dollars. There must be something pretty good here, with that type of growth! The plain simple fact, however, is that in our Plan you will never have idle money awaiting deployment. You have already seen, and in Section VI, which is now on our immediate horizon, you will see very specifically, that you will always have a debit balance in your margin account and all moneys available will go to reduce that debit balance. Simply put, it is better to pay off 12% debt than to enjoy 5%, or even 9%, total return.

MORTGAGE-BACKED SECURITIES

You have read that there have recently been periods of consecutive months when the Seasoned Veteran worked exclusively with these securities, selling them to financial institutions of many types. I have made more than a few commission dollars in this activity, and I suppose I should view them in a more friendly fashion.

These are the most complicated securities in the entire investment spectrum. They have more bells and whistles than the Toonerville Trolley and the Queen Elizabeth combined. I would wager that if all the tens of thousands of individual (as opposed to institutional) investors who have purchased them since GNMA pass-throughs were first introduced twenty years ago (followed in the Seventies by FNMA and FHLMC, or Freddie Mac, pass-throughs) were lined up, and were asked if they were glad they bought them, fewer than 25% would raise their hands. And if the same group were asked if they truly understood them, fewer than 5% would raise their hands.

One of the best things about these securities is that many hundreds of recent MBA's and Ph.D's in finance, mathematics, and computer science have been put to work at good salaries in quasi-federal agencies and investment banking firms to analyze the gigantic real estate mortgage industry, create securities with the mortgages, and thereby create liquidity so that banks, S&L's and mortgage companies can sell their mortgages to investors and thus have the wherewithal to make new mortgages. There is absolutely no doubt that our very important housing industry has significantly benefited.

The basic security, of course, is one of many thousands of pools of "securitized" single family real estate first mortgages, with from ten or so mortgages to a pool — up to many thousands of mortgages to a pool. The monthly payments to principal and interest that the mortgagor makes are "passed-through" to the investor, so that the investor gets a monthly check.

Here is problem number one: The monthly check contains a return of *principal*, which, if the investor does with it as he might do with an interest or dividend check (i.e. spend it), he will eventually have lost all his capital.

Problem number two: The checks frequently contain pro-rata shares of principal *prepayments*, whether they be made voluntarily (by the mortgagors' houses being sold or mortgages being refinanced, among other reasons) or involuntarily as a result of foreclosure, whereby the GNMA, FNMA, or FHLMC makes up any shortfall or deficiency. Not only might these be spent, as above, but they might create a very quick capital loss. Suppose you buy a 12% GNMA at the current price of about 108. There are 20 mortgages in the pool. Suppose next month four of the mortgages are paid in full. That means you will receive, several months from now, a very large check with about twenty percent of your principal in it. This principal is coming back to you at *100*, and you have a very quick

8 point loss. Further, there is not much chance that your investment at 108 will ever go up, because in the required scenario that interest rates are going down, most of the mortgages will refinance at the then available lower rates and you will receive more payments at par. Institutional investors are aware of this, and they will not bid these prices higher. Now you are thinking: OK! I will buy an 8% pool that's listed in the newspaper at 88, and on prepayments I will make a quick 12 points. Fine. The problem is that these pools, of course, tend *not* to prepay because the mortgage rates are low to begin with, and those that the computer boys identify as fast payers (a "speed pool" with fast PSA, an acronym for "pool speed assumption") are not going to be available to buy at 88; they will be more like 92 or 94. And, sure enough, as fast as you pay 92 or 94, the PSA will change downward and the speed premium vanishes and you have about a 5 point computational loss.

Then there are CMO's (Collateralized Mortgage Obligations) and REMIC's (Real Estate Mortgage Investment Conduits). Today's *Wall Street Journal* indicates there were three newly formed issues of these securities sold yesterday, totaling $650 million, and $40 billion were sold in the first half of 1989. Again, there must be something good about them. They are a way of taking mortgage-backed securities, or even raw mortgages which are called "whole loans", and prioritizing the principal payments into classes. These classes are called *tranches*, which derives from a French word meaning "slice." The Seasoned Veteran has asked at least a dozen very intelligent veteran bond people, "Why this word? Why not plain English?" I have been met with just as many blank stares and shoulder shrugs! Anyhow, these securities are based on all principal payments being applied to the first class, until all four or five classes are sequentially retired when the last mortgage is paid. The investor buys whatever *tranch* he thinks will satisfy his maturity requirements, using the PSA as the basis for estimating the maturity. The investor is at the PSA's mercy, and it frequently is revised after you buy the darned thing.

But *you*, as a participant in our Plan, are *not* that investor! And if you were one in the past, and still own mortgage-backed securities, you might well consider liquidating them as a source of capital for our Plan.

FIXED INCOME MUTUAL FUNDS

I made a very strong recommendation in the last Chapter *for* equity mutual funds of most categories, and have even included in my recommendation balanced funds that contain both equities and fixed income securities.

I now wish to make just as strong a recommendation *against* mutual funds that contain only fixed income securities.

There is nothing subjective about my feelings. They are based entirely on the performance records regarding total return.

In the last Chapter we saw that, according to Wiesenberger's *Management Results* dated June, 1989, an unweighted average of 381 equity funds (including balanced funds) produced a total return of 91%, for the 5 1/2 year period starting January, 1984 and a 403% total return for the 10 1/2 years starting January, 1979. The ranges for the four categories of equity funds were 79% to 108% and 355% to 436% respectively.

The same *Management Results* shows that for the same 5 1/2 year period 74 U.S. Government funds (including GNMA funds and funds using hedging strategies) had an unweighted average total return of 73%, and for the 10 1/2 year period 158%. 110 corporate bond funds (including high yield, or junk, funds) showed total average returns of 78% and 211% for the two time frames, and the figures for the 173 tax-exempt bond funds were 76% and 124%, respectively.

These total return comparisons make the point unarguable. The case is sealed by stating that the absolute largest fixed income mutual fund, a GNMA fund that grew by *over ten billion dollars* from 1983 to 1988 (virtually all of it new money from investors, with many of the dollars coming from high-yielding instruments that were purchased 1979 to 1982 and were now maturing) had a total return of 78% and 139% for the two time frames. Considering the difficulties inherent in managing a mortgage-backed securities portfolio, this is not too bad, but for our Plan it is not good enough!

Our UST/FIPS strategy would have made these figures look down-right puny.

INDIVIDUALLY SELECTED CORPORATES AND MUNICIPALS

Chapter 11 virtually covered this subject, with the decision resolved in favor of UST.

The Seasoned Veteran believes the yield spread between UST and AAA and AA corporates and taxable equivalent municipals would have to widen from the current 30 to 100 basis points to something on the order of 300 to 400 basis points before I would consider changing my thinking. And I can't foresee that anything will take place to make this happen.

Incidently, the formula to convert a tax free yield to a taxable equivalent yield is a simple one: divide the tax free yield by (1.00 minus the tax rate) to get the taxable equivalent yield.

STRAIGHT PREFERRED STOCK

These securities trade almost totally on a current yield basis in accord with the money market and have no place in our Plan.

Very, very occasionally a situation will come along where a cumulative preferred issue will have been in dividend arrearage and its market price will be very low. The company's earnings substantially improve, and the arrearage is made up in one large payment. Such a situation occurred with Chrysler in 1982 and with Long Island Lighting in 1989. If you are able to anticipate such an occurrence before the stock's price totally reflects it, it is a nice play. A very nice play.

CONVERTIBLE BONDS & PREFERREDS

John Heywood was a sixteenth century English dramatist who put together a collection of pithy sayings from the colloquial language. One of them was "Would ye both eat your cake and have it, too?" This describes the attempt that investment bankers make when they devise and issue these securities. They are not bad, but we can do better by using straight equity and straight debt as means to our Plan's objective.

ZERO COUPON BONDS

It is amazing to me that these securities have had their inception only in the past 10 years. Yet during this short period, the zero coupon marketplace has expanded by many hundreds of millions of dollars, mostly in U.S. Treasuries where they are almost entirely a manufactured product. The manufacturers in this case are large investment banking firms, who create them by separating the "coupons" from the bond "corpus" and the subsequent non-interest paying securities are generic "Strips" (Separate Trading Registered Interest and Principal) or proprietary "CATS" (Certificates of Accrual Treasury Securities), "TIGRS" (Treasury Investment Growth Receipts), "TR's" (Treasury Receipts), and a few others.

There are also municipal zero coupon securities, mostly original issue discount, and a few corporates, mostly junk.

I recall asking a very intelligent and seasoned banker, back in 1965, why the U.S. Treasury issued discounted obligations only in the form of one year or shorter Bills or low denomination Savings Bonds. I said it seemed to me there would be a market for longer maturities as growth vehicles, at severe price discounts where compounding would be put to work. I was told to forget it; no institutional investor would ever buy a bond beyond one year in maturity that didn't throw off cash interest every six months. It is too bad that I did "forget it." I might, if I'd continued forward on the idea, have "invented" what has proven to be a gigantic industry and put the Icahns and Trumps to work as my houseboys. Alas, and alack.

I am not recommending zero coupon securities for our Plan.

There are some good advantages, mainly that the reinvestment rate of the unpaid but accruing and compounding (semi-annually) interest is locked in at the same yield basis as purchased. However, the accruals are "phantom" income that create, under current and foreseeable tax law, a current tax obligation without a "throw-off" with which to pay it. This is not true on most municipal zeroes, so there is an advantage on these.

Another thing: since there is no interest "throw-off," the inside market is usually about 20 to 50 basis points higher (which makes the dollar price commensurately lower) than equivalent interest-paying securities. This gives brokers the opportunity to offer zeroes to their unsophisticated customers at much higher than normal percentage markups, because these customers are usually looking only at the published yield curve for interest-bearing UST.

I would not consider zeroes for our Plan unless the interest rate scenario was a UST Long Bond at 16% or higher. And then I would want to think about it.

One area where zeroes do have a place: gifts to young children and grandchildren for educational purposes. The 1986 Tax Reform Act has complicated the tax treatment of these investments under the various state Gifts to Minors Acts, but they still should be considered and you should discuss them with your tax advisor. A 15-year UST zero at 9.00% yield basis costs about 26 cents on the maturity dollar.

And Chapter 15, upcoming, will discuss zeroes in tax-deferred IRA's and Keoghs.

LIMITED PARTNERSHIP INVESTMENTS

These are investments designed to allow investors to participate in everything from wildcat oil drilling to "mezzanine" LBO financing, from real estate of all types to cattle feeding programs.

The Seasoned Veteran is going to exert real discipline in this section. I am going to limit myself to a list of no more than ten single sentence paragraphs to give the reasons why these investments do not fit into our Plan:

They are illiquid.

They no longer afford any real tax shelter.

There is a better chance with this type of investment that you have fallen in with "bad guys" than any other type.

The sales commissions, general partner's fees, expert fees, etc. are horrendous, almost always at least 15% on the front end, frequently up towards 25%; there are a lot of fingers in the pie.

The proforma cash flow and internal rate of return projections are frequently plucked almost from thin air.

The general partner will make a profit in more cases than will the limited partners, and he will usually have a low or zero cash investment; the cards are almost always stacked in his favor.

The illiquidity lasts a long time — five, seven, ten years, if it ever ends.

Coupled with the illiquidity is the long-term absence of a way to determine current market valuation.

The person selling you this investment will not really understand it, nor have a means of following it. You will have no way, short of the general partner, to get your questions answered; he will nearly always be unavailable — he will, according to his secretary, be "out in the field this week, looking after your investment."

The prospectus will weigh more than this book. And that should be enough reason without the first nine!

PRECIOUS METALS — COIN AND BULLION

These are supposed to be the most conservative of investments, and in an Armageddon scenario I suppose value would be realized in spades.

In the meantime, they are best used in a runaway inflation setting. I've already given you a technique in Chapter 12 that will allow you to make a very nice return if and when we climb toward and into double-digit CPI increases and levels.

Further, if you are so inclined, there is nothing precluding you from buying common stock in a precious metals company as one of your FFF equities. In an inflationary scenario, these are frequently nice plays and the SSS will get you out just right.

But I do not recommend the metals themselves. I suppose if you want to keep a few American Eagle coins in your safe deposit box, no harm is done, but they are not included in our Plan.

Pure gold has been in a nine year bear market; had you bought bullion at the average 1980 dollar price of $613 per oz. and sold it in the Summer of 1989, you would have experienced a negative annual total return of about 4.5% average for each of nine years, with zero cash "throw-off."

Let me pause here and tell you a short story about a man I know quite well. He is the man I mentioned very early in this Chapter. He is a professional man in his late fifties. His professional practice has been extremely successful. He has earned well into six figures each year for over twenty years. He has paid his income tax. He saves a six figure amount every year. He does two things with his savings, which are truly capital. One half of it goes into UST bills, which he keeps rolling over every three or six months. The other half goes into gold coin and bullion, which he keeps in a very large (and heavy!) safe deposit box. He also has vast amounts of insurance: malpractice, disability, and term life. It is hard for me to fault this man, although I doubt I would invest the same way were I he. He, unlike most of us, has been able to grow his capital by his day-to-day labor. He has a low-eight figure net worth. He has not really needed portfolio power. He sleeps very soundly at night. He frequently asks me, with a nice smile on his face, how my investments are doing.

LOW-PRICED UNSEASONED OTC STOCKS

In today's newspapers are listed many hundreds of NASDAQ and "other OTC" stocks that closed yesterday at prices below $3 a share. There are also hundreds of OTC stocks that don't make the newspapers; these are listed daily in the "pink sheets." The market for these stocks is discussed in a newspaper called the *Penny Stock Journal*, which is well written and enjoys a fine circulation.

In Chapter 9, I discussed the category of NASD member firms that specializes in these stocks. While I have never worked in one of these firms, several of my good friends have.

I am going to dissuade you from buying these stocks by telling you an absolutely imaginary story that at the same time has great verisimilitude:

It is 8:30 A.M. at the branch office of Able and Baker, members of NASD. The twenty-nine year old branch manager has called a ten minute meeting of his fifteen brokers, all but one or two five or more years younger than he.

"Troops," he will say, "yesterday afternoon the firm took down a position of 250,000 shares of XYZ Fermented Spirits Co. You will recall this fine company well. It is the company with the process for fermenting wine in thirty minutes. We brought it public last fall at $1.00. Today we are quoting a market of 1 1/4 bid, 1 3/4 asked." (The Seasoned Veteran: They bought the shares yesterday for 7/8 or lower, most probably.)

"Our branch office has been given, because we are all working so hard, 75,000 shares exclusive until 4:00 P.M. today. You can offer it to your clients at 1 3/4 net, minimum order 2000 shares. For every share you sell, your next paycheck will be increased by 35 cents." (The Seasoned Veteran: 35¢ to the broker, and at least 52 1/2¢ to the firm, a total real spread of 100%.)

Fifteen smiles turn into broad grins. Winks are exchanged.

The branch manager continues: "Joe, this will give you down payment money on the BMW you crave. Art, this will pay your American Express charges on the trip to Europe last Spring. I'm tired, incidentally, of the calls you get here at the office from their collection department. Bob, here is your chance to pay for that divorce. And Sam, this will put you into six figures for the year. OK. I don't want any lunch breaks, and I want all the tickets as they are written. 4:00 this afternoon is the deadline. And the person among you who sells the most shares gets a steak dinner for two tonight, with a bottle of champagne, at whatever restaurant you choose. On me! Now let's HIT THE PHONES!!"

That day, fifteen brokers "dial for dollars" in such a way that their dialing finger develops an even larger callus than the Seasoned Veteran is getting with the writing of this book!

Onward!

15
IRA's, Keogh's, and 401 (K)'s

I talked briefly about these accounts in the early pages of this book, and provided some caveats on the likelihood of your being able to include these funds as capital in your Investment Plan.

There are problems.

First of all, we must rule out 401 (K) programs entirely. These are excellent tax shelters for employed people, and I strongly urge those of you who are 401 (K) plan participants to continue with them. The problem revolves around the fact that your employer has control over where your vested interest in the 401 (K) plan is invested. It frequently happens that you have *some* choice, usually within a family of mutual funds that is selected by your employer. My strong recommendation to you, if this is the case, is to elect an investment vehicle that is an equity or balanced mutual fund that has long term growth of capital as an objective. In the previous Chapter, you learned quite a bit about my thinking on mutual funds, and the same thoughts are applicable here. You may certainly consider your 401(K) plan as an excellent vehicle for growing capital. It is, however, in no way an integral part of the Investment Plan promulgated by this book. It must be considered aside and apart from your Plan.

That leaves us with IRA's and Keogh's.

You have learned that your margin account at Murphy & Carroll is primarily a vehicle to use UST and FFF as securities that can make a consistent total return. By leveraging these securities and their total return, funds can be provided to participate in MFLS. It is a Plan that is simple in its structure, and its basic simplicity is one of the things that allows it to work so well.

The core problem is that neither IRA's nor Keogh's are marginable. They must be maintained in separate accounts, with Murphy & Carroll as legal Custodian. These accounts are identical to cash accounts in connection with IRS regulations and other rules that pertain to them. Even though it is possible to set up a "self directed" account for both IRA and Keogh plans at a brokerage firm, there is no way that the assets in the plans can be used as collateral for loans of any type, from anybody.

Another problem, applicable only to Keogh plans, is that there may be an employee of yours, or several of them, who are participants. This requires certain liquidity provisions which must be met in the event the employees leave your employ.

With full knowledge that many of you have built up considerable tax-deferred equity in IRA's and Keogh's, it is difficult to find a direct place for them in the UST/FIPS, FFF/SSS, and MFLS categories. They simply muddy the Plan's waters.

Nonetheless, here are some ideas for you!

You can (if you have not done so already) set up your IRA or Keogh in an equity account or balanced growth mutual fund, or several funds, using the same selection techniques and holding strategies that have just been outlined in Chapter 13. All of the mutual funds have specific IRA custodial plans, and many of them will help you with the formalities of the Keogh. One of the advantages is that the cash distributions can be reinvested in additional shares without current income tax consequence. This mutual fund holding can be considered an adjunct to your Plan, although not an integral part of it. Do not reduce your Plan's five MFLS holdings; consider the IRA or Keogh mutual fund(s) as supplemental holdings.

Here is another idea: You can consider setting up an IRA or Keogh custodial account at Murphy & Carroll, a self-directed account, and use it as a vehicle for the same type of common stock investing that is included as FFF/SSS in the Plan. This will be an account totally removed from your Plan, but if you consider common stock selection to be your forte this will have an appeal for you. A decided advantage is that your net realized capital gains, and any dividend "throw-off," will not currently be income taxable. Until you begin making withdrawals after age 59 1/2, you will be able to grow capital on a tax-free basis. A disadvantage is that the cash "throw-off" must stay in the self-directed account, and if the amounts are small they must go into a companion IRA or Keogh money market fund at a relatively low rate of return until they build up to an investable amount. You may, therefore, wish to concentrate on low-yielding common stocks in this activity, although this should not be the sole criterion.

One last idea: UST zero coupon securities have an appeal because annual income accretion is not taxable in an IRA or Keogh. If and when the yield curve goes up to a point where UST zero coupon securities can be purchased at an 11.50% or higher yield basis (correlative to 16.00% mentioned in the last Chapter, because 11.50% is the after-tax equivalent) in a maturity that corresponds to your age bracket, 59 1/2 to 70 1/2, the Seasoned Veteran feels this would be an attractive holding. Again, it is not an integral part of your investment plan. And be sure that your Customer's Person gives you an execution at a yield basis reflective of the true inside market for UST zeroes, per the discussion in Chapter 14.

I believe your journey is progressing smoothly. We are now at the end of a very important section, a point where you might wish to take a short rest stop. Perhaps you wish to go back over some of this material to be certain that you are comfortable with it; now is a good time to do that. When you are ready to go, I am! We will now really start to put it together, to finalize the plan that is *best for you*.

SECTION VI.
THE PORTFOLIOS

16
Choosing the Proper Lane

I am going to spend a little time with this introduction to your Plan's portfolio management, in order to explain the basic thinking and structural background for the four Chapters that follow. By doing this, the "ground rules" for your portfolio will be established. These rules will be applicable to every portfolio.

THE BROAD HIGHWAY: THE AGE FACTOR

You may have noticed from the Table of Contents that the next four Chapters discuss the portfolios in terms of the investor's age. The reasoning for this is in the realm of "how much time does the investor have to grow capital and still enjoy its fruits in his (or her) lifetime?"

To answer this question is an obvious challenge, because every investor has a different circumstance. Obviously, I can't know every investor's specific circumstance. So it is therefore necessary to set up a structure that will pertain to a "typical" investor of a certain age, and presume that this investor fits certain socioeconomic and other demographic characteristics. Assumptions must therefore be made, and these assumptions will be described and explained at the beginning of each of the next four Chapters.

The Seasoned Veteran nevertheless believes that a fairly wide latitude must be allowed the individual investor. In this area, you can travel on a broad highway. You can even switch lanes from time to time!

For example, a 41-year-old investor who is planning on totally retiring at age 50 will be very interested in the strategies outlined not only in Chapter 18 but also those in Chapters 19 and 20, which pertain to older categories. Or a 56-year-old investor who plans on producing income from employment until he or she is past 70 will perhaps wish to employ strategies that are slightly more aggressive, those that are intended for younger investors and which are explained in Chapter 17.

But in a general way the Chapters are targeted to investors as follows:

Chapter 17 presumes income from employment sufficient to cover *all* living expenses. It is hoped that cash additions to the Plan's capital can be made from time to time.

Chapter 18 presumes continued employment, but provides for your possible desire to make some major expenditures in the area of college tuition, expensive vacations or automobiles, things of this sort that might be paid for by withdrawals from the Plan.

Chapter 19 again presumes continued employment, some major expenditures, and a desire to prepare for total retirement at age 65.

Chapter 20 presumes no employment income and the desire to allow a majority of living expenses be met by "income" from the Plan. You will also have Social Security and perhaps a pension, either from your employer and/or from yourself, through your IRA, Keogh, or 401(K) plan.

The Plan is designed to grow capital from age 20, or younger, to the day your physician signs a pretty personal death certificate. This fact, too, puts you on a very broad highway.

THE HIGHWAY NARROWS:
THE BASIC PORTFOLIO STRATEGY

Every portfolio will contain UST/FIPS, FFF/SSS, and MFLS (which will be phased out in Chapter 19, although the mutual funds will remain without the leverage).

Interest and dividends received in cash from UST and FFF will *always* be credited against the Murphy & Carroll debit balance.

During the calendar year, *all sales* of UST and FFF will be treated as follows: if a profit is realized, the net before-tax profit will reduce the debit balance and the replacement purchase will be in a dollar amount equal to the original cost of the security sold; in this way profits will reduce the debit balance during the year. If a loss is incurred, the replacement purchase will be in a dollar amount equal to the net proceeds of the security sold. An individual holding of UST will always be in multiples of $1000 par value, or multiples of $5000 par value if your total portfolio size permits. An individual holding of FFF can be in any number of shares, *e.g.* 158 shares is perfectly satisfactory. There is no need for "round lots" of stock. The objective of all FIPS and SSS sales during the calendar year is to reduce the debit balance. If profitable sales are made in amounts that *eliminate* the debit balance and produce a credit balance, a January Review (see below) is immediately occasioned.

The mutual funds purchased under MFLS will stand aside and apart from the Murphy & Carroll UST and FFF portfolio. *All* cash distributions on the mutual fund shares, be they dividends or realized capital gains distributions, will be used under automatic reinvestment plans to purchase additional shares of the same specific mutual fund. This will never change.

During the calendar year, any addition of new cash to the Plan will simply reduce the debit balance. Any withdrawal of cash will simply increase the debit balance. If the new cash addition eliminates the debit balance and produces a cash credit balance, a January Review is immediately occasioned.

A VERY NARROW HIGHWAY:
THE JANUARY REVIEW

Every year, the month of January will be the most important time in your Plan's year. You will use this month to set a goal of maximum total return for the year at hand. You will focus only on the Magic Number. In this regard, you will be traveling a very narrow highway.

You will review the preceding year. You will attempt to identify your mistakes, analyze them, and attempt to set up techniques that will not repeat them. You will identify your bright spots, and attempt to expand upon them. You will review the world and its economy, and make a forecast for the next 12 months which will influence your FFF selections. You will set a conscious goal that no matter what your results for last year, this year will do even better!

By about January 5, you will have received your month-end December statement from Murphy & Carroll. You will use it to perform the analysis that will be described in Chapter 22 at the end of this book. And you will immediately use it to structure your portfolio for the year at hand. This will require two actions, and every attempt should be made to do them simultaneously, so they are completed by January 31 at the latest.

(1)   All 12 Murphy & Carroll monthly statements from last year should be photocopied in their entirety and packed off immediately to your tax advisor, together with photocopies of all mutual fund statements showing cash distributions. (Even though these distributions were used to purchase additional shares, income taxes must unfortunately be paid on them.) You must ask, even demand, that your tax advisor give you during January an "approximate but accurate" figure on what your Plan's income tax liability due April 15 will be. If you determine your Plan must undergo a cash withdrawal to pay it, this must be factored in. Perhaps at this time of year you might have lump sum "other income" of some sort - an employment bonus, a Christ-

mas gift, etc. - that can meet your tax liability. Remember: a cash withdrawal has the same impact on your Plan as a capital loss.

(2)   You will determine where your Plan stands with regard to the debit balance as a percentage of UST and FFF market value.

If the debit balance on January 1 is a higher percent than the recommended Chapters 17 to 19 percentages (which means you have had a bad year), you will adjust the FFF section of your Murphy & Carroll portfolio by selling from individual FFF holdings, with the sales proceeds being used to reduce the debit balance to the recommended percentage. If you have a need for tax money, this will be factored in. One example: You want a ratio of debit balance to total UST and FFF market values of 50%. On December 31 your UST was $20,000, your FFF was $70,000, and your debit balance was $50,000, equal to 55.55% of total market value. It was $5,000 more than 50% of total market value. Further, your tax advisor called on January 20 to say you have a tax liability from your Plan of $2,000. You determine this $2,000 must come from the Plan, so you withdraw it and set it aside for April 15 income taxes. Now your debit balance is $52,000, and you have a $7,000 "problem."

You will identify $7,000 from your $70,000 FFF market value that is the $7,000 that looks to you like it is the worst bargain (remember that word!) and sell it, with proceeds going to reduce the debit balance. This might well involve several stocks from the FFF, or portions of several stocks. This FFF sale will not impact taxes until next year, so the $2,000 tax liability is unchanged. You will never sell a UST or a mutual fund to bring your debit balance to the recommended level; you will only sell FFF. Once the debit balance level is adjusted, you will not do anything further with it until next January except attempt to reduce it by UST/FIPS and FFF/SSS profits. Do not worry about a margin call. The borrowing strategy is so conservative that the likelihood of a margin call is equivalent to building a snowman on my favorite Florida beach! And if there *ever* should be a margin call, the mutual fund shares can be used to meet it.

If the debit balance on January 1 is a lower percent than the recommended Chapters 17 to 19 percentages (which means you have had a good year), you will take a new loan from Murphy & Carroll in an amount that will bring the debit balance back up to the recommended percentage of UST and FFF market value. The proceeds of this new loan will be used to purchase new shares in one or more of the five mutual funds you own under the MFLS. The selection of *which* mutual fund or funds should receive the addition is left to you, with the amount of new money from the loan a factor. If the amount is small in relation to your overall MFLS portfolio, the Seasoned Veteran would select only one mutual fund, the one that you believe will do best in the year at hand, the one that seems to be the best bargain. If you have had a very good year just past and the amount of borrowed funds is large in relation to your overall MFLS portfolio, select two to all five mutual funds for the new investment, perhaps using some balancing concepts to even out the respective dollar holdings. If the selections are front-end or 12(b)1 load funds, use your Murphy & Carroll cash account so your Customer's Person can earn a commission. Be sure to set up your new shares on automatic reinvestment plans.

One example: You again want a 50% debit balance ratio to total UST and FFF market values. On December 31 your UST was $32,500, your FFF was $87,500, and your debit balance at $37,500 was 31.25% of total market value. You want your debit balance to be $60,000, which is 50% of $32,500 plus $87,500. You therefore borrow $22,500 from Murphy & Carroll ($60,000 minus $37,500), deposit it to your cash account, and buy the mutual fund(s) you deem appropriate. If you are buying no-load mutual funds you do not use your cash account but instead deal directly with the mutual fund. In this example, I did not include an income tax need. If cash is needed for this unpleasantness, the $22,500 borrowing would be the same but some of it would go to the tax bill and the rest to MFLS.

Your January Review will *not* include an analysis of the quality of your UST and FFF holdings *unless* there is a need to adjust the debit balance by selling FFF. The FIPS and SSS strategies will otherwise dictate the holding period. This is not true for the MFLS; the holding or selling strategy for the five mutual funds has already been discussed in Chapter 13. It, too, is an integral part of the January Review and it will prevail without regard to debit balance levels or anything else. The only time a mutual fund will be sold is when its performance is found lacking.

You will need to exert some self-discipline to complete your January Review by January 31 at the absolute latest. There is no better time than during the New Year's Day football games to start getting organized. The only reason the Seasoned Veteran has picked January 31 rather than January 15 is in consideration of your tax advisor's schedule. Perhaps if you are especially nice to him or her, your fee for his or her services might be lowered!

Chapter 22 will further address the January Review, and some of the loose ends that you are perhaps experiencing will be tied together at that time.

Early on, the Seasoned Veteran promised concepts, techniques, and strategies designed and well chosen to grow capital by compounding a total return, by using the Eighth Wonder of the World and a Magic Number. You are seeing them now! Your "driving skills" have improved enormously! We are approaching the end of our journey.

17
Ages 20-39: The World Is Your Oyster

Why, then the world's mine oyster
Which I, with sword, will open.

Our old friend Will Shakespeare put these words into the mouth of one of his characters in *The Merry Wives of Windsor* in 1601. He was at the top of his own game that year; he wrote *Hamlet* just after he completed *The Merry Wives.*

Back in the Fifties, during college, the Air Force, and getting started in the investment business, the Seasoned Veteran had a handful of friends and contemporaries who could put their hands on investable amounts of capital. Without exception, these were scions of very wealthy families, and their financial circumstance was the result of inheritance or other family largess. I recall being stationed in the Air Force in San Antonio in April, 1956, with my college classmate, Bill Mellon of the Pittsburgh Mellons. One Saturday afternoon we walked into a Ford dealership and Bill Mellon bought a 1956 Ford Thunderbird with currency from his wallet. I was mighty impressed! (And, believe me, so was the salesman! The entire transaction took no more than 20 minutes.) And there were other friends in similar circumstances. But I did not know anybody my age who could invest $10,000 or more as a result of his or her own labors. I was aware that maybe the Shirley Temples and Mickey Rooneys of the world were "making big bucks," but they were an infinitesimal percentage of the younger population. My observations on this point continued on into the Sixties. I was a bank vice president with a salary in the mid teens, and I became friends with and banker to several of the world-champion Green Bay Packers. I was privy to their salaries. An All-Pro offensive lineman made $27,000, and two members of the backfield who are still household names a quarter century later were making $75,000 and $80,000, respectively.

Now all is changed. Professional athletes of a dozen sports, rock stars, movie stars, professional people of every specialty, entrepreneurs, investment bankers, corporate executives, TV stars, and even public servants in the various political subsectors, along with others, are enjoying many six figure, some seven figure, and even a few eight figure (!) annual incomes while they are in their twenties and thirties, and in a few cases while they are in their teens. These people number in the hundreds of thousands. And, believe the Seasoned Veteran, the world is indeed their oyster! Their oysters are filled with the largest pearls one could imagine!

Please go back and review page 46, which shows how $1,000 grew at 15% compounded annually. Remember our Magic Number!

For a 25 year old person who comes into our Plan with $100,000, and achieves the Magic Number on average for 40 years, and retires at the conventional 65 years of age, he will have something more than a gold watch to admire in his newly acquired leisure time. If he wants, he can spend his 65th birthday opening a bank account of $26,786,400.

Or a 30 year old person who has $100,000, and decides he would like to quit the "rat race" at age 50, and successfully implements our Plan today. He will have $1,636,800 on his 50th birthday, which maybe then he would like to convert to a 30 year AAA municipal bond portfolio at 7.5% tax-free, giving him spendable income of $122,760 every year until he is 80.

Or a 35 year old lady who has just inherited $250,000. She plans on growing capital only for 10 years, when she will need it for family reasons.

Her successful implementation of our Plan will provide her $1,011,500 to meet her objective.

Or let's take the 39 year old corporate CEO who just got "displaced" in a corporate reshuffle. He has after-tax severance pay (a golden parachute!) of $220,000, his former company's stock worth $160,000, and a vested employee benefit plan of $70,000. He immediately finds another job, so the full $450,000 is available to him to join our Plan. He signs on for 25 years, because he is a businessman who wants to work even beyond age 65, if he can. But he won't really need to. If the Magic Number is attained by him, his $450,000 will turn into $14,813,550.

Or let's take the person with the very largest pearl in his oyster. The 22 year old first-round draft pick of the Seasoned Veteran's favorite pro football team just signed a four year contract with a large six figure annual salary, plus a $400,000 signing bonus. Suppose he takes his signing bonus capital, sets aside $120,000 for income taxes, and puts $280,000 into our Plan and successfully implements it for 43 years, until age 65. This strapping young man would be in pretty good shape to face the "perils" of the retirement years. He would be worth just over $114,000,000. (I believe I will send this young man a copy of this book. I have read he is getting investment advice from his agent!)

I hope these little stories have given those of you who are in your twenties and thirties , and who have incomes from employment in medium to high five figures, the incentive to accumulate the required capital to commence our Plan. It can be your Plan. Back in Chapter 2, I indicated this was not a book to teach you how to save money, and it (as you have seen) is not. But let us just spend a second or two with it. If you can save something like $70 per month, and put it into money market accounts or C.D.'s that will average 7.00% compounded semi-annually over a 10 year period, and pay the taxes on your interest as you go along, you will have accumulated $10,000 in 10 years. Suppose you start this savings program at age 30, and come aboard the Plan with $10,000 capital at age 40. Assume you successfully achieve the Magic Number every year until age 65. You are worth $286,250 at that time! The world is your oyster, too! To then put this capital in a different plan, designed to produce tax-free income at 7.50% and protect (but not grow) capital, would give you $21,469 per year with which to make wagers with your golf buddies until you are 85. Think about it! The Eighth Wonder of the World is available to you without charge, and the Magic Number *is* attainable!

Here is how you go about attaining it while you are in the 20 to 39 age category.

PORTFOLIO STRATEGY

On whatever date you commence the Plan, you will allocate 40% of your capital to UST/FIPS and 60% of your capital to FFF/SSS. This will provide you a loan value (based on 90% UST margin and 50% FFF margin) of 66% of your capital. You will not use all of your loan value. You will only use 40% of your capital. This 40% loan will be used to purchase the five mutual funds that are MFLS.

These percentages will apply for the balance of the calendar year that you start the Plan and all of the next calendar year.

Let's use an example, with $100,000 as starting capital.

You commence the Plan on April 20, 1989. Let's say hypothetically that the Long Bond yield on that day is 9.60%. You will, in accord with UST/FIPS, buy $40,000 par value of the UST Three Year Maturity Note (or Bond). You will simultaneously buy $60,000 of FFF, with $4,000 going into each stock. Once this is done, you will have a $66,000 loan value, from which you will borrow $40,000 from Murphy & Carroll and under MFLS you will buy five mutual funds with $8,000 invested in each. In January, 1990, you will conduct a January Review and adjust your debit balance to 40% of UST and FFF total market values, as discussed in Chapter 16.

In January, 1991 you will, as part of the January Review, change your percentage allocations, and these percentages will continue until the

January Review of the year that you turn 40 years of age.

The new percentage allocations will be 30% UST/FIPS and 70% FFF/SSS. This provides a 62% loan value. The debit balance is adjusted upward to 50% of UST and FFF total market values (80.6% of loan value) and this will be your January Review debit balance goal until age 40.

You will notice that the Seasoned Veteran has you starting your Plan in a somewhat more conservative fashion than you finish it, in the 20 to 39 age bracket. There is good reason for this. The first one and a fraction years you will be "getting the hang of the Plan." You might make a mistake or three in your FFF selections. You might choose a mutual fund that is a disaster. You and your Customer's Person will be getting to know one another, and how the Plan works in real life. You will, for the first year and a fraction, probably enjoy a lower cost to your cash "throw off" vs. interest-on-debit balance equation. For example, suppose your UST "throws off" 8.00% in interest and your FFF "throws off" 3.00% in dividends. And your Murphy & Carroll debit balance costs 12.00%. Based on the 40% UST, 60% FFF, and 40% debit balance levels of the first year and a fraction, your net cost works out to be no cost at all! You actually make 0.20% on the equation, and every little bit helps toward getting your Plan off on the right foot. Then when your percentages are changed after one year and a fraction, the same income and cost assumptions and the same arithmetic on 30% UST, 70% FFF, and 50% debit balance produces a net cost of your MFLS of 1.50%. Using this approach, you are leveraging 50% of your capital at a cost of 1.50% to grow mostly computational total return in long-term double digits on your MFLS. This is really a pretty nifty situation!

The 30% UST, 70% FFF, and 50% debit balance toward MFLS is the most aggressive strategy the Seasoned Veteran will permit you in your use of the Plan.

In this Chapter, I am not going to discuss any rationale or strategy for taking capital out of the Plan. I am presuming that you will be in a position to grow your capital and even add to it without subtracting from it by cash withdrawal. Remember: a cash addition is equal to an after-tax capital gain while a cash withdrawal is equal to an after-tax capital loss. And you should always remember that compounding a total return, by definition, works best with the largest possible amount of capital in each compounding period.

The most successful implementation of this Plan, which is again a means to achieve a Magic Number on the average over many years to take advantage of the Eighth Wonder of the World, *demands rigid discipline*. I cannot emphasize this enough. There is no room to outguess yourself. You are not in a position to second-guess the UST and the FIPS percentages, and the MFLS that goes with them. You are not in a position to second-guess the economy and the markets. You will maintain your UST, FFF, and debit balance percentages, and MFLS, and your January Review, in every single solitary unique scenario that our Higher Power chooses to throw at you. You cannot succumb to the manic-depressive syndrome; you cannot become a trader; you cannot give up on your ability to select good FFF; you cannot be impatient; you cannot "sit out this year and try real estate, or gold, or antiques;" and believe me, you cannot say, "I am young enough to take some extra chances. If it doesn't work, I can always earn it back in my employment."

You must trust the Seasoned Veteran, who knows whereof he speaks, when he says "The World is Your Oyster!" and "This Investment Plan is a Winner!"

Onward! The years do pass, and we approach the dreaded, inevitable, and wonderful years of Middle Age!

18
Ages 40-59: The Top of Your Game

I well remember the evening of my 40th birthday. I was a newcomer to Florida and was attending the Casino Night at the local Yacht and Racquet Club that I had joined. We were using "play money" and everybody was having a good time. I was having a very good time! I have always liked roulette. It is essentially a "no-brainer" and my moderate interest in casinos is enhanced by not having to work too hard while enjoying them. At roulette I always bet the number that was my prep school jersey number in football and basketball. The evening of my 40th birthday, in no more than 100 spins of the wheel, my number came up about 15 times, significantly beating the odds. I had two thoughts: why was I not in a real casino, and perhaps this was a harbinger that life really did begin at 40.

The 20 years of your life that this Chapter addresses should be the best years of your life. You should be approaching and attaining your maximum earning power in your career. You will normally go from a maximum expense posture in relation to your family responsibilities to a minimum expense posture. You will perhaps make the last mortgage payment on your dream house, perhaps then selling it (which might provide capital for your Plan) and moving to a smaller place that is less demanding of your time, attentions, and checkbook. You might receive an inheritance. And in non-monetary realms you have developed some wonderful qualities in the areas of self-analysis, patience, and a general awareness of what is going on in the world around you. All of these ingredients of middle age will enhance your abilities to successfully implement your Investment Plan.

How excellent it would be if you are celebrating your 40th birthday in a context where it is the year 2005, and you came into the Plan with $100,000 15 years ago and have, on the average, attained the Magic Number and compounded it each year. You spend 15 minutes doing a little arithmetic and see that your Plan is worth nearly $815,000. And since you do not plan on retiring until age 65, and your career is now blossoming, the world will continue to be your oyster!

But let's suppose that scenario, alas, is not yours to enjoy. You are 53 years old right now, and you started an investment program some years ago that today adds up to about $125,000. And you are absolutely fed up with working, figuring that under any and all circumstances you will bow out of the labor force at age 60. Well, if you get started with our Plan today, bringing into it your $125,000 of capital, in seven years of successfully attaining the Magic Number you will have over $330,000. And in Chapter 20 upcoming, the Seasoned Veteran will show you how you can take $30,000 per year out of the Plan to live on and still grow capital such that at age 70 you might well have nearly $600,000 of capital in the Plan. I am sure you will like this new scenario, and so will your heirs!

Or suppose you are 45 years old, and have been a real estate developer for 25 years. You are tired of it. The absence of high inflation and supportive tax laws have adversely impacted some of your deals and holdings, and you are fed up with serving your many masters, who have been not only customers and bankers, but now more than ever the public officials who are making your life miserable in terms of zoning, impact fees, and dozens of permits that take longer to get and more sweat to get them. You have $80,000 in the bank and you can liquidate your real estate holdings for an after-tax $720,000. You determine that you will keep

$300,000 in the bank to live on for five years. So you will have $500,000 available for the Plan without withdrawal for five years. You believe you can attain the Magic Number on the average for these five years. You will implement whatever strategies the Seasoned Veteran will explain in Chapter 20, because you will consider yourself retired at age 50. Well, you will have just over $1,000,000 going into your early retirement, and Chapter 20 will be a pleasure for you to read!

Here is one last scenario. You are a career woman, age 48, and you are earning $50,000 per year. You plan on working to age 55. You have $85,000 in the bank, and have just received a $200,000 inheritance from your mother's estate. You keep $50,000 (one year's salary) in savings, and come into the Plan with $235,000 for seven years. You are able to compound the Magic Number on the average for these seven years, so you then have $625,000. Chapter 20 will give you advice on how you can continue with a spendable $50,000 per year lifestyle every year past age 55. If you live to be 80 you will have nearly $3,400,000 to pass on to *your* daughter!

If by any chance the power of the Eighth Wonder of the World has previously been eluding you, the Seasoned Veteran hopes you are now becoming a true believer!

Here is the specific manner in which your Plan is to be worked in the 40 to 59 age category.

PORTFOLIO STRATEGY

If you commence the Plan in the years that you are between 40 and 59 years old, you will allocate 45% of your capital to UST/FIPS and 55% of your capital to FFF/SSS. This will provide you a loan value of 68% of your capital, based on 90% UST margin and 50% FFF margin. Again, you will not use all of your loan value. You will use 45% of your capital, and this 45% loan will be used to purchase the five mutual funds that are MFLS.

Also again, these percentages will apply for the balance of the calendar year that you start the Plan and all of the next calendar year.

A quick example: $100,000 starting capital; $45,000 to UST with the specific maturity selection dictated by FIPS; $55,000 to FFF, with $3,667 in each stock; loan value of $68,000; debit balance of $45,000, with five mutual funds getting $9,000 each. Cash "throw-off" is $5,250 and debit balance interest cost is $5,400 (based on the same 8.00%, 3.00%, and 12.00% assumptions made in Chapter 17), so the MFLS cost is 0.15% of your capital to enjoy the additional compounding that the mutual funds will provide.

At the second January Review, or if you have been participating in the Plan from the ages below 39, you will adjust your percentage allocations in the following manner (and these allocations will continue at every January Review until the one in the year you turn 60 years of age):

The new percentage allocations are 40% UST/FIPS and 60% FFF/SSS. This provides a 66% loan value. The debit balance is adjusted upward to 50% of UST and FFF total market values (75.8% of loan value) and this will be your January Review debit balance goal until age 60.

Your UST and FFF allocations of 40% and 60% will also stand until that time.

Again, you have started the Plan for one year and a fraction in a more conservative posture, and the reasons are the same as those given in Chapter 17. Your cash "throw-off" vs. debit balance interest cost equation (using the same percentage assumptions as before) has improved slightly from the 20 to 39 portfolio. Your cost is 1.00% of your capital to enjoy the MFLS leverage. If it was a nifty situation at 1.50%, it is one-third niftier now!

In Chapter 16, I promised that I would provide the rationale and strategy to provide for your meeting some significant major expenses out of your Plan during these years of middle age. The Seasoned Veteran, throughout this book, has put forth numerous cautions on the subject of cash withdrawals and their extremely negative impact on the Plan and its basic concepts: the Eighth Wonder and the Magic Number. So I will presume that even against these warnings you have determined to enjoy some of your fruit. At this point I can only hope the fruit has had time to somewhat ripen!

The strategy is a very simple one. You simply borrow the amount of cash you want from your unused loan value at Murphy & Carroll. At the time of your next January Review, you adjust the debit balance to 50% and your UST and FFF to 40% and 60%, respectively. Let us look at several examples.

You are 55 years old. You started the Plan nine years ago with $180,000, and you have done on average better than the Magic Number; you have averaged 19% compounding each year for nine years. Last December 31 your Plan was worth $860,000, of which $230,000 was UST, $345,000 was FFF, and $570,000 was MFLS, and in your January Review you adjusted your debit balance to $285,000. On March 1, you determine you want to withdraw $60,000 from your Plan to buy a new luxury automobile, and give your present Honda to your daughter as a gift. On March 1 your Plan has improved somewhat. Market value of UST is $235,000 and market value of FFF is $360,000. Your debit balance stands at $290,000 (because $5,000 interest was added on in January and February). Your total loan value, at 90% UST and 50% FFF, is $391,500. You have $101,500 of unused loan value, so your new $60,000 loan (taken in cash for the automobile) still leaves you with $41,500 of unused loan value. Expressed another way: If you assume that this year's Magic Number will be attained, and your last December 31 Plan value of $860,000 would increase this year to $989,000 without the withdrawal, your $60,000 withdrawal and the $6,000 extra interest for ten months has taken 51% away from the Magic Number. Your Plan this year will grow by only 7.35% instead of 15.00%.

Another example: You are 46 years old. You started the Plan only three years ago with $100,000, and your performance has been negatively impacted by a moderate bear market that lasted 11 months. You have only had 7.00% average annual compounding, and your Plan after the last

January Review had $122,000 in net worth: $43,000 in UST, $56,000 in FFF, $72,000 in MFLS, and a $49,000 debit balance. In this example it is July 31, and you need to withdraw $10,000 to meet the expenses of your son's junior year in college. There have been no market value changes since January and your loan value at Murphy & Carroll is $66,700, so with your debit balance on July 31 at $50,000 (up $1,000 since January because interest charged is slightly more than cash "throw-off"), you have $16,700 of unused loan value and the $10,000 tuition requirement is no problem. The problem is that if you continue growing your Plan at only 7% per year, and make a $10,000 cash withdrawal every year, you will be walking slowly backward on your journey each year until soon you will be running backward and falling down!

When cash withdrawals of this sort are made, you must be certain to adjust your debit balance to 50% of UST and FFF total market value at your next January Review, in accord with the detailed instructions provided in Chapter 16.

You have observed that the basic strategy in the 20 to 39 age bracket was 30% UST and 70% FFF, with 50% MFLS.

And in the 40 to 59 age bracket it was 40% UST, 60% FFF, with the same MFLS percentage.

The Seasoned Veteran is very excited about the premise that those strategies will produce the Magic Number. And the Magic Number, coupled with the Eighth Wonder, produces dollars. Many dollars.

Now we must protect our lead. Seasoned veterans on the gridiron do not throw long passes when they are ahead in the fourth quarter in a tough game. Right now, we are ahead by more than touchdown, and the two minute warning whistle just sounded!

19
Ages 60-64: Pulling It In

Another analogy lies in the world of Izaak Walton.

I have never been a serious fisherman. I recall going out onto a Wisconsin lake in about 1940 with my grandfather, in a flat-bottomed rowboat with a cement-filled coffee can used as an anchor. We had bamboo poles, string, and hooks my grandmother made from safety pins. We would use earthworms as bait for perch and bluegills, and it was not unusual to bring in 40 or 50 in an afternoon. They were so small we would need that many to feed the three generations of my family that were vacationing together. Then in about 1970 I would carry on the same exercise with my children, this time casting for pike and bass. I have even spent weekends trying for muskellunge in northern Wisconsin and steelheads in northern California, but found them very evasive. In Florida I have been deep-sea fishing many times, once bringing in a 38 pound dolphin.

While I am far from an expert angler, I do know one very important thing. For all the attention given to tackle, bait, location, trolling and casting technique, and now even electronic devices to find the fine finned fellows, it is totally up to the individual holding the fishing rod to bring the fish to gaff or net. Without the strength and talent to pull them in, fishing is really a frustrating sport.

In this Chapter we will develop a strategy that will not let the big one get away!

As most people approach their 60th birthday, they are inevitably thinking of their retirement years: an opportunity to do some of the things that the time spent in their employment has precluded. Financial considerations play a large role in this. These people are also aware of their own mortality, and estate planning rightly becomes an even more important consideration.

The recommended strategy for living well and simultaneously growing capital during retirement will be explained in detail in the next Chapter. Right now, the Seasoned Veteran will recommend an adjustment in your UST and FFF portfolio mix and MFLS to put you into position to really enjoy your 65th birthday and all those that follow it.

THE PORTFOLIO STRATEGY

You are beginning your January Review in the year that you are turning 60. You have a margin account that is right on target: 40% UST, 60% FFF, a large MFLS, and because you have just completed a very good year in terms of realized UST and FFF profits, your debit balance is only 25% of UST and FFF current market values. Normally, you would again increase your debit balance to 50% of UST and FFF values, and use the proceeds of the 25% loan to increase MFLS.

No! In this year you will have only a 45% debit balance (age 60).

And in the next year, when you are turning 61, you will have only a 40% debit balance (age 61).

And in the third year, a 30% debit balance (age 62).

And in the fourth year, a 20% debit balance (age 63).

And in the year you become age 64, your January Review will permit only a 10% debit balance.

And then, in the year you turn 65, in your January Review you will eliminate your debit balance entirely, and you will change your portfolio mix to 50% UST and 50% FFF.

All of these adjustments to your debit balance will be accomplished in the same manner as was explained in Chapter 16.

If realized UST and FFF profits from the previous year have reduced your debit balance *below* the prescribed levels, you can borrow from Murphy & Carroll up to the prescribed level and add the loan proceeds to MFLS.

If your December 31 debit balance is above the prescribed level, your January Review will include sales from FFF to bring it down to the correct percentage.

Your requirements for cash withdrawals will be met as outlined in Chapter 18, with the important provision that the recommended debit balance percentage levels not be exceeded.

Your UST and FFF percentage allocations of 40% and 60% will continue through the January Reviews ages 60 to 64. They will be revised at the January Review in the year you turn 65, as will be explained shortly.

One example: You are in the January Review of the year you turn 63. On December 31 you had UST of $450,000, FFF of $625,000, MFLS of $800,000, and a debit balance of $200,000. Your Plan's worth is $1,675,000. You are now permitted a debit balance of 20% of UST and FFF total, which would be 20% of $1,975,000, or $215,000. You will therefore borrow $15,000 from Murphy & Carroll and add it to one of your five MFLS holdings. On August 15 of this year you determine you would like to help your granddaughter go to prep school, where the tuition is $10,000. On August 15, because you have been having a good year, your UST is $460,000 and your FFF is $690,000, and your debit balance (because several profits have been taken between January and August 15) is $195,000. You may have a debit balance of 20% of ($460,000 plus $690,000), which is $230,000.

You could borrow $35,000 if you wanted to, and still be within your Plan's parameters, so the $10,000 tuition requirement is no problem. Now suppose you do not have the borrowing power available under the 20% limit, and you still want to help your granddaughter. You will then sell

FFF to a point where your requirement is directly met by the sales proceeds. You will not let your debit balance exceed, as a result of your withdrawals, the 20% of UST and FFF current market values. Only UST and FFF market depreciation will be permitted to allow a debit balance above 20%.

Onward! The Golden Years are at hand!

20
Retirement: The Battles Are Won

Every week for 30 years I have been involved, in one way or another, in helping retired people with their money. This help has taken dozens and dozens of forms, but I am not going to provide a lot of biographical anecdotes. Someday I might in another book, because some of them are quite interesting, but I feel you are perhaps satiated on these for now.

The common thread of most retired peoples' thinking on the subject of retirement finances is to protect capital and produce a return from it for the purpose of meeting living expenses. This is not a new phenomenon. It has been going on for hundreds of years.

Several trillions of dollars around the world are invested in this manner. These dollars are invested risk-free in insured deposits in the banking system and in bonds issued by sovereign governments with the highest quality ratings. With only a very moderate degree of risk, these dollars are also invested in highest quality corporate and municipal bonds in every country and in life insurance annuity policies issued by the strongest life insurance companies. With progressively more risk, higher returns are sought by those investing their dollars in lower quality and lowest quality bonds issued by corporations and municipalities, and a variety of other income-producing financial instruments, many of which were discussed in Chapter 14.

In every case, the retired person asks to get interest from the issuer along the way, and then 100 cents back on each invested dollar when the obligation matures.

That is a fair enough request, *but it is never met!* You will soon see why.

As this is written, the interest rate spectrum available to those who will commit their capital for from one to five years in a risk-free investment is roughly 8.50% taxable. In the same maturity range, high grade risk investments reward the investor with about 75 basis points more, lower grade risk investments about 175 basis points more, and most of the lowest grades perhaps 400 basis points more.

For those who commit their capital to the vagaries of the world and its marketplaces for ten years, today's inverted yield curve provides risk-free yields of about 8.40% taxable, with roughly the same increments for riskier investments as are indicated in the paragraph above.

And for the 20 to 30 year investor the risk-free yield curve provides about 8.25%, with approximately the same increments for lesser quality securities. The average for long-term junk bonds is about a 15.00% proposition today.

In the Chapters just preceding, I showed several examples of how capital can be invested in long-term fixed income securities to produce significant annual incomes, if the investor so chooses. I believe one such example spoke of $286,250 invested at 7.50% tax-free producing $21,469 per year, and that plus Social Security is not a bad sum to live on. Not bad at all. But this is a retirement strategy that is *not recommended!*

Please take note of the fact that all of the preceding four paragraphs mentioned investment returns that *do not exceed our Magic Number!* That is extremely important, and we will come back to it in a moment.

It has been many, many pages in this book since we talked about *inflation*. And we have spent really very little time talking about *income taxes*.

Both of these nasty things can ravage your retirement years.

Both inflation and income taxes negatively impact your cash "throw-off," or interest, on a deposit or debt obligation of any type other than a municipal security, where federal income taxes do not play a role (but inflation does); if you buy a municipal obligation issued in your state of residence, the income is usually free of state taxes as well.

Let the Seasoned Veteran now address the hundreds of investors who have told me "I must buy municipals. I am in a tax bracket that precludes anything else." One hundred percent of these people are dead wrong!

Please let me repeat the formula for converting tax free yields to taxable equivalent yields. It is:

$$\frac{\text{Tax Free Yield}}{1.00 \text{ minus Tax Rate}} = \text{Taxable Equivalent Yield}$$

The *Wall Street Journal* of September 20, 1989, page C23, tells us that the current Merrill Lynch Index has tax-free G.O. municipals of 20 year maturity issued by State governments at 7.05%, and the same maturity high quality corporates are 9.28%. Let's now apply the formula, assuming a 28% tax bracket. We see that the taxable equivalent yield on the municipals is 9.79%. So the investor insisting on the tax free yield is only 51 basis points better off, and here we are truly comparing apples vs. apples as to quality and maturity. The 20 year UST in the same newspaper was 8.30%, so the corporate investor has a yield spread advantage of only 98 basis points and the municipal investor only 149 basis points as consideration for the credit risk and relative illiquidity they are choosing to assume. The Seasoned Veteran does not think this is much of a deal. Expressed another way, the corporate investor is only 11.8% better off (98 basis points as a percentage of 8.30%) and the municipal investor is only 17.9% better off than he would be in UST on a before-tax basis.

The bottom line is that the marketplace will *always* adjust the price of a municipal to reflect the prevailing tax laws, so that similar quality and maturity corporates are almost identical to the same yield as municipals on a taxable equivalent basis.

Now let's analyze the affect that taxes do have on the cash "throw-off," again assuming a 28% tax rate.

Suppose you invest $10,000 in a corporate bond at a 10.00% coupon interest rate, with interest payable semi-annually. You will receive $500.00 every six months, or $1,000.00 annually. After paying your federal income taxes you will have $720.00 left to spend ($360.00 every six months). This is an after-tax yield of 7.20%, very close to what you would have received on a municipal security. Presuming no tax rate change, this will be the case every year until the obligation matures.

Now let us factor in inflation; it impacts *both* principal and cash "throw-off" on a fixed income investment.

Suppose inflation is at a moderate 4% annual level. That means 2% inflation every six months. Your first after-tax $360.00 is impacted by 2%, so you will only have $352.80 in buying power compared with what $360.00 would have purchased on the day you made the investment. And your second after-tax $360.00, at the end of the first year, will only buy $345.74 of goods and services compared with $360.00. Taking it out five years, your tenth semi-annual check for interest payment will be $500.00, but after taxes at 28% and five years of inflation at 4% it will have a true value of $288.26. Annualizing this, it is a "real" current yield of 5.77% on your $10,000 investment. And if the investment continues for another five years, your $720.00 after-tax income will purchase $486.43 of goods and services, a "real" current yield of 4.86% at the end of the tenth year as opposed to 10.00% on the face of it.

And the above example considers only interest!

Let's now look at your principal. Fortunately, there is no income tax to be paid on the $10,000 that the obliger pays back to you at maturity. But the 4% inflation takes a toll! If it was a five year investment, your $10,000 has turned into $7,865 in purchasing power. If it was a ten year investment, $6,413 is being returned to you to buy things with, or very importantly to reinvest in a new instrument, as compared to $10,000 when you made the investment. If it was a 20 year investment, the figure is $4,263.

And this is with inflation at the "low" level of 4%. If we were to double it to 8%, the five year figure is $6,591, the ten year figure is $4,344, and in 20 years your $10,000 will be returned to you worth $1,887 in purchasing power.

The Seasoned Veteran believes that for participants in our Investment Plan to invest in fixed income securities of any sort on a "buy and hold" basis during retirement years is absolute financial suicide and should be avoided under any scenario except absolute deflation, which the Seasoned Veteran believes will never happen in the foreseeable future.

You will continue with the Plan very much as before! I am not going to recommend much of a change!

You will *not,* as you might be guessing, be converting your UST to corporates or municipals of lower quality and liquidity. You will *not,* as you might be guessing, be converting your FFF to electric utility common stocks exclusively, although they might play a role in your FFF selections (using the Moody average of High Grade Electric Utility Common Stocks as an index, these stocks produced an average annual total return of about 10.50% for the ten years from 1978 and about 13.50% for the five years from 1983; dividends accounted for 7.60% and 8.65%, respectively). You will *not,* as you might be guessing, be putting your five mutual funds on automatic monthly withdrawal plans.

The only thing that will radically change is that you will not be carrying a debit balance for MFLS purposes (you will not be adding cash at all to your mutual fund sub-portfolio). You will instead be using your debit balance to live on!

PLEASE! Do not leave me. *You will be delighted with how it works!*

THE PORTFOLIO STRATEGY

As we outlined in Chapter 19, your January Review in the year you reach your 65th birthday put you in a Murphy & Carroll portfolio mix of

50% UST, 50% FFF, a "sub-portfolio" of five mutual funds held by the mutual funds' custodians, and a zero debit balance.

For all the years you have been a participant in the Investment Plan, your annual objective has been to grow your capital at an after-tax minimum annual compound growth rate of the Magic Number, 15.00%.

This will continue to be your Magic Number every year during your retirement years!

Your portfolio strategy during each of these years will be to adjust your Murphy & Carroll portfolio mix during each January Review to 50% UST and 50% FFF. You will continue to let all UST and FFF cash "throw-off" be credited to your Murphy & Carroll margin account. Your FIPS and SSS strategies, which determine the holding periods for UST and FFF, will remain absolutely unchanged. You will have your mutual fund "sub-portfolio" continue with the same automatic reinvestment plans for cash distributions that have been in effect since the day you first bought each mutual fund. Your mutual fund selling strategies will be unchanged, the same as were discussed in Chapter 13.

Here is the one important difference in your portfolio strategy: During each January Review, you will determine how much of your total December 31 market values (UST plus FFF plus mutual funds) you wish to spend in the present calendar year, *to a maximum of 9.00%*. You may consider this figure as you formerly considered your take-home salary! You will advise your Customer's Person that you would like to effect a loan from Murphy & Carroll for one-twelfth of this amount each month, on a day of the month that best suits you (the first check, for January, should be sent immediately), and you will hold your Customer's Person responsible for setting up a tickler (or whatever other internal system Murphy & Carroll might have) to insure the check is sent promptly and automatically so that you will have it in hand on the specified day each month. In this fashion, you will be incurring a debit balance each month of (a maximum of) 0.75% of your last December 31 total Plan market values. (It will be larger than 0.75% of your Murphy & Carroll UST and FFF, because they do not hold your mutual funds.) For the entire year, the *average* debit balance will be no more than 4.50% of your December 31 total Plan market values. On next December 31 it will be no more than 9.00%.

In this fashion, if you achieve the Magic Number each year, your capital will grow at 6.00%, which should cover (year in and year out but probably not every year) the negative impact that inflation will have on your dollars of capital.

And there is absolutely no income tax effect on the monthly withdrawal from the Plan! It is not the number on which your income taxes are based. The income tax, as before, will be a function of the UST and FFF cash "throw-off," cash distributions on your mutual fund shares, and realized net capital gains (or losses) on your sales of UST, FFF, and mutual funds.

There are several options available to you regarding your treatment of the retirement years' debit balance that will be incurred at Murphy & Carroll.

Before detailing these options to you, let's examine the cash flow situation in your Murphy & Carroll margin account. Let's continue using the cash "throw-off" estimates of 8.00% on UST and 3.00% on FFF. That means that your margin account, with 50% UST and 50% FFF, will "throw-off" 5.50% in cash. You are borrowing an amount that averages 4.50% of UST, FFF, *and mutual funds*. Let's presume the breakdown is 25% UST, 25% FFF, and 50% mutual funds. That means 9.00% of Murphy & Carroll assets are being borrowed against on a daily average. At a cost of 12%, this is 1.08%. So the *net* cash "throw-off" at Murphy & Carroll becomes 4.42% (5.50% minus 1.08%). Therefore, for you to spend 9.00% when your net cash "throw-off" is 4.42% requires 4.58% from "capital." The market values of your UST, FFF, and five unleveraged mutual funds will need to increase by at least 4.58% during the year, or you will be "in the hole" or in a "deficit total plan" on December 31 this year compared with December 31 last year. And anything over 4.58% appreciation in market values will represent net appreciation on your total Plan. If you achieve the Magic Number, it will mean you will have 10.42% from appreciation, both realized and computational, and 4.58% from the net cash flow at Murphy & Carroll. This is before-tax. The UST and FFF income at Murphy & Carroll will be taxed at 28%, so the 5.50% becomes 3.96%, and there will be taxes on any net realized capital gains as well as on cash distributions from the mutual funds, even though they are reinvested.

Here are your options on the treatment of any "deficit total Plan" situation that occurs in the next year's January Review:

(1) You may sell from FFF to eliminate whatever debit balance remains on December 31, so that you will be starting this year's monthly cash withdrawals from a zero debit balance level.

(2) You may elect to continue with the previous year's debit balance for one more year, but no longer than that. It *must* be brought to zero by every third January Review, under all circumstances.

(3) You may elect to reduce your monthly cash withdrawal from Murphy & Carroll in the second year.

(4) Or you may use a combination of all three of the above.

In summary: You will continue with your Plan's major components. You will have 50% UST and 50% FFF at Murphy & Carroll in all market scenarios, with FIPS and SSS as explained in Chapters 11 and 12. Your mutual funds will be managed as before, with all cash distributions used to purchase new shares. You will live on a maximum of 9.00% of your Plan's market value each year, without direct regard to the cash "throw-off" which will continue to be credited directly to the margin account. The maximum 9.00% spending level will be achieved by borrowing from Murphy & Carroll. The achievement of a total return level over 9.00% enhances your total Plan value. Your objective will be to continue to grow capital at or above the Magic Number and live on 9.00% of capital each year.

Now let's look at how capital grows at 6.00%. Incidentally, there is a very thick book available in most public libraries called *Financial Compound Interest and Annuity Tables* (Financial Publishing Co., Boston, MA) which gives compounding for 120 periods for all rates up to 30%, and for ten year periods for increments of five percentage points from 35% to

100%. Here, according to this fine book, is how $1,000 will grow at 6.00% compounded annually:

At end of:		
5 years	$1,338	(age 70)
10 years	$1,791	(age 75)
15 years	$2,397	(age 80)
20 years	$3,207	(age 85)
25 years	$4,292	(age 90)

Let's now take an investor who retires at age 65 with $1,000,000 in the Plan. Let's say there are market values of $300,000 UST, $300,000 FFF, and $400,000 in the mutual fund subportfolio on December 31 of the year before the investor turns 65, and the January Review has eliminated the very small MFLS debit balance. The investor determines to withdraw $90,000, or $7,500 monthly, from the Plan by borrowing from Murphy & Carroll. He will have cash "throw-off" of UST $24,000 and FFF $9,000, a total of $33,000. His debit balance borrowings will cost $5,400, so the positive cash flow is $27,600. This investor must have appreciation on his UST, FFF, and mutual fund subportfolio of $62,400 during the year to avoid being in a "deficit total Plan" situation. If his appreciation, both realized and computational, is less than this, the investor will utilize one of the four options which were provided on the preceding page. If the appreciation is more than $62,400, the investor can and should still utilize the four options to reduce or eliminate the debit balance. The investor should always have a zero debit balance every two years.

Let's look at the same investor, this time assuming he has achieved a 15.00% after-tax total return consisting of net Murphy & Carroll margin account cash flow and both realized and computational appreciation in his UST, FFF, and the five mutual funds. This investor has utilized his withdrawal option to the maximum 9.00% level, so after one year he has grown his capital at 6.00%. And let us suppose he continues this every year for five years. He has available for spending something over $450,000 during the five years (it is more than $90,000 after the first year because the 9.00% is computed each year on an appreciated figure) and he has a Plan market valuation of $1,338,000. This is better than not bad!

Now let's consider the investor who came aboard the Plan at age 60, with $100,000 original capital. He has achieved the Magic Number, on average, and is retiring at 65 with just over $200,000 in the Plan. He elects to withdraw 9.00%, or $18,000 per year, for spending purposes in the first year. He does this every year (achieves the Magic Number and spends 9.00%) until he is 90 years old. He has had well over $450,000 to live on (plus his Social Security and possibly a pension) and he is able to leave his heirs over $850,000. If this investor had, at age 65, determined to invest his $200,000 in tax-free 25 year municipal bonds, he would have had nearly the same spending capacity but his $200,000 principal would have been totally ravaged by inflation, and his heirs might end up with the price of a new car to split between them.

The retirement years' portfolio strategy is a simple matter of (going back to our friend John Heywood) having your cake and eating it, too!

To analogize again: We are coming into the outskirts of the journey's destination. We have seen the entire panorama of roads and highways, motels and restaurants. We have learned how to continue on through storms, bad roads, and unwanted hitchhikers. We have discovered there are a few places to speed up, although certainly not every day or even every year. We have had an excellent guide, and he or she will hopefully, now that we are near our destination, choose to stay on for a while as a friend and helpmate. Our vehicle has been well serviced along the way, and will be excellent transportation for us for as long as we choose to keep it.

It is one of those excellent machines that seems to get better with age!

SECTION VII.
ALONG THE WAY

21
Reading the Menu

The Seasoned Veteran believes that you should consciously earmark ten hours per week for reading that will significantly improve your chances for success in consistently attaining the Magic Number.

I am a person who likes to read. I have an interest in many subjects. I like to read newspapers and magazines of all sorts. I like to read books of every conceivable description. I have learned a lot from my reading. I have also wasted a horrendous amount of time with it!

The purpose of this Chapter is to help you, as you travel on your journey, focus on the type of reading that will be of maximum benefit to you in reaching your objective: to Grow Capital.

I believe that ten hours per week is sufficient. This is an average of just under one and one-half hours per day, seven days a week.

I believe you should attempt to discipline yourself and actually set up a schedule that will allow this activity at certain set times each week. I am aware that for some of you this will be a struggle. Some of you probably just plain do not like to read. To you I say: "No pain, no gain!" Others of you are terribly busy. To you I say simply: "You can find the time!" A solitary lunch at a fast food restaurant with a magazine or newspaper can be a very pleasant hour. When you take your children to the park, keep one eye on them with the other eye on a Murphy & Carroll stock research report. It can be done!

In a general way, I would recommend you break your ten hours of weekly reading into three sections.

One section, taking up 25% of your reading time, should simply be a sincere effort to know what is going on in the world on a daily basis, with particular emphasis on the part of the world that concerns itself with business and finance. This can best be accomplished with a daily newspaper, and we have already discussed the *Wall Street Journal* in Chapter 8. There is very little of major importance that will escape the "What's News" Column on the first page. The business sections of the two major news magazines are excellent and so is *Business Week* and *U.S. News and World Report*. In this type of reading you will have to discipline yourself. There are fascinating accounts of robberies and murders in your daily hometown newspaper, and the weekly newsmagazines have dozens of interesting articles on great varieties of subjects; you cannot read them all and still have time for reading that focuses on the many aspects of growing capital.

The most important decisions you will make are in the area of selecting FFF and mutual funds that will attain the total return numbers that you are looking for. The balance of your weekly reading time, over seven hours, should be specifically earmarked for reading in this area.

The Seasoned Veteran believes this reading should take two different forms.

At least two hours each week should be devoted to what I call "broaden your horizons" reading. This will nearly always involve magazines. You are looking for investment ideas, where the investment idea can be determined to ally itself with a company that has publicly traded common stock, where the common stock meets all the parameters of FFF. You are looking for the GM, IBM, and Xerox of tomorrow. You might get the idea for it in magazines such as *Harpers, National Review, GQ, Guns & Ammo, Harvard Business Review, Vogue, Rolling Stone, Humanist, Motor Trend, Modern Maturity, High Fidelity, Sunset, Town & Country, Radio Electronics, Sea Frontiers, Penthouse, Popular Photography, Inc.,* or *Ebony.* You should scan magazines of this type for ideas, getting them not only from the articles but also from the advertisements. You are looking for an FFF possibility that has not been written up yet in a big way by Wall Street. You can then discuss it with your Customer's Person. (Remember: This type of activity is his or her *Specialty!*) Do not buy the stock unless it meets all FFF/ESG criteria. You will be surprised how many good ideas you will get. You will also probably be surprised at how few of them will survive your "winnowing out" process. Do not be discouraged! It took Thomas Edison thousands of experiments before his electric light bulb would last more than a few seconds.

Five hours per week, one half of your reading time, should be specifically devoted to FFF and mutual fund selecting. The thrust will be toward FFF. You have read Chapter 12. You know the FFF/ESG parameters. You know the word *bargain*. You know that you are seeking bargains that will go up 60% in price in two years. You know that you are seeking bargains that must be considered to be bargains by other investors within two years at prices 60% higher than today. You know that you will have turnover every year in your FFF, and the entire FFF will turn over every two years. You must always have FFF in each of the seven categories "waiting in the wings."

Your reading emphasis in this area should be on the stock research reports that Murphy & Carroll publishes. You should have an understanding with your Customer's Person that these reports will be mailed to you *promptly* upon publication. These reports almost always make a strong case for buying the stock. In this instance you must be a "second-guesser." You must check the stock out in Standard & Poor's *Stock Reports*. Look at the bar chart. How has the stock performed in other market scenarios over the past six years? Look at the ten year Per Share Data. How does the EPS trend look? What about dividend payout ratios? What about P/E ratios over the past compared with today? Do Murphy & Carroll's EPS forecasts look realistic? Flip the page. How do finances, debt ratios, ROE, etc. look to you? Do institutions own a significant share percentage? Ask the same question for insiders. Ask yourself these questions: Have I read about this company elsewhere, in *Forbes, Barron's* or *Value Line*? How much sponsorship is there from *all* of Wall Street? Is it likely to increase and really fire investors' imaginations in the next two years? Might it be a takeover candidate? What would John Templeton think of it? Or Carl Icahn? Or Peter Lynch? Or the Seasoned Veteran?

Before I get carried away, I will stop.

The bottom line is clear. Before buying an FFF stock, or a mutual fund, you must ask and affirmatively answer literally dozens of questions.

The bulk of your ideas, and probably your selections, will come from Murphy & Carroll. That is not to say that you cannot get ideas that will turn into FFF and mutual fund selections from other sources. The *Wall Street Journal*, your hometown newspaper's business section, *Time, Newsweek, Forbes, Barron's, Value Line, Fortune*, and other publications that highlight individual companies and their common stock are all sources for FFF ideas. A good idea is to keep a notebook. Jot down the idea, the date, the current price, the source of the idea. Start some independent research. Have your Customer's Person do the same. Cross off the ones that fail to pass muster, that don't make the cut. Keep working on the ones that do. Always have specific Category FFF ready to go!

Once an FFF stock, or a mutual fund, is purchased you do *not* need to be an expert on it. That is one of the great things about the selling strategies from Chapters 12 and 13. You will hold these instruments only until they are no longer bargains, and this will be mathematically determined in accord with FIPS, SSS, and MFLS with no room for error.

One last thing. You do not need to be a professional, or even a serious amateur, economist. You should have a good general grasp of the economy and its direction, and this will influence your FFF and to a lesser extent, your MFLS selections. But you do not need to be an accurate forecaster of interest rates (FIPS is market directed), you do not need to worry about next month's trade deficit report, and you do not need to concern yourself with last month's report on leading economic indicators. If you want to concentrate on anything, try to be an inflation expert. That will govern most of the rest of it for the foreseeable future.

22
Enjoying the Meal

You have seen the Investment Plan. You have all but completed the journey.

You have discovered a way to compound a total return in the investment markets. You know every nook and cranny of what it is and how it works.

You are in position to take advantage of what is happening in the world to make you, over years and decades, a wealthy person. The Eighth Wonder of the World is an immutable force, and the Magic Number *is* attainable.

You must keep score on an annual basis to see how you are doing toward the objective of the Magic Number, the 15.00% annual total return. You must annually determine how fast your vehicle is going.

I recall being taken by the father of one of my friends to a White Sox baseball game in Comiskey Park in 1941. We watched Luke Appling and Ted Lyons, and for the other team an outfielder known some days as the Yankee Clipper and other days as Joltin' Joe, who was, as we watched, in the process of putting together one of the most outstanding personal records in American sports: 56 consecutive games with a base hit. On the way into the ballpark my friend's father got a scorecard and a pencil. He was a very nice man. For the entire nine innings, however, he was so intent on keeping an accurate and detailed scorecard that it seemed to me he missed the fun of the game.

I do not think it is a good idea for you to figure out your position on a weekly or monthly basis. If you do this, you will be so close to the trees that you will not see the forest.

If you want to keep a quarterly or semiannual scorecard, I suppose I would not strongly object. You will, after all, be getting monthly statements on your Murphy & Carroll margin account, and you will be looking up your FFF prices in the Sunday newspapers, and you will be conducting regular six-month-from-date-of-purchase reviews of your FFF, and you will know what the bond markets are doing because you will always know the UST Long Bond yield. And you will be getting statements from your five MFLS holdings, although these generally are mailed only when a cash distribution is made and additional shares are bought, and even then the total dollar valuation is usually not given; only the total number of shares that the custodian holds in your account. Nonetheless, you will at all times have a pretty fair mental grasp of how you are doing.

The Seasoned Veteran believes that you should keep, on one piece of paper that will be good for six years, an Annual Scorecard and January Review Worksheet. And then, after six years, you will start another piece of paper.

Here, very specifically, is how you do it:

Your local office supply store will sell you a pad of 13 column accounting paper. The individual pieces of paper measure 11" by 17". There are two irregular columns to the left side of the paper, and then 13 one inch columns extending all the way to the right. The one inch columns have nice vertical lines to keep digits separate. There are 35 lines horizontally. You will use 18 of these lines, so you can skip lines if you want to give yourself a nice neat format. You will use the wide column to the left to list your captions. If you wish, the small column at the very left edge of the paper can be used to number the captions. The regular one inch columns will be designated with dates that will be December 31 and

January 31, the former column being used for exact numbers as they existed on December 31 from your Murphy & Carroll month-end statement and from your calculations on what your five MFLS holdings' market values were on that date; the latter column will be exact numbers representing your holdings on January 31 after your January Review actions have been completed.

On the next page you will see a sample form that the Seasoned Veteran has developed and successfully used.

INVESTMENT PLAN

ANNUAL SCORECARD AND JANUARY REVIEW WORKSHEET

		12/31/88	12/31/89	1/31/90	12/31/90	1/31/90	12/31/90	1/31/91	12/31/91	1/31/92	12/31/92	1/3/93
	Age: 36		37	37	38				39			40
(1)	VST	44000	39500	29500	36000	41000	38000	43000	46000	66000
(2)	FFF	60000	66000	76000	97000	92000	104000	99000	114000	99500
(3)	Other	0	500	200	0	0	2000	2000	1000	1000
(4)	Sub-total	100000	106000	106000	133000	133000	144000	144000	146000	166000
(5)	Debit balance	40000	33000	52750	37000	44500	61000	71000	58000	82500
(6)	Equity at Murphy & Carroll	60000	73000	53250	106000	64500	83000	73000	108000	82500
	MFLS									
(7)	Fund #1	8000	9000	13500	18200	26100	37700	36000	45300	51425
(8)	Fund #2	8000	9900	13200	19300	27200	37800	37800	46000	52225
(9)	Fund #3	8000	19300	13450	16500	24400	29800	33200	43200	49335
(10)	Fund #4	9000	9800	13700	18500	24400	31200	34500	38000	44725
(11)	Fund #5	8000	9600	13500	19000	26700	40200	40200	53900	53900
(12)	Total MFLS	40000	48200	67950	91500	131000	171700	181700	227700	351600
(13)	Total Plan	100000	121200	171200	197500	197500	254700	254700	335100	335100
(14)	Magic Number Bogey	N/A	115000	N/A	132200	N/A	152000	N/A	174900	N/A
(15)	Total Plan % Change	N/A	+21.2%	N/A	+63.0%	N/A	+29.0%	N/A	+31.6%	N/A
(16)	DJIA	2000	2350	2925	N/A	N/A	3450	N/A	4080	N/A
(17)	DJIA % Change	N/A	+12.5%	+30.0%	N/A	N/A	+17.4%	N/A	+13.3%	N/A
(18)	VST Long Bond	9.50%	10.10%	2.05%	N/A	N/A	9.75%	N/A	8.50%	N/A

I believe all of the captions are self-descriptive, except possibly two of them. Caption (3) is simply called "Other." This will be the total market value of call options on takeover stocks, index option puts, or gold, crude oil, and/or Treasury Bond futures contracts that you might own in accord with strategies outlined in Chapter 12. Caption (14) is called "Magic Number Bogey." Bogey is a word that has several meanings beyond golf; among banking professionals, a bogey is a balance sheet standard, or objective, that represents where a specific asset (or liability) should ideally be at a given date. Our Magic Number Bogey is simply where the Investment Plan should be, as measured in dollars, if the Magic Number of 15.00% is being attained. Calculate this number and put it on the form, in advance, for each year.

The sample form, you have observed, is filled in with some hypothetical numbers. Hopefully, time will prove that they have a good measure of reality! For teaching purposes, the example presumes that there are no market value changes between December 31 and January 31. This is, of course, unrealistic in the real world.

The assumption is that in mid-December, 1988, a 36 year old investor commences the Plan with $100,000 cash capital. For teaching purposes, this investor is "you." Also for teaching purposes, the assumption is that the DJIA on December 31, 1988, was 2000. (It was actually 2169.) By December 31, 1988, you have purchased 40% UST and 60% FFF. With the UST Long Bond at 9.50%, your UST is entirely in Three Year Maturity Notes or Bonds. Your FFF is in holdings of $4,000 each. You have $66,000 in loan value, and borrow $40,000 to buy MFLS, which are equally distributed in $8,000 holdings.

There is nothing for you to do in the January, 1989 Review because you have just gotten started, and your portfolio is perfectly allocated.

DECEMBER 31, 1989
ANALYSIS AND JANUARY REVIEW

At this time, because you have been aboard the Plan for over one year, the initial "conservative" strategy of 40% UST and 60% FFF is replaced by the 30% UST and 70% FFF allocations explained in Chapter 17. To accomplish this, $5,000 par value of the UST Three Year and $5,000 par value of the UST Five Year are sold, and the proceeds are invested in FFF issues already owned, with the allocations determined by you in terms of "What are the best bargains today?"

You noted in the last sentence that $5,000 par value of the UST *Five* Year was sold. During the year, the Long Bond crossed over 10.00%, so 50% of the initial $40,000 par value UST Three Year was sold at that time and replaced with $20,000 par value UST Five Year, in accord with FIPS. The small loss incurred in this transaction has been absorbed by the debit balance, which even then has gone down by $7,000, reflective of cash "throw-off" and FFF net realized profits (the DJIA was up 12.5%) being that much greater than the UST loss and debit balance interest costs. All of the five mutual funds have done better than the DJIA, with gains ranging from 16.2% to 23.7%. The $500 in Caption (3) "Other" represents call options on a takeover stock.

In the January Review, the first calculation is to determine 30% of UST and FFF combined, after the $10,000 par value UST sale and FFF purchase. It is 30% of $105,500, or $31,650. This compares with $29,500 UST actual, or $2,150 more than owned. Because UST/FIPS calls for owning UST only in $5,000 par value increments, nothing is done. However, if the difference was $2,501 or more (more than 50% of $5,000) a $5,000 par value UST Five Year Note or Bond would be purchased, with the funding to come from the partial sale of several of the lowest-rated bargain FFF stocks. So it is determined no change is to be made in UST/FFF allocations. Once determined, the loan value is calculated at $64,055 ($500 is being used for the takeover stock call option), and 50% of UST/FFF is $52,750.

So the debit balance is increased by a $19,750 loan, which allows $3,900 to be allocated to four of the mutual funds and $4,150 to a fifth mutual fund. Mutual Fund #3 gets the extra $250 because it seems to be the best bargain. You have been pleased to note that in your first year you have exceeded your Bogey by $6,200, or 6.2% in a year that the DJIA did not go up by a percentage amount equal to your Bogey.

DECEMBER 31, 1990
ANALYSIS AND JANUARY REVIEW

During this year interest rates went down by over 200 basis points on the Long Bond and the stock market had an excellent year, up 30.0% on the DJIA.

Your Plan, by virtue of its position in Three Year and Five Year UST securities, fifteen well-selected common stocks, and five growth-oriented mutual funds owned with borrowed money, did a lot better!

Notice how the debit balance decreased, going down $25,750. This is mostly a reflection of FFF net realized profits, as many of your original FFF hit the "plus 60%" price.

Presuming that the 8.05% Long Bond Yield on December 31 is as low as it has gotten, you still own 50% Three Year and 50% Five Year UST. You have nice paper profits in these, and if the Long Bond yield goes down another six basis points, below 8.00%, you will sell all UST and go into UST-Bills, thus realizing the approximate $6500 profit accrued on paper during the year. You have, however, a situation where you must buy an additional $5,000 par value of the Two Year UST. 30% of the $133,000 amounts to $39,900, and your $35,000 owned is more that $2,500 short of what your Plan dictates. So, based on the Long Bond at 8.05%, the Two Year UST is called for. If it should be sold within the next few days when the Long Bond might go through 8.00%, you will make a few dollars. The $5,000 required comes from the sale of the lowest-rated bargains among the FFF. Once this is done, loan value totals 90% of $41,000 plus 50% of

$92,000, or $82,900. Of this, you can borrow $66,500, or 50% of $133,000. This allows a new loan of $39,500 ($66,500 minus $27,000 already owed). To allocate $39,500 among five MFLS means $7,900 to each. However, first we must sell Mutual Fund #3. In its second year it must do 15% better than the DJIA, and it has not. 15% better than the DJIA would be up 34.5%. It has only gone up 22.7% ($16,500 vs. $13,450). The new replacement mutual fund is purchased in an amount of $24,400, representing $16,500 sales proceeds plus $7,900 from the new loan. $7,900 also is added to the other four MFLS.

It is interesting to note that two years ago, upon starting the Plan, your mutual funds were 40% of the Total Plan. After one year they were, after the January Review, 56.1%. Now, after the second January Review, they are 66.3%. The leverage is working!

DECEMBER 31, 1991
ANALYSIS AND JANUARY REVIEW

Here you are, watching the football Bowl Games on New Year's Day, 1992. You are thinking "What a run! What a tackle! What a reception!"

But you are also thinking, "What is going on in the markets? Interest rates on the Long Bond never did go through 8.00% early last year. Instead they started climbing, up to 9.75% yesterday. And the stock market! Even with interest rates heading skyward, and the CPI showing significant movement toward 8%, or higher inflation, the DJIA was still up by almost 18% on the year. It must be earnings! Yes, corporate earnings *do* seem excellent. The Dow Jones Industrial Average Stocks probably did earn $300 last year, and even at that the market is only about 11.5 times those earnings. Maybe the Seasoned Veteran was right in Chapter 7 of his book when he said the well-managed corporations of the world can handle 10% to 12% borrowing costs and 5% to 8% inflation and still make good money. Maybe the Nineties are really going to be something to behold!"

During the year your UST, which is now $20,000 par value Three Year and $15,000 par value Five Year, went down about 7% in market value, and the $5,000 par value Two Year purchased a year ago had to be sold at a very tiny loss when the Long Bond went through 9.00%, and it was replaced by $5,000 par value UST Three Year. Nonetheless, the FFF produced some realized gains that significantly helped reduce the debit balance, down $5,500 to $61,000, and nice computational gains are showing in the FFF portfolio, up $12,000 to $104,000. Further, since inflation measured by the CPI shows an alarming trend, you have put in place your inflation hedge with one gold futures contract, worth $2,000 if it were sold on December 31.

In your January Review, you must first sell $5,000 of your lowest bargain FFF and buy $5,000 of Three Year UST. That is because 30% of $142,000 is $42,600, and your UST December 31 market value was only $38,000. This done, you have a loan value of $88,200. You can borrow a total of $71,000, so there is $10,000 in new borrowing available to you. This would normally provide $2,000 for each of five MFLS holdings. But you have noticed that there are some disparities among the market values of the five; you determine to add $3,300 or $3,400 to the three that are lowest. You have also noticed that Mutual Fund #4 did not have a particularly great year. It was up 18.2% vs. 17.9% DJIA, not nearly as good a performance as in its first two years. You will keep an eye on it for another year. You also notice that your MFLS is now over 71% of your Plan. Upon discovering this, you say "Wow!" Then you discover that in three years the DJIA is up 72.5%. Your Plan is up 154.7%. You find yourself saying something you don't want your 12 year old daughter to hear, except that she might understand because you have a pretty wide smile on your face when you say it!

DECEMBER 31, 1992
ANALYSIS AND JANUARY REVIEW

This is the year that you, our investor, turns 40. You will, in accord with

Chapter 18, change your allocations from 30% UST to 40% UST, and from 70% FFF to 60% FFF. Your 50% MFLS strategy is unchanged.

Let's see what happened in the year just ended. It was a good year. Interest rates went down year-to-year by 125 Long Bond basis points. They did not go down far enough to occasion any UST profit taking, but there was about a 7% computational gain on the UST holdings of $25,000 par value UST Three Year and $15,000 par value UST Five Year (which now, because time goes by, have about 1 1/2 years and two years to go before they mature). The DJIA was up 18.3%, over 4000 now, and you did even better: Year-end FFF was up 20.2%, and profits realized during the year were a strong factor in a debit balance decrease of $13,000. All of the MFLS holdings except Mutual Fund #4 did better than the DJIA. Mutual Fund #4 will now be sold.

The most important part of this January Review is the acknowledgement of the investor's becoming age 40 by increasing UST and decreasing FFF. The numbers dictate the sale of $20,000 of the lower bargain-rated FFF and, with the Long Bond at 8.50%, the purchase of $20,000 par value UST Two Year. This will make UST exactly 40% of UST plus FFF. The $1,000 in "Other" represents call options purchased on a takeover stock. (Last year's $2,000 in commodity futures as an inflation hedge is not anything you wish to talk about! Fortunately, it did not hurt even badly enough to say "ouch!") After the new UST purchase, you can use $82,500 of your total $108,900 loan value which means you can have $24,500 in new money for MFLS. You determine that Mutual Fund #5 has enough market value in relation to the others, so you divide the $24,500 by four to get $6,125 for each of Mutual Funds #1 to #4, keeping in mind that Mutual Fund #4 is a new one replacing the one that was sold. After the mutual fund allocations are made, you observe that 75.1% of your Plan is now in MFLS.

And you think "I walked into Murphy & Carroll only four years ago with $100,000 in my pocket. I used it to buy UST and FFF to the tune of *all* my $100,000. Where in the world has over one-quarter of a million dollars of mutual funds come from? *This is the darndest thing I ever saw!*"

Back in the first pages of this book I told you that during the Seventies I was a student for two weeks each of three summers at the Stonier Graduate School of Banking at Rutgers University. The course in Bank Portfolio Investments was taught by Professor Paul Nadler.

Paul Nadler probably knows more about the banking industry than any other human being in the world. He writes and lectures far and wide and has done so for three decades. Every state and county banker's association in the country attempts to get him for their annual dinner meetings and conventions. He is both an absolute expert and a wonderful public speaker. I introduced him in 1981 at my own Banker's Association dinner.

When Paul Nadler lectures at the Stonier Graduate School, he has a wide stage and a large blackboard. He paces and shouts. He breaks at least ten pieces of chalk per lecture. He makes his point and yells "Onward!," moving then on to the next point (Does that sound familiar?). He covers wide areas, both on the stage and in the lecture's content. His course at Stonier is ten two-hour lectures. It is the highlight of the School's curriculum.

At least once in every lecture Paul Nadler would explain an excellent concept in bank portfolio investing that was somewhat unique and different. Then he would shout "TINSTAAFL!" and explain the risks that were involved, the scenarios under which it might not work, why it might be necessary to approach the concept with caution. All of us wondered what "TINSTAAFL" meant. It was a word, we quickly determined, that was not in the dictionary.

It was not until the last 15 minutes of the last lecture that Paul Nadler explained what "TINSTAAFL" meant. It is an acronym for a nine word sentence that we have all heard many times. The sentence has a world of truth to it. It is in the realm of Absolute Fact. The sentence is:

There Is No Such Thing As A Free Lunch.

Your Investment Plan has risks. It will demand your time. There will be distressing moments and even discouraging years. You will make mistakes. Your Customer's Person will give you bad advice. You will try to think and live by "This, too, shall pass!" but it won't right now and you will have to wait longer. You will see recessions, inflation, extremely volatile markets on the wrong side, and probably again a Crash. You will see budget deficits and trade deficits and economic ineptitude on the part of the politicians. You will see domestic and international happenings that will make your hair curl and your blood boil. There will be times you wish you were elsewhere. You will think maybe this lunch is *too* expensive!

But these are things that we have seen before!

If you keep the faith, and maintain rigid adherence to UST/FIPS, FFF/ ESG/SSS, MFLS, January Reviews, diligent reading, and all the rest, you and your Investment Plan, and the Eighth Wonder of the World and the Magic Number, will prevail! You will enjoy the lunch and agree its price is worth it.

You will have more mutual fund shares surrounding you than Averill and Archibald had Indians!

There is no such thing as a free lunch, but there is such a thing as a good Investment Plan. And now your journey toward learning it is complete. Your vehicle is in the garage and its engine is turned off.

It is ready to go again, whenever you are!

EPILOGUE
"WHERE ARE THE
CUSTOMERS' YACHTS?'

I have told you a bit about my early years as a stockbroker, starting in 1959. And I have told you that my *modus operandi* was usually to research a growth stock, sell it to my clients, hope it went up, sell it for a happy client, and move on to the next stock.

This was an office of a national NYSE member firm in San Francisco, and there were about 25 brokers. I was in my late twenties, and there were about a half dozen brokers who were exact contemporaries of mine. Without exception, they were wonderful people and we had a lot of camaraderie. We all had a good sense of humor. And we shared the same way of running our brokerage businesses.

I have also told you that there was a short but very severe bear market in May and June, 1962, when the market went down about 23%. It was not much fun watching the NYSE ticker tape on the translux screen that ran across a long wall in the office. We each had little cubicles with four foot walls on the trading floor, and we could stand up and talk to each other over the walls of our cubicles. Jim Murphy did not like us to do this, but we did.

As we watched our favorite stocks plummet on the tape, we developed an inside joke to keep our spirits up. It was a sort of a sick joke. We tried our best not to let clients who sat watching the tape hear it. We would slowly, very slowly, say to ourselves and to one another: "Where are the customers' yachts?"

There came to be many follow-ups: "My customers won't be able to afford rowboats." "My customers were seen on deck this morning blowing up their Mae Wests!" "My customers won't have yachts—they'll have lockers—Davey Jones' Lockers!" "Thirty five footers are being sold at the wharf today for $100!" "Yachts? They'll be lucky to have enough money for a pair of water wings." And more of the same ilk.

I first visited southeast Florida in 1947, on a family vacation. I developed a love affair with the beaches. One of the reasons I moved to southeast Florida in 1973 was to be near the beach. Today I live one hundred yards from the Atlantic Ocean.

Virtually every Saturday and every Sunday, fifty two weeks a year, I go to the beach. I position my beach chair and beach blanket about twenty yards from the water's edge. I read. I walk. I swim and body-surf. I doze. I watch the seagulls, sandpipers and pelicans. I play frisbee and kadima. I watch the parasails, jetskiers, Hobiecats, and windsurfers. It is an altogether pleasant way for me to spend the day.

In recent years, at the two beaches I frequent the most, there has been a new development. From fifty to one hundred yards offshore nautical vessels will anchor, for the day or for the afternoon. These are not rowboats. They are not even runabouts. They are *yachts*. Their size ranges from thirty to eighty feet. The prevailing easterly wind causes the bows to point seaward, the transoms toward the shoreline. There will be five to twenty-five people aboard. They will be partying. They will swim from the boat, sometimes coming ashore. There will be stereo music. There will be snorkeling. There will be, perhaps, a fishing line wet. There will be the tinkling of ice. There will be, in short, people having lots of fun. They will be involved in the pursuit of happiness.

I fully expect that you, if you have the portfolio power I expect you will have, will have one of these yachts, at least if you want one. It will probably be an eighty footer.

And when that happens, someday you will be cruising in Florida waters. And perhaps you will anchor, with your family and friends, directly in front of me.

Look for me — give me a call. It will be great meeting you! Perhaps you'll give me a Coke Classic with lots of ice, and you can show me around your yacht. We will have a few laughs, and you can introduce me around. We might even talk for a moment or two about *The World's Most Valuable Investment Strategy*.

But the real Investment Strategy is not in italics, it is not any longer just a book.

It is yours, and I hope you will use it well. It will not disappoint you.